VOLUME 586

MARCH 2003

THE ANNALS

of The American Academy of Political
and Social Science

ROBERT W. PEARSON, *Executive Editor*
ALAN W. HESTON, *Editor*

Community Colleges:
New Environments, New Directions

Special Editors of this Volume

KATHLEEN M. SHAW
Temple University

JERRY A. JACOBS
University of Pennsylvania

SAGE Publications ⑤ Thousand Oaks · London · New Delhi

#51750098

The American Academy of Political and Social Science

3814 Walnut Street, Fels Institute of Government, University of Pennsylvania,
Philadelphia, PA 19104-6197; (215) 746-6500; (215) 898-1202 (fax); www.aapss.org

Origin and Purpose. The Academy was organized December 14, 1889, to promote the progress of political and social science, especially through publications and meetings. The Academy does not take sides in controverted questions, but seeks to gather and present reliable information to assist the public in forming an intelligent and accurate judgment.

Meetings. The Academy occasionally holds a meeting in the spring extending over two days.

Publications. THE ANNALS of The American Academy of Political and Social Science is the bimonthly publication of the Academy. Each issue contains articles on some prominent social or political problem, written at the invitation of the editors. Also, monographs are published from time to time, numbers of which are distributed to pertinent professional organizations. These volumes constitute important reference works on the topics with which they deal, and they are extensively cited by authorities throughout the United States and abroad. The papers presented at the meetings of the Academy are included in THE ANNALS.

Membership. Each member of the Academy receives THE ANNALS and may attend the meetings of the Academy. Membership is open only to individuals. Annual dues: $71.00 for the regular paperbound edition (clothbound, $108.00). For members outside the U.S.A., add $24.00 for shipping of your subscription. Members may also purchase single issues of THE ANNALS for $21.00 each (clothbound, $29.00). Student memberships are available for $49.00.

Subscriptions. THE ANNALS of The American Academy of Political and Social Science (ISSN 0002-7162) is published six times annually—in January, March, May, July, September, and November— by Sage Publications, 2455 Teller Road, Thousand Oaks, CA 91320. Telephone: (800) 818-SAGE (7243) and (805) 499-9774; FAX/Order line: (805) 499-0871. Copyright © 2003 by The American Academy of Political and Social Science. Institutions may subscribe to THE ANNALS at the annual rate: $454.00 (clothbound, $513.00). Add $24.00 per year for subscriptions outside the U.S.A. Institutional rates for single issues: $88.00 each (clothbound, $98.00).

Periodicals postage paid at Thousand Oaks, California, and at additional mailing offices.

Single issues of THE ANNALS may be obtained by individuals who are not members of the Academy for $33.00 each (clothbound, $46.00). Single issues of THE ANNALS have proven to be excellent supplementary texts for classroom use. Direct inquiries regarding adoptions to THE ANNALS c/o Sage Publications (address below).

All correspondence concerning membership in the Academy, dues renewals, inquiries about membership status, and/or purchase of single issues of THE ANNALS should be sent to THE ANNALS c/o Sage Publications, 2455 Teller Road, Thousand Oaks, CA 91320. Telephone: (800) 818-SAGE (7243) and (805) 499-9774; FAX/Order line: (805) 499-0871. *Please note that orders under $30 must be prepaid.* Sage affiliates in London and India will assist institutional subscribers abroad with regard to orders, claims, and inquiries for both subscriptions and single issues.

Printed on recycled, acid-free paper

THE ANNALS

Editorial Office: 3814 Walnut Street, Fels Institute for Government, University of Pennsylvania, Philadelphia, PA 19104-6197.

For information about membership° (individuals only) and subscriptions (institutions), address:
Sage Publications
2455 Teller Road
Thousand Oaks, CA 91320

Sage Production Staff: Paul Reis, Barbara Corrigan, and Paul Doebler

From India and South Asia, write to:		From Europe, the Middle East, and Africa, write to:
SAGE PUBLICATIONS INDIA Pvt Ltd		SAGE PUBLICATIONS LTD
B-42 Panchsheel Enclave, P.O. Box 4109		6 Bonhill Street
New Delhi 110 017		London EC2A 4PU
INDIA		UNITED KINGDOM

°Please note that members of the Academy receive THE ANNALS with their membership.
International Standard Serial Number ISSN 0002-7162
International Standard Book Number ISBN 0-7619-2830-8 (Vol. 586, 2003 paper)
International Standard Book Number ISBN 0-7619-2841-3 (Vol. 586, 2003 cloth)
Manufactured in the United States of America. First printing, March 2003.

The articles appearing in *The Annals* are abstracted or indexed in Academic Abstracts, Academic Search, America: History and Life, Asia Pacific Database, Book Review Index, CAB Abstracts Database, Central Asia: Abstracts & Index, Communication Abstracts, Corporate ResourceNET, Criminal Justice Abstracts, Current Citations Express, Current Contents: Social & Behavioral Sciences, e-JEL, EconLit, Expanded Academic Index, Guide to Social Science & Religion in Periodical Literature, Health Business FullTEXT, HealthSTAR FullTEXT, Historical Abstracts, International Bibliography of the Social Sciences, International Political Science Abstracts, ISI Basic Social Sciences Index, Journal of Economic Literature on CD, LEXIS-NEXIS, MasterFILE FullTEXT, Middle East: Abstracts & Index, North Africa: Abstracts & Index, PAIS International, Periodical Abstracts, Political Science Abstracts, Sage Public Administration Abstracts, Social Science Source, Social Sciences Citation Index, Social Sciences Index Full Text, Social Services Abstracts, Social Work Abstracts, Sociological Abstracts, Southeast Asia: Abstracts & Index, Standard Periodical Directory (SPD), TOPICsearch, Wilson OmniFile V, and Wilson Social Sciences Index/Abstracts, and are available on microfilm from University Microfilms, Ann Arbor, Michigan.

Information about membership rates, institutional subscriptions, and back issue prices may be found on the facing page.

Advertising. Current rates and specifications may be obtained by writing to *The Annals* Advertising and Promotion Manager at the Thousand Oaks office (address above).

Claims. Claims for undelivered copies must be made no later than six months following month of publication. The publisher will supply missing copies when losses have been sustained in transit and when the reserve stock will permit.

Change of Address. Six weeks' advance notice must be given when notifying of change of address to ensure proper identification. Please specify name of journal. POSTMASTER: Send address changes to: *The Annals* of The American Academy of Political and Social Science, c/o Sage Publications, 2455 Teller Road, Thousand Oaks, CA 91320.

THE ANNALS

OF THE AMERICAN ACADEMY OF POLITICAL AND SOCIAL SCIENCE

Volume 586   March 2003

IN THIS ISSUE:

Community Colleges: New Environments, New Directions

Special Editors: KATHLEEN M. SHAW
JERRY A. JACOBS

FORTHCOMING

Assessing Systematic Evidence
in Crime and Justice: Methodological
Concerns and Empirical Outcomes

Special Editors: DAVID WEISBURD
                  CYNTHIA LUM
                  ANTHONY PETROSINO

Volume 587, May 2003

Islam

Special Editor: ASLAM SYED

Volume 588, July 2003

Misleading Evidence and Evidence-Led Policy:
Making Social Science More Experimental

Special Editor: LAWRENCE SHERMAN

Volume 589, September 2003

PREFACE

Community Colleges: New Environments, New Directions

Since their inception, community colleges have been expected to serve a number of roles in American society. As the entryway to college for groups of people who would otherwise have been excluded from higher education, community colleges provide the first step on the ladder toward a baccalaureate degree. As higher education institutions that are uniquely linked to their local communities, community colleges are asked to address the educational and civic needs of a wide array of local citizens. And as the educational institutions most attuned to the needs of the local business community, they are charged with equipping their graduates with the skills needed to succeed in the economy. In short, community colleges, at least in their idealized form, should be functioning as a democratizing force in American society—providing access to education and training where it would not exist otherwise, increasing the ability of people to engage in the civic life of American society, and providing the skills and training needed to gain employment.

Whether community colleges ever lived up to these ideals has always been in question. Yet as community colleges enter the new millennium, they are encountering a set of forces that are making it increasingly difficult for them to maintain a commitment to the diverse and sometimes competing missions that have always characterized this sector of higher education. Both internal and external forces are converging to steer these institutions away from important aspects of their historic missions—most notably, academic preparation for transfer to the four-year sector. Instead, they are increasingly adopting a more singularly market-driven mission that focuses on providing the skills demanded by the local economy. As a result, an equity agenda, which for so long has been at the forefront of the rhetoric surrounding the community college,

DOI: 10.1177/0002716202250198

has been eroded by a business model that emphasizes efficiency, outcomes, and the needs of employers.

This issue of *The Annals of the American Academy of Political and Social Science* is devoted to exploring the shift in both mission and function that is emerging among community colleges. By examining a series of important and interrelated developments in this sector of American higher education, we hope that this volume will inform scholars, community college leaders, and policy makers about the shifting and ever more complex economic, political, and social environment community colleges find themselves in.

Community Colleges as an Area of Study

Community colleges deserve more attention than they usually receive for a number of reasons. Perhaps the most important of these is the fact that from a structural perspective, they are situated as a bridge between the K-12 educational sector and higher education. Community colleges admit students who are the products of local public school systems, and they feed their graduates to local employers and four-year colleges and universities. Thus, these institutions are in many ways a reflection of the quality of the K-12 system and can affect the quality and functioning of the four-year system as well.

Second, the community college sector has grown rapidly in the past half century. Between 1965 and 1997, the number of community college students increased 4.6-fold, while the number of students enrolled at four-year institutions increased 1.9 times (U.S. Department of Education, 1999). Although the growth in all of higher education was extraordinary during this time period, the rise of community colleges signals a radical shift in the institutional makeup of American higher education.

As a result of this growth, community colleges are increasingly likely to serve as the entryway to postsecondary education for poor and minority students. Enrollments of Hispanics in community colleges tripled between 1976 and 1997, while African American enrollment increased 1.5 times during the same period. As of 1997, 56 percent of all Hispanic students and 42 percent of African American students were enrolled in two-year institutions (U.S. Department of Education, 1999).

The concentration of so many nontraditional students places a unique burden on community colleges and is in part a reflection of the stratification of this country's higher education sector. Indeed, many argue that stratification is increasing with emerging state policies requiring community colleges to be the sole deliverers of remediation in many state higher education systems. And the open-door policies that have characterized community colleges are being eroded by recent state and federal policies that are reducing access to community college for some populations. Clearly, this is a critical time in the history of community colleges in particular and in the history of American higher education more generally.

An Overview of the Contents of This Issue

As Steven Brint points out in his retrospective essay on the state of community college research, many of the issues that are discussed in this volume of *The Annals* were evident to varying degrees in 1989, when he and Jerry Karabel published their seminal book, *The Diverted Dream*. However, Brint and Karabel could not have foreseen the ways in which a variety of forces would have emerged to create pressures on the community college that are different in both scope and intensity than those that existed in 1989.

This issue of *The Annals* examines the community college using three separate but interrelated themes. First, recent changes in federal policy are described and discussed in terms of both their effects on access to postsecondary education via the community college and the types of education that are available to individuals. Overall, recent federal policy has reduced access to postsecondary education for recipients of such programs as the Workforce Investment Act (WIA) and welfare (Temporary Aid to Needy Families). Equally important, however, is the fact that the type of education available through federal programs has shifted away from degree-granting programs and toward short-term, noncredit programs often designed to meet the immediate employment needs of local businesses.

The second theme represented in this volume focuses on broader societal factors that have contributed to the movement of community colleges away from their traditional academic mission. The market-driven philosophy that is becoming increasingly dominant emphasizes efficiency, profit, and strong ties with the business community. Several of our authors illustrate the ways in which this philosophy operates within specific institutions and point as well to the ways in which these pressures are unequally felt among community colleges.

Finally, specific community college practices are critically examined in terms of how well they serve the academic and employment needs of students. Taking as a starting point the obvious and multiple limitations under which community colleges operate, the authors provide concrete suggestions designed to maintain these institutions' function as a path toward educational and economic self-sufficiency. Each of these three themes, and the articles that contribute to them, are described in more detail below.

Changes in federal policy

Perhaps the most notable new aspect of the community college environment has emerged from recent federal policy. While education and training have traditionally enjoyed wide support among lawmakers and the general public as a reliable avenue toward economic self-sufficiency, in recent years, this support has eroded, particularly with regard to low-income populations. What has emerged instead is a work-first philosophy, which emphasizes rapid job placement as the strategy of choice in achieving stable employment, rather than a longer-term approach that incorporates education and training along with work experience.

The work-first philosophy has driven the development of two major pieces of federal legislation—welfare reform and WIA. As a result, among both welfare recipients and WIA clients, there is far less college attendance, and when access is available, it is most often to short-term training programs rather than to credit-bearing courses or those that would count toward a degree. Whereas the halls of community colleges once remained accessible to these most disadvantaged populations, a large portion of them cannot even walk through the doors anymore as a result of these policies, and those who pass through these doors walk down different corridors.[C]ommunity colleges are increasingly likely to serve as the entryway to postsecondary education for poor and minority students.[C]ommunity colleges are increasingly likely to serve as the entryway to postsecondary education for poor and minority students.

[C]ommunity colleges are increasingly likely to serve as the entryway to postsecondary education for poor and minority students.

The articles by Christopher Mazzeo, Sara Rab, and Susan Eachus; Jerry Jacobs and Sarah Winslow; and Kathleen Shaw and Sara Rab clearly document the effects of federal policy on access to education via the community college. This trio of articles stems from a collaborative study of welfare reform and community colleges in six states. In their analysis of state-level variation in the effects of welfare reform on access to college, Mazzeo, Rab, and Eachus illustrate the ways in which this policy generally reflects a movement away from the long-held belief that education and training represent the surest route toward economic self-sufficiency. While traditional policy analyses focus on political or institutional factors, Mazzeo, Rab, and Eachus's unique contribution is in illustrating the importance of ideology in the response of states to federal welfare policy. They examine the beliefs that key policy makers and implementing agencies hold about welfare recipients and the role of education and training in their lives. The authors also point to the roles of state officials, welfare advocates, and community colleges themselves in explaining how access of welfare recipients varies across states.

The article by Jacobs and Winslow complements the Mazzeo, Rab, and Eachus article by examining the impact of welfare reform on enrollment over time and across states. They compile a variety of evidence from a variety of sources, including federal statistics, state data, and community college enrollment records, and they conduct original analysis of three national data sets. While some discrepancies between data sources are evident, most of the evidence points to a decline in the rate of enrollment in postsecondary education of welfare recipients. Moreover, some data suggest that young single mothers who might have been welfare recipients under Aid to Families with Dependent Children are less likely to enroll in higher education under Temporary Aid to Needy Families. Their results also indicate that welfare recipients in states with less favorable policies toward higher education are less likely to be enrolled in postsecondary education. This underscores the conclusion that state-level variation in policies does matter in terms of affecting the chances to pursue additional education. Finally, Jacobs and Winslow illustrate that the type of education available to welfare recipients has shifted considerably. Whereas access to degree-granting programs existed to some degree prior to welfare reform, the analyses provided by Jacobs and Winslow illustrate that this is no longer the case for the vast majority of welfare recipients after the 1996 legislation was passed. Not only has access to postsecondary education been significantly reduced, but the education and training that is available is, for the most part, short term and non–degree granting.

This trend mirrors a growing trend in the federal government away from utilizing education as a means to improve the economic status of low-income populations. As the article by Shaw and Rab points out, this trend is encouraged and reinforced by WIA, which has eroded the federal government's historic commitment to the retraining of displaced and laid-off workers in favor of an emphasis on rapid job placement. As is the case with welfare reform, both the quantity and quality of education available to most WIA recipients has shifted toward shorter-term, non-credit-bearing training programs. This reduction in overall support for education and training, when coupled with the onerous reporting requirements instituted by the federal government, has greatly reduced the incentives for many community colleges to participate in the training and education of WIA clients. And when they do, their customer is increasingly seen as the local labor market—not community college students themselves. Thus, as Shaw and Rab illustrate with examples from several states, community colleges, which were once the major portal through which individuals could receive training and education funded by the federal government, are no longer functioning in this manner.

Alicia Dowd's article on access and equity in the community college points to another major shift in the federal policy landscape—namely, changes in federal financial aid policy. Not only has the purchasing power of Pell Grants greatly decreased in recent years, but there is a clear trend toward loans, and away from grants, in financing community college education. Because community college students are most price sensitive, this trend has the clear potential to reduce access to education for the poorest students.

A sharp turn toward a market philosophy

Dowd situates her analysis of federal financial aid policy within a larger context that takes into account other broad shifts in American higher education. She argues that a number of trends are converging to challenge, and ultimately shift, the community college mission away from its traditional commitment to providing access to education that is the first step toward an associate's or bachelor's degree. In its place is an increasing focus on a market-driven mission which is more attuned to the needs of local industries than to the needs of individual students and whose success is measured in terms of economic, rather than educational, indicators. Of course, community colleges have always been attuned to their local context. Indeed, as Dougherty (1994) and Brint and Karabel (1989) have illustrated in their earlier work on community colleges, these institutions have a consistent need to be responsive to their local context, given the economic and political factors that affect them so directly. However, there is growing evidence that in the past quarter century, and in the past decade in particular, the needs of the business community, and economic concerns more generally, have become an increasingly prominent part of the landscape of community colleges. As a result, the historic commitment of community colleges to serve the needs of individual students, and the needs of the broader local community, has been eroded.

[T]his volume raises the important question of whether, and how, community colleges can serve the needs of this nation's most disadvantaged students.

What has driven these policy shifts? Several of our authors point to changes in dominant rhetoric and philosophy and suggest that these changes have important implications for community college mission and practice. Patti Gumport's revealing interviews of community college presidents document these forces in action. Gumport is in the unique position of having direct access to the experiences and reflections of the decision makers themselves. Her interviews suggest that there are two institutional logics that frame the response of community colleges to various environmental pressures. Until quite recently, the social institutional logic, which casts public higher education as primarily an educational enterprise, has guided the actions of community colleges. Yet her research suggests that an industry logic, which focuses on efficiency, profit, and strengthening the local economy, has become increasingly prominent in the past twenty-five years.

Gumport's analysis is consistent with that of other authors represented in this volume. Dowd points to a movement toward a capitalist ideology and market-driven mission that focuses on competition and profitability; Shaw and Rab, as well as Mazzeo, Rab, and Eachus, point to a work-first philosophy that conceptualizes students as prospective employees in the local labor market; and Grubb points to an erosion of the equity agenda. All of these analyses, although using slightly different terminology, are consistent in pointing to a shift away from educationally driven decision making and toward an economic model that emphasizes employment rather than education.

Yet Gumport's work suggests that despite the growing prominence of the industry logic and similar philosophies in the past quarter century, such frameworks do not wholly constrain the actions or decisions of community college presidents. Rather, they are still able to maintain a level of autonomy that allows them to respond to external pressures in a number of ways, although their scope of response has become more limited.

Kevin Dougherty's analysis of employer-focused training in community colleges also points to variability in the response of community colleges to external pressures. Dougherty's analysis is unusually thorough and convincing because he utilizes both quantitative and qualitative data in his analyses. Not surprisingly, he finds that there is a general trend in the direction of employer-focused training. However, this trend is neither wholly consistent nor uniform. Indeed, his research suggests that the demand varies by type of local employer, as well as by the size of the community colleges available and their proximity to business. For example, large manufacturers tend to utilize community colleges much more heavily than smaller employers in industries such as retail trade. Thus, both Dougherty and Gumport suggest that despite the presence of significant and sustained pressure from a variety of outside sources, these forces do not exert a uniform pressure on community colleges, nor does this sector respond to such pressures in a uniform manner. Rather, they exhibit a level of institutional agency that allows them at least some autonomy in their response to what are, admittedly, forceful external pressures to become more responsive to the business sector and decision-making frameworks that privilege economic concerns over educational issues.

Potential partial correctives

Despite the evidence presented by Gumport and Dougherty that community colleges are not completely uniform in their response to the pressure to adopt a market philosophy, it is fair to say that the articles in this volume cast a generally critical eye on community colleges as an educational sector and on their potential to serve as the democratizing force that they have been purported to be. There is a firm consensus among the authors that community colleges are, overall, increasingly responsive to the industry and the business sector rather than to the students, or potential students, who might enroll in their courses. Furthermore, with the notable exception of Deil-Amen and Rosenbaum, the authors would seem to be in general agreement that the increasing prominence of market philosophy and practice has had a negative effect on issues of access and equity. Indeed, this volume raises the important question of whether, and how, community colleges can serve the needs of this nation's most disadvantaged students.

However, several articles in this volume point to ways in which community colleges can improve their ability to respond to the needs of students and, in doing so, continue to be responsive to their historic mission. First, Norton Grubb examines the noncredit sector of community college courses in an attempt to explore how altering them in specific ways might better fulfill what he refers to as the equity agenda. Unlike most of the other authors in this volume, Grubb does not focus most of his attention on the external pressure and contextual factors that have shifted the community college mission. Rather, his article examines specific practices within the noncredit arm of the community college.

Grubb considers how noncredit education could be restructured to better serve the needs of students as well. This emphasis on community college curricula and its importance in achieving educational equity is an important but often overlooked dimension in studies of these institutions. While highly critical of the current state of noncredit education, Grubb contends that it is here to stay and thus it is important to determine how to improve its contribution to students' educational chances.

Like Grubb, Regina Deil-Amen and James Rosenbaum focus their attention on a concrete element of the community college—in this instance, the advising structure and, more specifically, the relationship between community colleges and the business sector in the job placement process. Whereas other authors in the volume underscore the dominance of business over educational considerations, Deil-Amen and Rosenbaum suggest that stronger linkages between education and the business sector would actually enhance the educational goals of community colleges. While community colleges engage in ever-increasing amounts of employment-related education and training, the authors argue that this sector stops short of providing the services and linkages needed to ensure that students actually obtain adequate employment. Deil-Amen and Rosenbaum suggest that the practices of proprietary institutions are also more effective in providing advising services to their students. Deil-Amen and Rosenbaum's article is invaluable because it examines in detail some of the important weaknesses that exist in community colleges. Moreover, they illustrate how the failure to provide more concrete linkages to the employment sector further disadvantages community college students who choose to acquire their employment training through these institutions.

Summary

As Steven Brint points out in his provocative article regarding the state of the literature on community colleges since the publication of *The Diverted Dream*, many of the trends that were on the horizon more than a decade ago have now become an integral part of the community college landscape. Brint and Karabel's argument that community colleges reinforce, rather than ameliorate, existing social inequalities has been generally confirmed, as in the case of transfer rates that continue to be much lower than the transfer aspirations of students and whose economic effects are exacerbated by the increasing premium placed on the baccalaureate degree. Low rates of economic return for most academic programs offered by community colleges also persist, and community colleges continue to enroll a disproportionate number of low-income students. Their original skepticism regarding vocational programs has been tempered to a significant degree by emerging analyses suggesting that selective vocational programs produce higher economic outcomes than many academically oriented programs at the associate's degree level. Yet, on balance, Brint and Karabel's original analysis regarding the role of community colleges in reproducing existing social inequalities remains convincing.

However, Brint and Karabel could not have foreseen all that has happened in the past quarter century. They did not, for example, foresee the seismic shift in the federal government's approach to the education and training of low-income and displaced workers—a shift that would so completely emphasize work rather than education as the path to long-term economic self-sufficiency. The shift in federal financial aid away from grants and toward loans has also had a chilling effect on community college enrollment and completion and has further challenged the ability of community colleges to serve this nation's most disadvantaged populations.

Nor could they have completely predicted the increasingly close relationship that has developed between community colleges and the employment sector. Through a series of complex economic, political, and social factors, community colleges are being pressured to act as the training arm of the employment sector to the increasing exclusion of other possible functions. And while these institutions are not passive in their response to such pressures, still, the pressure is real and growing, and many community colleges—perhaps most—have begun to de-emphasize their academic missions and, in particular, their historical commitment to serving as the first step toward the baccalaureate degree.

As Grubb argues, the equity agenda that has driven at least the rhetoric, if not the reality, of community colleges has eroded. An emphasis on education as the central mission of these institutions is being replaced with a market philosophy that emphasizes short-term, employer-driven training. Moreover, for those who are most disadvantaged—welfare recipients, those who have lost their jobs and are seeking retraining under the federal WIA, those needing financial aid—access to even short-term training is being eroded.

This volume of *The Annals*, when taken as a whole, provides several lenses through which to view contemporary community colleges as they respond to an emerging set of challenges. The degree to which community colleges either reinforce or ameliorate existing social inequalities remains an open question. It is our hope that the articles contained within this volume provoke discussion and debate about a critically important sector of the American educational system.

KATHLEEN M. SHAW
JERRY A. JACOBS

References

Brint, Steven and Jerome Karabel. (1989). *The diverted dream: Community colleges and the promise of educational opportunity in America, 1900-1985*. New York: Oxford University Press.

Dougherty, Kevin J. (1994). *The contradictory college: The conflicting origins, impacts and futures of the community colleges*. Albany, NY: SUNY Press

U.S. Department of Education. (1999). Retrieved from http://www.nces.ed.gov/edstats.

Few Remaining Dreams: Community Colleges Since 1985

In recent years, three schools of thought—human capital economics, sociological contradictions theory, and the new structuralism—have contributed to discussions of the role of community colleges in American postsecondary education. An evaluation of this work suggests that the circumstances of community colleges have, in several respects, changed for the worse in the years since publication of the author's book, *The Diverted Dream* (with Jerome Karabel). The community college student population has become more homogeneous in social class background and test scores, faculty work conditions have deteriorated, and dropout rates remain very high. One solution to the persisting performance problems of community colleges would be to split the colleges into three parts: one modeled on private-sector vocational training, another organized as two-year branches of four-year institutions, and a third as a community center for courses of avocational interest.

Keywords: community colleges; human capital economics; sociological contradictions theory; new structuralism

By
STEVEN BRINT

In 1989, Jerome Karabel and I published a book, *The Diverted Dream* (Brint and Karabel 1989), which proved to be a considerable provocation to community college leaders and researchers. Ours was a revisionist history; it argued that community colleges were initially promoted by leaders of elite universities to redirect students who might otherwise demand access to four-year colleges and universities,

Steven Brint is a professor of sociology and the director of the Colleges and Universities 2000 Study at the University of California, Riverside. In addition to The Diverted Dream, his books include In an Age of Experts, Schools and Societies, and The Future of the City of Intellect. He is currently at work on a study of continuity and change in American colleges and universities from 1970 to 2000.

NOTE: I would like to thank David Bills for initial encouragement. I would like to thank Charles S. Levy for research assistance and comments that greatly improved the quality of this article. I would also like to thank Kathleen M. Shaw and Jerry A. Jacobs for their very helpful comments.

DOI: 10.1177/0002716202250208

thereby diminishing the status of these institutions. This contrasted with then-current views of the two-year colleges as a great democratic experiment, the people's colleges. We argued further that neither student consumers nor businesspeople were at first very much interested in the vocational programs that became the center of the community colleges' mission. Instead, leaders of the colleges themselves saw vocational curricula as the best avenue for their students and for their own institutional survival. We developed an institutional argument to explain this choice, focusing both on the structural constraints on community colleges (notably, the lower status of their students and the monopolization of professional labor markets by four-year colleges and universities) and the open opportunity fields in which they operated (notably, the existence of potential training markets for many semiprofessional and technical occupations).

In addition to our doubts about historical studies based on the responsiveness of community colleges to consumer and employer demand, we raised a number of critical questions about community colleges. We characterized them as the lowest rung in postsecondary education, both in terms of student composition and student life chances, and we raised concerns about the effects of community college entrance on the life chances of students. We saw community colleges as one means by which student ambitions were softly lowered to fit with the opportunities actually available in the labor market. We speculated whether the colleges led to democratization of higher education—by bringing in students who would not otherwise have attended a postsecondary institution—or whether their primary function was to divert students who would otherwise have attended a four-year college. We presented evidence that otherwise comparable students had a better chance of completing their baccalaureate if they started at a four-year college than if they started at a two-year college. We also raised questions about the economic payoffs to vocational programs. We anticipated important differences by field, but we also argued that many vocational students did not obtain jobs in the fields in which they prepared. We found no evidence for a common argument of the time—that rates of return for vocational students were notably higher than for liberal arts transfer students who went on to complete a baccalaureate. Karabel and I did not argue that liberal arts programs in community colleges were economically superior to vocational programs, only that the B.A. was economically superior to the vocational A.A.

As a contributor to this volume, I feel a bit like the man who comes home after a fifteen-year seafaring absence. The neighborhood is still recognizable, but considerable building has been going on. In this article, I will try to take stock of what we have learned about community colleges in the fifteen years that I have been away and whether the neighborhood as a whole—that is to say, the community college sector—is better or worse off or about the same as when I left.

The succeeding cohort of scholars has greatly deepened our understanding of community colleges by providing more definitive answers to issues for which evidence at the time we wrote was fragmentary. It has also developed theoretical approaches to understanding the role of community colleges, which help to explain some of the dilemmas faced by community colleges. But it has not, in my view, greatly changed the portrait of community colleges presented in our book—and indeed certain developments in the community colleges since the publication of *The Diverted Dream* are cause for heightened concern.

New Schools of Thought

The scholarly literature on community colleges post–*Diverted Dream* can be divided into three major schools: the human capital economists, sociological contradictions analysis, and the "new structural critics." Considerable overlap exists between the latter two of these schools, and the distinction between the two is subtle. It is based on both attitude (the contradictions analysts are more ambivalent than critical) and theoretical stance (the contradictions analysts adopt a systems theory perspective, while the new structural critics are more eclectic). I will use the work of Thomas Kane and Cecilia Rouse as exemplary of the human capital school, the work of Kevin Dougherty as exemplary of the contradictions analysts, and the work of Regina Deil-Amen and James Rosenbaum as exemplary of the new structural critics. The educational economist Norton Grubb has contributed significantly to the first two of these schools, and I will discuss his work as well. I will focus on how this new work has contributed to an understanding of community colleges—and where it does and does not go beyond the conclusions Karabel and I reached in *The Diverted Dream*.

Human capital economics. It is exceptionally useful to have economists involved in a contested literature—as long as their perspective does not thoroughly dominate discussion. However blinkered they may be at times to forces of history, culture, and social structure, economists bring a high level of logical rigor to their studies. Human capital economists, led by Kane, Rouse, and Grubb, have greatly expanded our understanding of the economic returns to forms of two-year college education.

Both Kane and Rouse (1995) and Grubb (1996) argued that the comparison between two-year and four-year college students, which Karabel and I emphasized, is but a subset of the relevant comparisons. Community college students should be compared, they argue, also to those who obtain less education. Moreover, entrants, dropouts, and graduates should be systematically compared to one another, both in general and by field. Thus, they propose a series of comparisons—between high school dropouts and high school graduates, between high school graduates and those with some college, between those with some college who start at community colleges and those with some college who start at four-year colleges, between those with some college and associate's degree holders, between associate's degree holders and bachelor's degree holders.

Those who are familiar with this work, which thus far is based largely on analyses of the National Longitudinal Study of the High School Class of 1972 and the National Longitudinal Study of Youth, know that human capital economists have found that rates of return to the B.A. are nearly twice that of the A.A. for men, and nearly 60 percent higher for women sixteen years out of high school; that holders of associate's degrees do better on average than four-year college dropouts; and that two- and four-year college dropouts do not differ much from one another, if one holds constant the number of credits obtained. Family background and ability measures explain no more than one-fifth of the differences in rates of return (for representative work, see Grubb 1993, 1997; Kane and Rouse 1995, 1999).

This work can certainly be read as a story of human capital investments rewarded. The data can also be read in another way: in relation to what students say they want and what actually happens to them. From this perspective, our emphasis on differences between two- and four-year college students is understandable. The least restrictive (and I think most accurate) indicator of student aspirations shows that approximately 70 percent of two-year college entrants, and an even higher proportion of four-year college entrants, say their educational goal is to obtain a bachelor's degree (Kane and Rouse 1999, 70).[1] No wonder: the earnings differential between college and high school graduates climbed steadily between 1975 and 1995, and it has continued to grow since that time for women while leveling off for men. About half of four-year college entrants achieve this stated goal, but only about 15 percent of two-year college entrants do. Even when background and test scores are controlled, a significant differential between two- and four-year college entrants in B.A. completion rates—10 to 20 percent—remains.

I would raise questions also about the *ceteris paribus* assumption in comparisons of two- and four-year college dropouts. The vast majority of community college students do not take as many college credits as four-year college students. In fact, about 35 percent of community college entrants who say they are working toward a degree last a semester or less at a community college before dropping out. Labor market returns are negligible for students who accumulate only a small number of credits in a community college. Is it reasonable to hold credit hours constant in comparisons of two- and four-year dropouts when credit hours completed are far from comparable between the two groups in real life?

Kane and Rouse (1995) have recently acknowledged that factors related to weak social integration and limited academic support may help to explain high two-year college dropout rates. But their initial reflection on this problem remains closer in spirit to the human capital approach:

> A simple cost-benefit analysis shows that, over 30 years, the community college student who completes even one semester will earn more than enough to compensate him for the cost of the schooling. . . . Second, there is an "option value" to college entry if students are able to gain more information about the costs and benefits of further investments. When one is uncertain about the prospects of completing college before entry, there will be a value attached to enrolling in order to discover whether one is "college material." (Kane and Rouse 1995, 611)

In other words, when costs in terms of forgone earnings will not support a human capital argument, the tendency is to support the status quo by offering a self-sealing psychology of costs. In this view, community college students are in reality, if not in aspiration, latent terminal students—just as an early leader of the junior college movement, Walter Crosby Eells, asserted seventy years ago.

Because of these difficulties in properly interpreting the meaning of rates of return to different amounts of postsecondary education, economists' findings on relative returns to vocational and academic fields may be more valuable than their findings on returns to different amounts of education. These latter findings indicate that vocational degrees are now worth more than academic degrees, and that within the vocational domain, some fields perform very well and others not very well. Again using National Longitudinal Study of the High School Class of 1972 follow-ups, Grubb (1996) found much higher rates of return to vocational two-year degrees than academic two-year degrees, and indeed he found a small, though insignificant, earnings differential when comparing academic associate's degree holders and high school graduates. Moreover, "some fields of study, especially business and health occupations for women, and business and technical subjects

---

Approximately 70 percent of two-year college entrants . . . say their educational goal is to obtain a bachelor's degree . . . but only about 15 percent . . . do.

---

for men, have high returns" (Grubb 1996, 106).[2] This is close to what Karabel and I surmised based on fragmentary evidence, but it is very useful to have detailed empirical confirmation—and also to have the additional finding that those who take courses closely related to their fields of employment often gain especially high returns. Given the reigning assumptions of fifteen years ago, it is particularly interesting to contemplate that the more highly motivated community college students may now be studying vocational rather than academic subjects. If true, this would be a striking example of the motivational consequences of structural change.

The sociological contradictions analysts. Kevin Dougherty's (1994) *The Contradictory College* is a landmark work on community colleges. It contributes in a number of ways to our understanding of community colleges: it includes an interesting macro-level focus on state actors as agents of community college development and transformation. It includes a well-articulated, institutional-level critique of the colleges as overextended in goals and lacking the means by which to achieve many of their ends effectively. It deepens our understanding of the problems of transfer students, in particular, and of why the community college is so often harmful to their aspirations. Finally, it offers provocative policy suggestions, addressing the issue, for example, of whether community colleges should focus exclusively on vocational training or attempt to improve their transfer function by becoming two-year branches of four-year institutions.

Dougherty agreed with the argument Karabel and I made about the key role played by university leaders and the American Association of Junior Colleges (AAJC) in the early years but thought we underestimated the role of the state. Dougherty showed that local high school officials who became active in community college advocacy frequently wanted to provide themselves with new and higher-status jobs. He showed that local government officials thought of community colleges as a potential boon for their communities, that state government officials found community colleges appealing on opportunity and efficiency grounds, and that the state, in general, has an economic interest in providing trained manpower for private business. Drawing on theories of "the relative autonomy of the state," he showed that state actors have motives that both reflect and are autonomous from the motives of business leaders. Continuing this theme, Dougherty greatly improved on our rather cursory discussion of variation in state policies toward community colleges, emphasizing the potential influence of such variations as explicit articulation agreements and location of community colleges as branches of four-year institutions.

State officials do provide legislative authorization, organizational frames, and funding for community colleges. Their motives and interests are therefore very much worthy of close study, as are the variations in state provisioning and organization of community college systems. At the same time, I will defend our approach this far: I think that Dougherty (1994) underemphasized the role of cultural innovation, national-level promotional activities, and the borrowing by states of successful educational innovations (Brint and Karabel 1991; DiMaggio and Powell 1983). States and localities do not act entirely independently of one another, and they certainly do not develop new forms out of whole cloth. From this perspective, it makes sense to focus, as we did, on early sponsors of the junior college movement, such as the University of Chicago and the University of California; the work of conceptualizers such as Leonard Koos and Walter Crosby Eells; and the energetic advocacy of the AAJC.

Dougherty's emphasis on organizational dysfunctions (or contradictions) is indebted to Robert Merton's revision of structural-functionalism. Like Merton, Dougherty is more sensitive to the structured tensions that arise in complex organizations than to their smooth workings. For Dougherty, the major contradiction of the contradictory college is for goal diffusion combined with inadequate means to meet multiple goals. The community college tries to be all things to all people. It succeeds well at some of its purposes but not at others. Because transfer is a particularly complex task, given the greater interest of the colleges in vocational training and the weak academic preparation of most students, the transfer function is the most seriously affected by these problems. "The community college's desire to provide educational opportunity has been undercut by its other purposes of providing vocational education and saving state governments money" (Dougherty 1994, 8).

Dougherty's book brings a crisp logic and strong evidence to bear on a variety of questions concerning the opportunities provided by community colleges. Karabel and I raised several of these questions, but Dougherty has found the evidence to settle them in a more definitive way. He has, for example, provided a definitive review of studies concerned with the differing rate of degree completion of two-year and four-year students, controlling for family background and test scores (see also Dougherty 1987). Dougherty went beyond the numbers to consider in detail the mechanisms through which high dropout rates are produced in community colleges. Here he focused on students' difficulties in obtaining financial aid, low levels of socially integrative activities, discouragement of academic work by fellow students, and the low expectations of teachers. He broke down the problem of transfer students into three distinct phases—problems at the community college, problems entering a four-year institution, and problems at four-year institutions—showing how each step involves a distinct set of obstacles. Although his treatment of vocational education was less definitive, he did raise questions about the vaunted responsiveness of community colleges to changing labor market conditions. Programs once established tend to perpetuate themselves, he found, and adjustment to new conditions is usually relatively slow.

Grubb's work adopts a similar form of analysis. Indeed, Grubb (1996, xvi) noted that like Dougherty, he sees both "positive and negative consequences" of community colleges, and that the reasons for these "contradictory effects" are "largely structural." In particular, "the position of two-year colleges in the middle of the education system, between mass institutions of secondary education and the selective four-year colleges with their different traditions, causes various problems." These "structural effects" are presented as paradoxes. They involve noble impulses thwarted by scarce resources or rigidities due to perceived legitimation requirements. Thus, Grubb (1996) wrote, "Community colleges are given the most difficult teaching task . . . but (have) fewer resources to carry out that task . . . and rarely support or reward good teaching." In another passage, he wrote, "Even though (community colleges) include many non-traditional students, they largely act like traditional educational institutions" (pp. xvi-xvii).

Where Dougherty's signal contribution has been to the study of transfer students, Grubb's major contributions are to the study of vocational students and to the study of the quality of teaching in community colleges. With respect to vocational students, Grubb finds community colleges to be clearly a democratizing influence, bringing students who would not otherwise have attended college into postsecondary education. He finds significant rewards for investments in human capital development, particularly for those who complete vocational programs and study subjects in which they are already employed. At the same time, he finds that many fields have marginal returns, that completion of twelve credit units or less brings insignificant rewards, and that most vocational programs have few links to employers and do not articulate well with the skills that employers want.

Grubb is critical of *The Diverted Dream* for seeming to disparage vocational curricula and for encouraging its continued stigmatization. But a careful reading of the book shows that Karabel and I did not disparage vocational training, only narrow forms of vocational education that do not connect students to public life and do not encourage their future opportunities for upward mobility. As we wrote,

> The problem with community college vocational education is not . . . that it attempts to connect the educational system with the world of work. On the contrary, (we believe) in the desirability of linking, where possible, the process of education to the activities of work and community. (Brint and Karabel 1989, 228)

The problem with our approach to vocational programs was empirical, not ideological. While no one disputes our argument that two-year vocational programs are neither economically nor socially equivalent to the bachelor's degree, new evidence does suggest that we were wrong to consider community college vocational education as "the bottom rung" of higher education's tracking system. Economic rewards tend to be greater for vocational students than for academic students, if they complete the associate's degree, and vocational students are now as likely as academic students to transfer to four-year colleges. At the same time, our concern that community colleges' emphasis on vocational education came at the expense of comparable support for a rigorous academic culture seems to be borne out by Grubb's own work—and the work of others who have studied these issues.

Grubb's emphasis on assessing positive and negative consequences extends to the little-studied topic of teaching and learning in the community college setting. In a study of 260 community college instructors from a wide range of fields, Grubb and Associates (1999) found that small classes typical of community colleges provide a potential support for the community colleges' claims to provide superior teaching. They provide many examples of excellence in student-centered (or, as they call it, "constructivist") teaching practices, the dominant approach in community colleges. These successful practices are attuned at once to high content standards and the busy lives and hands-on learning styles of many students. The chapter on vocational classrooms is particularly valuable, for it provides strong evidence of the relative vitality of occupational education. "For many fields, occupational teaching turns out to be rich and complex, more so than teaching in academic subjects" (Grubb and Associates 1999, 99). At the same time, they report "collapsed" standards in approximately one-quarter of the classrooms visited, including quite a few of the vocational classrooms visited (see also Worthen 1997). In these classrooms, content was converted into simplified facts and slogans, anecdote swapping was used as a replacement for serious discussion, and humor was employed as a substitute for problem solving (Grubb and Associates 1999, 218-29). Perhaps most worrisome is the buried finding that community college reading lists "very common(ly)" total one five-to-eight-page article a week and required essays were often two to four pages long. These low expectations arguably undermine the generally positive portrait of community college teaching found in the book. Moreover, practices related to literacy skills are especially uncommon in vocational courses, leaving students unprepared to meet the literacy expectations of their employers.

New structural critics. Regina Deil-Amen and James E. Rosenbaum provide a somewhat bleaker assessment of community colleges than either Dougherty or Grubb. Their image of community colleges follows the neoinstitutionalist model of public schools (Meyer and Rowan 1978). In this view, community colleges primarily provide credentials to students rather than concrete skills. These credentials are symbols that students deserve a certain status in society. These credentials are meaningful in the labor market, and the colleges do not, therefore, feel the need to help their students more directly by developing direct ties either to gatekeepers in four-year colleges or to employers in the labor market. Community colleges are, moreover, large and complex institutions, considerably understaffed, and their counseling staffs have relatively little time to offer to individual students. A culture of inclusiveness, reinforced by high dropout rates, has become the norm, and counselors are consequently reluctant to deliver unwelcome news to students. Counseling is used to encourage and build students' self-esteem, not to "cool out" students.

Deil-Amen and Rosenbaum make effective use of proprietary and private, nonprofit colleges in much of this work. In contrast to community colleges, proprietary schools have been subject to high levels of regulation since 1992, due to abuses of the financial aid system, leading to hundreds of closures. With their legitimacy in question, proprietary schools have worked hard to capture a student market, help students complete their programs, and find jobs for those who do complete. National Center for Education Statistics data suggests that proprietary colleges do a better job than community colleges in bringing students to certificate or degree completion (Futures Project 2000). Compared to community colleges, the culture of proprietary colleges is far more results oriented. Because the demographic characteristics of community college and two-year proprietary students are similar, the contrast between the two is particularly effective.[3]

Based on this contrast, Deil-Amen and Rosenbaum criticize community colleges for their failures in networking with employers and communicating with students. In their view, faith in the power of credentials too often substitutes for concrete social contacts. Although advisory committees exist on paper to link community college vocational programs and local employers, these advisory committees are usually moribund, according to Deil-Amen and Rosenbaum, and instructors are not expected to be involved in placing their students. Nor do community college instructors query employers concerning the kinds of skills and abilities they require. By contrast, instructors in proprietary colleges are expected to build and maintain ties with employers and to provide reliable information about the qualifications of particular students. Ironically, proprietary schools have developed mechanisms that allow them to place students more effectively than their higher-status public sector counterparts (Deil-Amen and Rosenbaum 2001).[4]

Proprietary schools also succeed more often in building students' "social know-how" because they tell students exactly what they need to do to complete programs and because they limit the number of course and program options available to students. By contrast, community college counselors expect students to shepherd themselves through a bewildering number of course and program options. Student confusion and frustration is tied to both the scarcity of effective counseling and the proliferation of programs (Deil-Amen and Rosenbaum 2003 [this issue]). Deil-Amen and Rosenbaum argue that self-esteem building has replaced "appropriate redirection" as the central ethos of counseling in community colleges. Today, counselors no longer use testing to redirect students into more "appropriate curricula." Instead, they seek to encourage students by accentuating the positive features of their records, however weak those records may be. Because they fail to provide honest assessments, counselors do not provide students with the information they need to improve. This too can encourage confusion and frustration (Deil-Amen and Rosenbaum 2002).

Deil-Amen and Rosenbaum base their conclusions on qualitative studies of programs in five community colleges and four occupational colleges (two proprietaries and two independent nonprofits) in the Chicago metropolitan area. Are these Chicago-area colleges representative of the national picture? Some doubts are raised in my mind by the colleges' apparent emphasis on academic transfer programs. Nevertheless, much of the analysis rings true. *The Diverted Dream* (Brint and Karabel 1989) also discussed the curious lack of interest of "career-oriented" community colleges in developing ties with local employers or studying their skill needs. Neoinstitutional theory provides a way to understand this otherwise puzzling oversight. The failure of the colleges to develop their students' social know-how meshes nicely with Dougherty's emphasis on the tensions created by program proliferation combined with tight resources. Deil-Amen and Rosenbaum's emphasis on the unintended consequences of the self-esteem culture is consistent with recent work on socialization messages in public schools (Brint, Contreras, and Matthews 2001).

Although Deil-Amen and Rosenbaum are clearly critics of the community colleges, the overall thrust of this work is at odds with *The Diverted Dream*. It assumes a world in which occupational training, far from representing the lowest rung in postsecondary education, has become a generator of student engagement and the center of labor market reward. The issue for them is not, as it was for Karabel and me, how to "heat up" students so that they can realize upward mobility through B.A. completion but rather how to help students who are not likely to complete their B.A.s to find their way more effectively into the world of work. Theirs is a world in which the job-related needs of employers are primary but not well understood (see also Rosenbaum and Binder 1997). Ours is a world in which promises of upward mobility are primary but not very often realized.[5]

The Revisionists Revised?

Thanks largely to the work of researchers discussed in this article, we have much more clarity now on several issues raised in *The Diverted Dream*. But has this new clarity substantially altered the portrait we drew of the community colleges?

In my view, not much of the picture drawn of community colleges in *The Diverted Dream* requires emendation. Our emphasis on the interests of four-year college leaders in the birth of junior colleges has not been seriously disputed. Neither has our emphasis on the advocacy of the AAJC as a force in the institutionalization of the two-year college concept. Our critique of consumer choice and business influence models as explanations for the vocationalization of community colleges has not been challenged. Most scholars accept our notion that the colleges, led by the AAJC, were themselves primarily responsible for this transformation, although Dougherty rightly amplifies on the interests and motives of influential state actors. Most scholars also accept our sense of the organizational interest behind this transformation, namely, the constraints on and opportunities for monopolization of training markets. Nor is our view of the largely supporting role played by foundations, the federal government, and corporations beginning in the 1960s in dispute.[6] Many empirical studies have confirmed our emphasis on the continuing advantage of bachelor's degrees over vocational associate's degrees. Many studies have also confirmed the declining condition of academic programs in community colleges and the advantages that four-year college students hold over community college students in obtaining bachelor's degrees, even after background and test scores are controlled. Our emphasis on the high dropout rates typical of community colleges has not been challenged. Nor has our argument that high levels of dropping out reflect, in part, the subordinate position of community colleges in the American system of higher education. Our concerns about the flexibility of vocational programs and about the high variability of labor market returns to these programs have been confirmed by subsequent scholarship.

A few images and assumptions of *The Diverted Dream* do, however, require revision based on contemporary research. The most important correction has to do with our image of vocational education. Our assumption in the mid-1980s was that vocational education represented the lowest rung in postsecondary education. Today, this characterization must be considered incorrect. Vocational programs may indeed draw more motivated students and more effective instructors than do academic programs. Certainly, their labor market returns are not worse than the returns to comparable levels of academic course work. Some programs, such as nursing and electronics technology, have shown strong returns. Nor are these programs less prestigious today in the eyes of students. Partly because of the emphasis on vocational training, academic programs have fallen on very hard times. Students who do not successfully transfer to four-year colleges from academic programs face relatively unpromising job prospects, even if they obtain an associate's degree. One cause of this change is the preference of employers for students with practical skills; another is the increasing proliferation of parallel occupational programs in four-year colleges.

It is important to be careful about how seriously this change affects the findings of *The Diverted Dream*. The historical argument about vocationalization is not affected, because vocational programs have only recently gained the status advantage over academic programs. In the book, Karabel and I were skeptical of the promises of vocational education, but our main argument was that associate's degrees in occupational fields were not comparable to bachelor's degrees, either in prestige or in immediate or long-term earnings. This conclusion is even more true today than it was in 1989 due to the increased earnings gap between college graduates and those with lower educational attainments.

While no one disputes . . . that two-year
vocational programs are neither economically
nor socially equivalent to the bachelor's degree,
new evidence does suggest that . . . vocational
education [is not] "the bottom rung" of
higher education's tracking system.

Our emphasis on diversion requires some revision. Recent work suggests, as we did, that community colleges both divert students from attending four-year colleges and bring students who would not otherwise attend college at all into the postsecondary system. In our efforts to balance the picture, we were perhaps too prone to emphasize the first effect over the second (see also Rouse 1995, 1998). The consensus among researchers today is that most students attending community colleges would not otherwise attend any postsecondary institution. Again, it is important to be careful in judging how seriously this finding undermines our argument. Most students who are the beneficiaries of this democratization effect of community colleges do not complete many units and, consequently, show only very small or negligible improvements in their job prospects.

Our emphasis on diversion may have hindered us from grasping the significance of new approaches to counseling emerging at the time of the book's publication. We may have been generally correct about the mechanisms used by counselors to encourage "realism" among the students in the years before the late 1980s, but times have changed. Instead of encouraging student realism, many counselors now attempt to build student self-esteem. "Soft landings," those that do not threaten students' self-confidence, are highly desired today, although no evidence exists that landing sites themselves have changed greatly. Students who need encouragement may gain a bit from this change; students who need clear information about where they stand may lose out.

Karabel and I developed a version of historical institutionalism to explain the origins and transformation of community colleges (Brint and Karabel 1991). This perspective remains valid, but it does not foreclose the contribution of other theoretical traditions. State theory, as employed by Dougherty, does, for example, help to fill in the sources of support for community colleges, although it tends to obscure the significance of intellectuals like Koos and Eells, who created conceptual models for the community college movement, and the role of the AAJC, which effectively promoted these models to state legislatures.

With respect to processes of organizational transformation, our analysis was clearly weighted toward power factors. Karabel and I emphasized the colleges' resource commitments, managerial techniques, and media images of changing labor market conditions as factors influencing student choices in the direction of vocational programs. I do not judge this to be a significant shortcoming. Dougherty's main point is that in an organization with multiple goals and limited resources, some goals are more likely to be effectively institutionalized than are others. Our emphasis on the resources and ideas available to vocationalizing leaders helps to explain why certain functions became more effectively institutionalized over time; Dougherty's Mertonian approach cannot. By contrast, the neoinstitutionalism employed by Deil-Amen and Rosenbaum does help to clear up one puzzle we were unable to solve, namely, why explicitly career-oriented institutions spend so little time developing close connections to employers. Like other organizations with well-institutionalized charters, community college leaders assume that the credentials they confer will carry weight in the market—and that no further actions are necessary to link students and jobs.

Human capital theory also makes an undeniable contribution to our understanding of the economic consequences of different levels and types of educational attainment. At the same time, it is prone to unscientific rationalizations in support of the status quo. Because outcomes are for human capital theorists, by definition, based on rational choices, whatever exists must somehow be rational. Therefore, outcomes that look like failings to many sociologists are generally interpreted by economists as successes. Economists' treatment of high community college dropout rates shows the difficulty. In their view, many students come to a community college and mill about searching for a life course. Some come to the conclusion that they are not college material and therefore choose not to invest further in the educational system. Economists interpret high dropout rates as the result of rational choices, which have a beneficial effect both for individuals (who are saved from unrewarding investments) and society (which saves potentially wasted resources).[7] From a sociological perspective, this analysis neglects the influence of social structure on individual decision making. What of the social class milieu and institutional climate in which community college students are embedded? It is very doubtful that such dim views of students' capacities for achievement would be taken seriously if they were addressed to higher-status people, many of whom have also been known to show signs of fecklessness on occasion.

Have Community Colleges Changed for the Better?

This leads to a final question: How much has changed in the community colleges since the mid-1980s? Have the colleges changed for the better, have their problems increased, or are the institutions still following the same course?

In terms of growth, community colleges remain, as we wrote, the great success story of American postsecondary education during the last century. Although they enroll less than half as many students as four-year institutions, they have continued to grow at a faster rate. More than 300 new community colleges have been added to the postsecondary landscape since 1989, compared to 235 four-year colleges (U.S. Department of Education 2002). For the high school class of 1982, community college dropouts and associate's degree holders made up nearly as large a segment of the "sub-baccalaureate labor market" as those with high school degrees only (34 percent to 39 percent) (Grubb 1996, 56).

The colleges have also succeeded on their own terms. They are now clearly vocationally oriented. Approximately 60 percent of community college students are enrolled in vocational programs, and a comparable number say that their major interest relates to occupational preparation. Short-term contract courses with local businesses are now found at nearly all community colleges, and half of the colleges have one contract student for every five regularly enrolled students (Kane and Rouse 1999). And of course, community colleges are very much a part of their communities in other ways as well. They offer a wide range of recreational and avocational courses, bringing together widely scattered individuals around common interests in such topics as digital photography, Web site design, Native American dances, and the history of jazz. These include an increasing number of emeritus colleges serving retirees.

Indeed, a good case can be made that the community colleges have shown the face of the future to American four-year colleges much more than have the traditional Ivy League leaders in this sector. Increasingly, four-year colleges, too, have emphasized occupational programs, worked to accommodate part-time and nontraditional students through flexible scheduling and distance education, and reached out to their communities through extension classes and service to local business, government, and nonprofit organizations (Brint 2002).

Yet it is difficult to see the community colleges as stronger today than they were when we finished our research on them in the mid-1980s. A basic flaw in the human capital argument, as it applies to community colleges, is that noncompletion rates continued to grow and transfer to decline at a time when, using high school graduates as a reference group, the premium for a bachelor's degree among full-time workers ages twenty-five to thirty-four was growing from 40 to 60 percent (Ellwood and Kane 2000). Transfer rates have picked up in some states recently, but academic programs have apparently continued to deteriorate as institutional energy has shifted more decisively to the vocational tracks.[8] Few community colleges offer academic course work beyond the introductory level, and the concept of weekly assignments has been reduced to a bare minimum in many classes.

Faculty work conditions at many of the colleges have also deteriorated. Almost two-thirds of the faculty at public two-year colleges teach part-time, twice as many as at four-year comprehensives. Forty percent of community college faculty hold a rank of instructor or lecturer, and more than 10 percent have no rank, five times as many as at four-year comprehensives (U.S. Department of Education 2002). These

---

The major contradiction remains that community college students desire higher-level attainments than the colleges are able to help them realize. Under such circumstances, the community college cannot help but play the midwife to humbler dreams.

---

high proportions of adjuncts, in all likelihood, reduce institutional identification among instructors and perhaps also traditions of collegiality and shared governance. Two-year college faculty are much more likely than four-year faculty to be unionized (Rhoades 1998). Moreover, a study of student performance in sequential courses suggests that adjuncts are less effective in introductory courses than full-time instructors (Burgess and Samuels 1999). Community colleges claim to be teaching centered, but they usually do not provide support for good teaching. Most students come to community college with weak literacy skills, but literacy-building practices are uncommon (Worthen 1997).

Stratification has also increased. Between 1980-1982 and 1992, the proportion of students from the lowest income quartile who enrolled in community colleges increased by 6 percent (from 16 to 22 percent), while it declined very slightly in four-year colleges. The proportion enrolling from the highest income quartile stayed constant in two-year colleges (at just less than 20 percent), while it increased from 55 to 65 percent in four-year colleges (Ellwood and Kane 2000, 286). Family income has a strong effect on the distribution of students with similar test scores between two- and four-year colleges (Ellwood and Kane 2000; Kane 2001). Most college students today work while they attend school, but community colleges have become the primary home for part-time and older students. Today, two-thirds of community college students attend part-time. About one-half say that work is their primary focus, not school, compared to one-quarter of four-year college students (Horn, Becktold, and Malizio 1998).

Given the community colleges' emphasis on occupational training and the job-advancement interests of these student-workers, it is not surprising that vocational programs appear to be in good shape compared to academic programs. And yet even here, the situation may be not quite as rosy as it first appears due to changes in market conditions for subbaccalaureate labor. Instability and low-wage work (defined as earnings of less than $11 per hour in 1999 dollars) have increased markedly in the labor market, and this rise of unstable, low-wage work has hit workers with "some college" experience hard. According to Bernhardt et al. (2001),

> Those with the least amount of schooling, a high school diploma or less, have seen a strong rise in low-wage careers, more than doubling from 14.4% in the . . . cohort [that came of age in the mid and late 1960s] to 35.3% in the more recent cohort. Workers with some college experience were hit just as hard in proportionate terms—their percentage of low-wage workers more than doubled—from 10.5% to 25.4%. (P. 157)[9]

One result is that workers with some college—including the two-thirds of community college entrants who do not complete an associate's or bachelor's degree—now look more like high school graduates in their earnings profile than like college graduates.

Semiprofessional jobs tied to high-tech, medical, and business services are faring well, by and large, but most semiprofessional jobs are not tied to these sectors. Overall, the new economy looks less like Silicon Valley than Wal-Mart Valley. It is composed of more low-wage, unstable jobs in retail and other service industries, most of which are not unionized and carry minimal benefits. As Bernhardt and her colleagues (2001) concluded,

> Economic mobility has deteriorated in this new economy, so that workers now face the prospect of more limited and more unequal wage growth from ages 16 to 36. Job instability has also risen in recent years and this rising instability appears to play an important role in explaining mobility trends. (P. 174)

Community colleges' problems come into sharper relief if we look at the interaction of three structural characteristics: (1) the centrality of occupational training programs, (2) the weak academic preparation and part-time status of most community college students, and (3) the public collegiate identity of the colleges (including required general education courses and academic-transfer tracks). General education courses are required for all students, but they are difficult for students with weak academic skills and complicated schedules to complete. Difficulties in satisfying general education requirements, therefore, become an important source of structural blockage. Because transfer, vocational, and recreational users each have different needs and interests, instructors in general education classes have trouble knowing how to orient their classes. As a solution, many instructors lower standards in an effort to increase interest among vocational and recreational students and to reduce dropout. Whatever prophylactic effects this may have, this strategy fails to provide university-level instruction for prospective transfer students, thereby increasing the incidence of transfer shock. By contrast, occupational courses are popular but often do not often include the literacy-building activities that most students need. Not surprisingly, evidence is beginning to accumulate that the reformed, results-oriented proprietary schools are doing the better job of occupational preparation for job-oriented students, while residential four-year colleges continue to do a better job of academic teaching for comparable students aspiring to the B.A. The low cost and convenience of community colleges make them attractive, but their combination of multiple goals, limited resources, academically marginal students, and hefty general education requirements make them effective for only a relative few of those who enter with a degree objective in mind.

Let us assume that the goals of community colleges are to provide college-level transfer work for those students intending to transfer to four-year institutions and occupational training that will facilitate mobility for those students who are not intending to transfer. When institutional leaders persistently fail to achieve their stated goals, it is time to wonder whether the real interests served by the institution are those stated or something else. Perhaps community colleges serve democratic, capitalist societies very well by failing to achieve their stated purposes. Perhaps these societies would not be as well served if, let's say, half of community college students received bachelor's degrees, rather than the current 16 percent. How many B.A.-level jobs, after all, does the economy produce? Perhaps the jobs available to community college vocational students do not generally include job ladders. How important are high-level cognitive skills—the kinds of skills that allow for significant mobility—if job ladders are scarce? From this perspective, the high community college dropout rate may not be a problem; it may even be a benefit to the economy. The colleges can say, "We gave them another chance." And the economy is not required to absorb tens of thousands more educated workers than it has places for.

A question remains whether the failure of community colleges is due to social circumstances of students (i.e., their complicated lives and relatively weak academic preparation), to the lack of incentives for policy makers and business leaders to create more effective institutions, or to the organizational problems of the colleges themselves. No doubt all three are important and mutually reinforcing. The major contradiction remains that community college students desire higher-level attainments than the colleges are able to help them realize. Under such circumstances, the community college cannot help but play the midwife to humbler dreams.

An observer might conclude that the colleges would achieve their stated purposes more often if they were divided into three separate institutions: one using the techniques of the reformed proprietaries for purposes of job training, one linked as two-year branches of four-year colleges for purposes of academic transfer, and one projecting a community center approach for purposes of providing recreational courses. Yet such a differentiation is very unlikely to occur. Community colleges provide a maximum of perceived opportunities, and they do so at a minimum of cost. Moreover, many interests are vested in the continuation of the colleges, even if they do not work very well, and bigger institutions do enjoy certain economies of scale.

The Potential Contribution of Educational Reforms

The location of community colleges within the larger structure of American postsecondary education ensures that many of the problems discussed in this article will continue. Well-designed state and institutional policies can provide only partial solutions to the key problems of high dropout rates, low transfer rates, and uneven success in occupational training programs. Nevertheless, partial solutions are better than no solutions. In this last section of the article, I would like to draw attention to some of the more promising policies that have been developed by states and community colleges in recent years. I will also discuss some social scientific inquiries that would be valuable to future policy development.

Dropout and transfer. To help their students become better-informed consumers, community colleges might be required to post retention, transfer, and degree completion rates for their students four and five years after entry, comparing their own rates to those of other community colleges in their state and to national rates. These rates would be listed with estimates, based on state data, of the proportion of noncompleters and nontransfers who complete or transfer after moving to other institutions. If possible, these rates should be given by socioeconomic status, race/ethnicity, and gender. The difficulty with this proposal is that community colleges generally do not have the resources to conduct accurate follow-up studies. States would have to invest considerable funds and training time for such statistics to be collected effectively.

Even in the absence of funds to provide this comsumer information, community colleges could attempt to simplify requirements for degree-granting programs. In addition, mandatory meetings of those declaring for particular academic transfer and vocational programs could be held at least twice a year to discuss course-taking requirements for these programs. This would help to provide the social know-how that Deil-Amen and Rosenbaum find to be in such short supply among community college students.

Financial aid policies could also be improved. Because low-income and minority students are averse to taking out loans for fear of the financial burden they create, income-contingent financial aid policies can be developed to scale loan repayment amounts and timing to adult income attainments. Such plans have been proposed by respected economists, such as William Bowen, but they have not been implemented. State experiments with such policies would be welcome.

Current studies of structural diversity in the community college sector have rarely yielded definitive results. However, one clear finding appears to be that transfer rates are higher in states that have formalized and explicit articulation agreements between two-year and four-year colleges (Keith 1996). Efforts to establish such agreements in those states that currently do not have them could help boost transfer. This requires considerable cross-segment cooperation, which appears to be easier in states with state higher education coordinating boards (Keith 1996). The size and organization of the two-year and four-year sectors may also affect dropout and transfer rates, and these also vary considerably by state. So far, studies of state variation have not been conclusive. More studies should be conducted of the relationship between the size of the two-year and four-year sectors and B.A. production by state, controlling for factors such as per capita income, tuition and fees, and student demographics. In these comparisons, the differences between states with two-year branches of four-year institutions and those with separate community college systems should be a particular focus (see Dougherty 1994).

Vocational programs. Like dropout and transfer rates, placement rates in occupational programs should ideally be available to students. Some states require that colleges report placement rates, but these rates are reported to policy makers, not to students. A careful examination of the methodology of states requiring placement reports would be valuable. Follow-up surveys with students are not very reliable, and it is unlikely that many colleges have the resources to conduct such surveys very well. Nevertheless, several states have developed policies to monitor placement. Florida and Idaho both require proof of placement rates in the 70 to 75 percent level. Programs that fail to achieve this level of placement are subject to elimination. Tennessee reserves 5 percent as an incentive bonus for institutions with high placement rates (Grubb 1996, 106). Policies such as these, if they are based on reliable data (a big if), would improve the capacity of institutions to respond to changes in labor market demand for different fields.

Occupational programs are frequently more costly than academic programs. A number of states now provide differential funding for programs with different costs, either based on formulae or through negotiated budgeting. These efforts can improve performance by partially eliminating bias against high-cost programs (Grubb 1996, 106). Arum (1998) has found a relationship between higher graduation rates and higher levels of investment by states in vocational education at the secondary level. The connection between resources invested in occupational programs and educational outcomes should be investigated also at the postsecondary level. If higher levels of investment are strongly related to lower dropout rates, the case for higher base budgets would be substantially strengthened.

Deil-Amen and Rosenbaum (2001), among others, have suggested that proprietaries may be outperforming community colleges in recent years. More systematic studies of the relative performance of the two sectors would be valuable, given the possibility that their case studies are not representative. If Deil-Amen and Rosenbaum are correct, however, community college leaders should be looking more closely at the proprietaries for ways to improve their performance in occupational training and placement. One advantage of the proprietaries discussed by Deil-Amen and Rosenbaum needs no further study. It seems clear enough that institutional policies to encourage linkage between instructors and local employers would be helpful. At the moment, within community colleges, these linkages are haphazard and fortuitous for the most part. New policies might, for example, include a merit pay category for instructors who devote time to interviewing local employers and engaging in placement-related activities.

Notes

1. For an excellent study of alternative definitions of transfer students, see Bradburn and Hurst (2002).

2. Specific fields within these broad categories may be particularly highly valued in the labor market. Studies cited in Phillippe (2000) find particularly high rates of return, for example, in the following programs: digital systems, facilities technology and maintenance, manufacturing process technology, dental hygiene, and nursing.

3. For a useful overview of the history of proprietary schools and their relations with community colleges, see the articles in Clawes and Hawthorne (1995).

4. This theme of differences between charter and network-organized labor markets has a parallel in the work of Maurice, Sellier, and Silvestre (1986). Maurice and his colleagues compare the French charter system with the German network system and come to similar conclusions about the superiority of the network-organized system.

5. *The Diverted Dream* (Brint and Karabel 1989) roots these promises in the public character of community colleges and ultimately in the ideals of a democratic-republican polity. The public character of community colleges remains highly relevant, in my view, both for purposes of perspective and as a subject of empirical investigation. Empirically, community college attendance appears, for example, to be associated with higher levels of civic engagement than proprietary school attendance among otherwise comparable students (Persell and Wenglinsky 2002).

6. Foundations have continued to play an important, though contradictory, role in recent years. The Ford Foundation, for example, has funded studies of community colleges with high transfer rates, while the Sloan Foundation has funded projects aimed at encouraging the rationalization of community college activities in a direction compatible with business interests and practices.

7. Community college leaders have long proposed a number of similar explanations for high dropout rates: students choose alternative pathways through college, stopping out, temporarily dropping out, or switching between a variety of schools as they go along. No doubt, this is empirically true for many students today (see Adelman 1995). The conclusions drawn from this empirical truth, however, depend on the observer. Where economists see signs of hidden rationality in students' lack of clarity or motivation, educators see a chance to clarify and motivate, and sociologists see structural barriers that can, at least at times, be overcome.

8. Some exceptions exist to this trend in the deterioration of the academic transfer function. For useful case studies of academically oriented community colleges in urban areas, see Shaw and London (2001) and Roueche, Roueche, and Ely (2001).

9. The study addresses changes in the labor market between the early 1980s and the early and mid-1990s. It compares the work experiences of two cohorts from the National Longitudinal Studies—one aged twenty-eight to thirty-six in 1981 and another aged twenty-eight to thirty-six in 1994.

References

Adelman, Clifford. 1995. *A new college course map and transcript files.* Washington, DC: U.S. Department of Education.

Arum, Richard. 1998. Invested dollars or diverted dreams? The effect of resources on vocational students' educational outcomes. *Sociology of Education* 71:130-51.

Bernhardt, Annette, Martina Morris, Mark S. Handcock, and Marc A. Scott. 2001. *Divergent paths: Economic mobility in the new American labor market.* New York: Russell Sage.

Bradburn, Ellen M., and David G. Hurst. 2002. Community college transfer rates to 4-year institutions using alternative definitions of transfer. *Education Statistics Quarterly* (fall): 1-9.

Brint, Steven. 2002. The rise of the "practical arts." In *The future of the city of intellect: The changing American university,* edited by Steven Brint, 231-59. Stanford, CA: Stanford University Press.

Brint, Steven, Mary F. Contreras, and Michael T. Matthews. 2001. Socialization messages in primary schools: An organizational analysis. *Sociology of Education* 74:157-80.

Brint, Steven, and Jerome Karabel. 1989. *The diverted dream: Community colleges and educational opportunity in America, 1900-1985.* New York: Oxford University Press.

———. 1991. Institutional origins and transformations: The case of American community colleges. In *The new institutionalism in organizational studies,* edited by Walter W. Powell and Paul J. DiMaggio, 311-36. Chicago: University of Chicago Press.

Burgess, Larry A., and Carl Samuels. 1999. Impact of full-time versus part-time instructor status on college student retention and academic performance in sequential courses. *Community College Journal of Research and Practice* 32:487-98.

Clawes, Darrel A., and Elizabeth M. Hawthorne, eds. 1995. *New directions for community colleges.* San Francisco: Jossey-Bass.

Deil-Amen, Regina, and James E. Rosenbaum. 2001. How can low-status colleges help young adults gain access to better jobs? Applications of human capital v. sociological models. Paper presented at the annual meeting of the American Sociological Association. Anaheim, CA, August.

———. 2002. The unintended consequences of stigma-free remediation. *Sociology of Education* 75:249-68.

———. 2003. What social know-how do colleges require and can college structure reduce the need for it? *Annals of the American Academy of Political and Social Science,* 586: 120-43.

DiMaggio, Paul, and Walter W. Powell. 1983. The iron cage revisited: Institutional isomorphism and collective rationality in organizational fields. *American Sociological Review* 48:147-60.

Dougherty, Kevin J. 1987. The effects of community colleges: Aid or hindrance to socioeconomic attainment? *Sociology of Education* 60:86-103.

———. 1994. *The contradictory college: The conflicting origins, impacts, and futures of the community college.* Albany: State University of New York Press.

Ellwood, David, and Thomas J. Kane. 2000. Who is getting a college education? Family background and the growing gaps in enrollment. In *Securing the future: Investing in children from birth to college,* edited by Sheldon Danzinger and Jane Waldfogel, 283-324. New York: Russell Sage.

Futures Project. 2000. *Policy for higher education in a changing world: A briefing on for-profit higher education.* Providence, RI: Futures Project.

Grubb, W. Norton. 1993. The varied economic returns to postsecondary education: New evidence from the class of 1972. *Journal of Human Resources* 28:365-82.

———. 1995. Postsecondary education and the sub-baccalaureate labor market: Corrections and extensions. *Economics of Education Review* 14:285-99.

———. 1996. *Working in the middle.* San Francisco: Jossey-Bass.

———. 1997. The returns to education in the sub-baccalaureate labor market, 1984-1990. *Economics of Education Review* 16:231-45.

Grubb, W. Norton, and Associates. 1999. *Honored but invisible: An inside look at teaching in community colleges*. New York: Routledge.

Horn, Laura J., Jennifer Berktold, and Andrew G. Malizio. 1998. *Profile of undergraduates in U.S. postsecondary education institutions: 1995-96*. Washington, DC: National Center for Education Statistics.

Kane, Thomas J. 2001. Assessing the U.S. financial aid system: What we know, what we need to know. In *Ford policy forum: Exploring the economics of higher education*. New York: Ford Foundation.

Kane, Thomas J., and Cecilia Elena Rouse. 1995. Labor market returns to two- and four-year college. *American Economic Review* 85:600-14.

———. 1999. The community college: Educating students at the margin between college and work. *Journal of Economic Perspectives* 13:63-84.

Keith, Bruce. 1996. The context of educational opportunity: States and the legislative organization of community college systems. *American Journal of Education* 105:67-101.

Maurice, Marc, Francois Sellier, and Jean-Jacques Silvestre. 1986. *The social foundations of industrial power*. Cambridge, MA: MIT Press.

Meyer, John W., and Brian Rowan. 1978. In *Environments and organizations*, edited by Marshall Meyer and Associates, 78-109. San Francisco: Jossey-Bass.

Persell, Caroline Hodges, and Harold Wenglinsky. 2002. For-profit post-secondary education and civic engagement. Unpublished paper, Department of Sociology, New York University.

Phillippe, Kent A., ed. 2000. *National profile of community colleges*, 3d ed. Washington, DC: American Association of Community Colleges.

Rhoades, Gary. 1998. *Managed professionals: Unionized faculty and restructured academic labor*. Albany: State University of New York Press.

Rosenbaum, James E., and Amy Binder. 1997. Do employers really need more educated youth? *Sociology of Education* 70:68-85.

Roueche, John E., Susanne D. Roueche, and Eileen E. Ely. 2001. Challenge of the heart: Pursuing excellence at the community college of Denver. *Community College Journal of Research and Practice* 71 (3): 30-34.

Rouse, Cecilia Elena. 1995. Democratization or diversion? The effect of community colleges on educational attainment. *Journal of Business Economics and Statistics* 13:217-24.

———. 1998. Do two-year colleges increase overall educational attainment? Evidence from the states. *Journal of Policy Analysis and Management* 17:595-620.

Shaw, Kathleen M., and Howard B. London. 2001. The role of culture and ideology in maintaining a commitment to educational mobility via transfer: Case studies of three community colleges. *Review of Higher Education* 25:91-114.

U.S. Department of Education. 2002. *Digest of education statistics, 2002*. Washington, DC: National Center for Education Statistics.

Worthen, Helena H. 1997. Signs and wonders: The negotiation of literacy in community college classrooms. Paper presented at the annual meeting of the American Educational Research Association, Chicago, April.

The Demand-Response Scenario: Perspectives of Community College Presidents

PATRICIA J. GUMPORT

Community colleges are often characterized as the segment of U.S. public higher education most responsive to environmental demands. During the past two decades of the twentieth century, community colleges faced expectations to expand their purposes beyond transfer and occupational education, to serve employers' needs for training, and to accommodate more students in need of basic skills. Drawing on focus group data, this article examines what community college presidents characterize as the demand-response scenario for their colleges, the ways they work within it, and how they seek to move beyond it. The analysis focuses on their accounts of appropriate organizational responses, showing how institutional logics embedded in the wider context allowed for a range of legitimate responses yet also fostered ambiguity about their identity and societal role.

Keywords: community colleges; presidents; environmental demands; institutional logic; public higher education

Community colleges have long been seen as the solution to an ever-changing set of societal expectations for American higher education. External pressures have emanated from national, state, and local levels as well as from K-12 education and four-year colleges and universities. Throughout the twentieth century, community colleges in the aggregate have responded. They have extended their activities beyond the twofold mission of preparing students for transfer to four-year colleges and universities and for occupations. Today, community colleges offer a variety of credit and noncredit

Patricia J. Gumport is an associate professor of education at Stanford University. She serves concurrently as director of the Stanford Institute for Higher Education Research and executive director of the National Center for Postsecondary Improvement.

NOTE: I received helpful comments on a draft from Michael Bastedo, Bernadine Chuck Fong, John Jennings, Stuart Snydman, and the editors. Judy Dauberman and John Jennings provided research assistance. The study was supported by a grant from the Educational Research and Development Center program of the U.S. Department of Education.

DOI: 10.1177/0002716202250210

courses not only as preparation for transfer and careers but also for remedial education, customized training and certification, general education, and other areas of interest to local communities.

Indeed, of all segments of public higher education, community colleges have been characterized as most responsive to external pressures. The general pattern of swift adjustment to legislative, employer, community, and student demands has been facilitated by a legacy of service that allowed for a multitude of interpretations over time (Gumport 2001). The result is a heterogeneous landscape of more than 1,100 community colleges, enrolling students with a wide range of skills and interests, and maintaining organizational structures that have been among the more flexible and varied in higher education.[1] While responsiveness has been a source of pride among community college leaders throughout the twentieth century, it has been accompanied by persistent ambiguity in terms of the mission—who should be served, and how?

Some community college leaders and researchers have raised pointed questions about the presumption that community colleges should do whatever is asked of them. One concern is that community colleges are cast as unduly passive, presumed to acquiesce to the demands of their many constituencies. In demonstrating eagerness to diversify their activities based on changing demands, community colleges appear to lack a central core. A related concern questions the cumulative effects of responsiveness. Pragmatically, incremental adjustments result in a fragmentation that hinders organizational effectiveness (Bailey and Averianova 1998). Beyond operational considerations, at stake are profound consequences for the identity of the community college as an educational institution. Observers worry that the increased prominence of terminal training programs and noncredit courses is detrimental to the transfer function and detracts from the liberal arts curriculum that constitutes lower-division undergraduate education (Dougherty 2002; Eaton 1994, 1995). Others question whether access to community colleges should even be seen as access to higher education; rather than facilitating upward mobility as "democracy's colleges," critics assert, community colleges reproduce social and economic inequalities (Karabel 1972; Brint and Karabel 1989; Dougherty 1994). From this perspective, a cumulative effect of responses to contemporary demands is to further weaken the role of the community college as a key entry point for higher education.

As evidence potentially mitigating these concerns, researchers have captured some of the characteristics and effects of today's community colleges. One line of research shows that both students and employers reap substantial benefits from expanded vocational and technical skill training programs (Grubb 1999). In addition, by providing workforce training, the community colleges themselves gain essential financial and political support from state and local funders as well as from business leaders (Grubb et al. 1997; Dougherty 2002). Another line of inquiry documents that the distinction between courses for training and courses for transfer has become blurred since some technical programs include transferable units (Townsend 2001). Finally, there is evidence that community colleges show no decline in commitment to the liberal arts. Data on associate's degree and prebaccalaureate certificate production in 1998 show that liberal arts fields represent a larger share than they did in 1980.[2] Moreover, initiatives to offer baccalaureate degrees in a viable market niche (Levin 2002) signal that some community colleges aim to extend their reach to upper levels of higher education rather than secede from it.

These disparate accounts substantiate the need to explore further community colleges' responses to contemporary environmental pressures. Two questions in particular warrant attention both for their theoretical foundation and their practical significance: How do community college leaders perceive the pressures brought to bear on their colleges and the options that are available to them? What are the implications of these changing pressures and organizational responses for the identity of the community college as an educational institution?

. . . [T]here is uncertainty over which organizational priorities and practices to pursue, given multiple external pressures and a range of behaviors among successful peers.

From a sociological perspective, community colleges can be understood as organizations situated within a wider institutional environment that defines their goals and prescribes the means by which goals are determined and legitimately pursued. In highly institutionalized environments, organizations that align with external pressures enhance their prospects for long-term survival (Scott 2001). The concept of institutional logic, drawn from neoinstitutional theory, provides a powerful lens for understanding how widely shared beliefs and values are embedded in multiple levels external to organizations yet are also enacted locally to obtain legitimacy. As defined by Friedland and Alford (1991, 248) and developed by Scott et al. (2000), institutional logic refers to "a set of material practices and symbolic constructions—which constitutes its organizing principles and which is available to organizations and individuals to elaborate." Accounts by organizational actors make evident the prevailing logic that constrains or enables their organization to undertake particular priorities and practices within parameters set by the wider environment.[3] Although a logic is structurally embedded, it may have historical limits and thus the potential to change.

In my current work, I apply the concept of institutional logic to examine continuity and change in public higher education.[4] I propose that the last quarter of the twentieth century was an era of transition in which two dominant logics were in use in public colleges and universities (Gumport 2002). Specifically, I argue that an industry logic gained momentum at the macro level, supplementing and in some circumstances becoming a viable alternative to a social institution logic. An industry logic puts a premium on economic priorities, valuing most highly those contributions that directly strengthen the economy and organizational practices that attend to market forces. Entrepreneurial initiatives, strategic thinking, cultivating new revenue sources, and managerial authority are organizational behaviors that move to the foreground as suitable solutions to external pressures. This logic is also evident when economic costs and benefits are invoked as driving decision making about program offerings (what to create, consolidate, or eliminate and based on what criteria). Several political and economic conditions have contributed to the ascendance of an industry logic: increased public and legislative scrutiny with performance-oriented mandates to demonstrate efficiency and productivity, increased competition at the state level for public funds, the growing legitimacy of market forces to reshape the priorities and practices of nonprofit organizations and government agencies, and the emergence of academic management as a professional class and ideology (Gumport 2000).

In contrast, a social institution logic casts public higher education as primarily an educational enterprise, serving the changing educational needs of the nation-state in addition to a broader spectrum of related functions, such as enabling upward mobility, providing the means for occupational advancement, socializing citizens, fostering critical thinking and intellectual pluralism, and transmitting the nation's intellectual and cultural heritages. Public colleges and universities show signs of this logic in material or symbolic commitments that display educational and civic values. While both logics acknowledge an institutional interdependence between the educational system and the economy, they espouse divergent priorities and value sets. An industry logic circumscribes purposes and practices within an economic rationality, while a social institution logic enables the legitimate pursuit of a broader range of activities under the rubric of educational and democratic interests.

With two dominant logics in use for public higher education, there are alternative bases of legitimacy with regard to both means and ends. Thus, organizational leaders face a context of ambiguity that poses both a challenge and an opportunity. On one hand, there is uncertainty over which organizational priorities and practices to pursue, given multiple external pressures and a range of behaviors among successful peers. On the other hand, the availability of two logics permits organizational actors to invoke more than one vocabulary and value set, as they pursue what is possible within wider institutional parameters. From this perspective, it is worth examining the conditions in which one or more logics came into use, as well as the dynamics between coexisting logics. As a first step, my aim in this article is to demonstrate the more general pattern of two logics in use, how they manifest and how they diverge. I analyze focus group data for the ways in which community college presidents depict environmental pressures alongside their organizations' objectives and activities. The analysis will show organizational actors invoking educational values from a social institution logic in contexts where an industry logic dominates. In addition to being of interest conceptually, the analysis has practical significance for community colleges—to consider the pressures that constrain them, the options that are available to them, and what these changing pressures and responses imply for community colleges' role in society.

Community Colleges in a Changing Context

To provide some context for the study, I sketch the changing contours of community colleges. During the first half of the twentieth century, two-year colleges provided transfer and career education, enhancing access to higher education by making education available locally and at low cost. In the post–World War II period, federal initiatives, such as the GI Bill and the Truman Commission on Higher Education, contributed to the transformation of junior colleges into community colleges, signaling additional expectations to serve their local communities. During the 1950s and especially the 1960s, dramatic increases in enrollments and the founding of community colleges reflected pressures to extend access to higher education for returning veterans and new segments of the population. Community colleges expanded and diversified their vocational programs and began to play a central role in training the workforce.[5] Yet they continued to offer lower-division undergraduate courses that enabled transfer to four-year colleges and universities as well as general education courses as preparation for civic life. During the last quarter of the twentieth century, two additional expectations crystallized. Community colleges were looked upon to meet new training demands, as the economy shifted from defense-related work to new industries (e.g., computer technologies) valued in the knowledge economy. They were also expected to expand instruction in basic skills to students who were not ready for college. While the emphasis among these purposes varied from one college to another, by the end of the century, the mission of community colleges had changed.

Contemporary observers tend to characterize the decades of the 1980s and 1990s as an era of increased and rapidly changing demands for public higher education (Gumport 2001). However, relative to the decades of dramatic expansion following World War II, this period for community colleges shows remarkably less enrollment growth and fewer new colleges.[6] Nonetheless, other measures of change are noteworthy, particularly heightened economic pressures and pointed expectations to meet directly the training needs of industry. Both of them added momentum to the ascendance of what I call an industry logic.

In terms of finances for community colleges in the aggregate, state appropriations as a proportion of total revenue declined from 48 percent in 1980 to 34 percent in 1995 (National Center for Education Statistics 1980, 1995). The decline for all public higher education was slightly less, from 44 percent in 1981 to 32 percent in 1997 (National Center for Education Statistics 2001). An equally revealing trend shows not only that community colleges have received the lowest state funding per full-time equivalent student of all levels of public higher education but that this already-low funding level declined by 6 percent between 1975 and 1995 (Gumport and Jennings 1999).[7]

These conditions and changes notwithstanding, community colleges have been faring well in the eyes of employers and legislators. As one indicator, according to the National Employers Survey conducted in 2000, 96 percent of employers found the community college graduates they hired to be at least somewhat prepared or better, and 41 percent of them found them to be either well prepared or very well prepared for employment (Institute for Research on Higher Education 2002). A recent study indicated that state legislator views of community colleges' performance are similarly positive, with high marks for developing new programs and making curricular changes that are "in tune" with business and industry (Ruppert 2001, 12-13).

[T]he challenge needs to be reframed from one of keeping up with changing demands to considering which demands need to be heeded under what circumstances.

One explanation for the satisfaction expressed by employers and elected officials is that community colleges have contributed to workforce development, economic development, and community development (Grubb et al. 1997). Training activities in particular have gained greater visibility in recent years, with community colleges offering courses in specific skills needed for growing industries, such as applied health and information technology.[8] Community colleges have even provided training directly for employees of specific companies, including certificates in networking and data communications, telecommunications, and programming for Microsoft, Cisco, Novell, and Oracle.[9] More than 90 percent of community colleges have taken on contract education—also referred to as contract training and customized training—which is usually fee based and generates revenue from private companies (Dougherty and Bakia 2000). When such courses are open to the public, whether or not they are offered for credit, the college can count the enrollment toward their state funding. In addition to these activities, some community colleges have extended their economic development role to offer small business assistance (e.g., advice, training, space) and to help with local economic planning (Dougherty and Bakia 2000).

Even as community colleges have expanded these activities, much to the satisfaction of employers and legislators, community college leaders report that economic and political pressures compel them to search further for cost savings and new revenue from nonstate sources.[10] The increased weight given to these objectives has sparked concern among both community college leaders and researchers about this trajectory and its potentially detrimental effects. They have questioned the educational value and quality of these new activities and whether they negatively affect transfer rates, general education, and the perception of community colleges as a site of lower-division undergraduate education.[11] The time is ripe for taking stock of these incremental adjustments, not only the array of programmatic and management practices that community colleges are expected to undertake but also what their responses signal about the character of the enterprise. Has the expansion of short-term training activities for companies become part of the core mission? Have courses in basic skills and English as a second language become major functions? Are these activities appropriate for the ways they develop the workforce and strengthen the economy or because they are consonant with educational values and the societal imperative to extend access to higher education? Under what conditions are these value sets compatible or in conflict? While beyond the scope of this article, these are the types of questions that can be explored for all segments of higher education.

Presidents' Perspectives

I now turn to the focus groups with community college presidents to illustrate how they have perceived and responded to the changing expectations of the 1980s and 1990s. Presidents are in a key position to depict pressures on their organizations as well as how their organizations consider what is feasible and appropriate.[12] My data derive from an exploratory study in which I conducted five, day-long focus groups with thirty public college and university presidents. I used a semistructured protocol to obtain their perceptions of environmental demands, organizational responses, and ensuing consequences.[13]

The presidents identified a wide array of expectations from external groups, including the presumption that the community colleges will adapt. Legislators and employers look to community colleges to train the workforce, and companies seek instruction in specific skills so their employees will be more productive. Policy makers look to community colleges to provide remedial education for underprepared students. Students of all ages assume community colleges will offer low-cost courses, whether basic skills or credit courses eligible for degrees or transfer, in a wide range of fields such as foreign languages, biology, and computer science. Immigrants turn to community colleges as the gateway to society, to provide the language skills they need to survive and get a job. This is what the community college presidents characterize as the demand-response scenario.

A key reason why community colleges are seen as demand driven is the presumption that they are money driven, not only in adapting to fluctuations in state funding but in seeking new revenue. As a president stated succinctly, "Money drives change. Community colleges will do what is asked and whatever sells."

Another president also attributed the motivation to acquire both public and private funds: "the stress on the organization is to survive economically. . . . It has brought an analysis within the college in terms of what is going to sell, so that we are designing programs to feed the demand."

However, several presidents proposed that simply meeting demands is not sufficient to satisfy their many constituencies. They pointed out that community colleges may attempt to do all that is asked of them, yet they are still open to criticism for not doing it well enough or fast enough. "They pay a price," reflected one president. One form of paying a price is that their role becomes filling in wherever a void is identified, whether it be training for a company or providing basic writing skills. Another price is hybridization. As one president said,

> There are a lot more opportunities in how you want to frame education within a community college. . . . We have a youth program on our campus, but we also offer postbaccalaureate certificates. We offer ESL classes. . . . And we are just now starting to help with professional development for teachers.

Declaring her college's intention to become involved in teacher professional development in the late 1990s, she attests to her college's eagerness to get on board with priorities on the public agenda, especially since other segments of higher education have not been quick to recognize their own obligation to help improve the quality of public schools. She noted that the flexibility to offer a wide range of activities may give the appearance of being unanchored: "It has to do with our being hybrids. We are part K-12 influenced and we are part traditional four-year institution. Who is in charge? Who has authority to guide us?" Here, *hybrid* refers to both their organizational form and their governance.

Extending the point that simply responding to demands is not enough, another president urged community college leaders not to accept the demands as givens:

> The philosophy of responsiveness, I submit, is inadequate. It is incomplete. . . . Individuals are responsible for guarding the values, and that is really difficult. That means you don't always yield to political pressure if you can survive. That means sometimes you say no to money, sometimes you are going to be a bad gal, or guy, or group of folks.

From her perspective, no doubt, being "bad" by saying "no to money" is more than offset by the good associated with "guarding the values." Other presidents concurred, and one identified several questions for them to consider:

> Are we going to say being demand-driven is adequate? . . . Are we going to be proponents of values? If we think there is something to preserve around certain general education values and the long-range public interest, then what do we need to do? We face the issue of what do we think is worth preserving and under what conditions.

In posing these questions, the presidents assert that the challenge needs to be reframed from one of keeping up with changing demands to considering which demands need to be heeded under what circumstances; rather than simply falling in line with whatever is feasible, they should be selective and question what is appropriate.

As the presidents reflected on changes in their colleges during the last two decades of the twentieth century, their discussions included numerous examples of the demand-response scenario and the ways they sought to move beyond it. They spoke of how the constellation of pressures at any specific time permits some leeway in how their organizations respond, yet there are also nonnegotiable constraints. In terms of response to pressures, the presidents offered instructional technology as an example of how community colleges are out in front, self-proclaimed gazelles who carefully monitor their surroundings and tap their agility to quickly reposition, in contrast to the dinosaur-like inertia of research universities. In terms of genuine constraints, they cited extensive regulations. One president characterized her situation in California:

> The UC system is governed by something like 700 or 800 statutes. CSU has 1,500. And the community colleges have 17,000! In spite of this heavy, heavy regulation, there are still ways to do things.... You know, how can we still get what we need and do it with the legislation or do it in spite of the legislation and ask, How out of the box can you be?

Acknowledging that their organizations are situated within such a regulatory environment, several presidents cast their stance as out of the box and themselves as entrepreneurs, while others spoke of the need for their organizations to be creative and weave together economic and political considerations with educational goals. Some presidents conveyed the challenge more dramatically and in more personal terms, calling on themselves as leaders to imagine goals and values not currently prescribed and to ignite discourse about them on their campuses.

It is not uncommon for presidents to define the terrain and articulate challenges in these terms. In fact, the higher education literature has reinforced the notion that colleges and universities, as well as their officials, pursue strategic responses. Research from the 1980s and 1990s reflects their potential to develop strategy (e.g., Cameron 1983; Keller 1983; Chaffee 1985; Hearn 1988), to manage environmental uncertainty and resource constraint (e.g., Leslie and Fretwell 1996; Gumport and Sporn 1999), and to respond to economic and political pressures through restructuring (Gumport and Pusser 1997, 1999). Extending this lens cross-nationally, Clark (1998, xvi) characterized case-study universities in Europe as facing "demand overload," resulting in "a deepening asymmetry between environmental demand and the institutional capacity to respond," in spite of the universities' efforts to be "aggressively entrepreneurial."

While the above works represent critically important lines of inquiry, they present an image of higher education organizations as engaged in formulating rational and informed responses to a changing mix of internal and external contingencies. How the institutional environment defines and legitimates this range of actions has received less attention. In the remainder of my data analysis, I apply the construct of institutional logic to show how the wider environment offered alternative rationales for framing what is demanded as well as what is possible, honorable, and necessary (Meyer and Rowan 1977; Meyer and Scott 1992). Within an industry logic, campuses are cast as purposeful actors, encouraged to make wiser choices and take risks. Yet in a social institution logic, the imperative to fulfill their responsibility as an educational institution underscores that higher education is expected to enact what is both morally and politically compelling in an age of unprecedented diversity and inequality. So in accentuating how American community colleges are embedded in wider belief systems, I propose that the presidents' self-ascribed potential for their organizations to move beyond the demand-response scenario points to the availability of more than one constellation of legitimate goals, rationales, and responses. Specifically, I suggest that the content of their accounts emanated from coexisting logics and, furthermore, that educational and civic values were invoked as a necessary corrective under conditions where an industry logic predominated. I support this interpretation with illustrations that emerged in their discussions of two domains: remedial education and workforce training.

The presidents identified a wide array of expectations from external groups, including the presumption that the community colleges will adapt.

External pressure to provide remedial education[14] increased during these two decades as more students were leaving high school without the basic math and literacy skills required for college-level work. Community colleges have had strong political and educational reasons to offer remedial courses to all who seek them since proficiency in basic skills is required for access to courses in general education, degree programs, and transfer programs. Yet some colleges put a cap on enrollments in remedial courses. Presidents offered two insights about this practice. One is that some campuses do not want their colleges overrun by students in these typically noncredit programs. Another is that certain resource allocation practices dictate a predetermined number of sections for remedial classes, even if they fill up weeks before registration closes.

At the same time, the presidents cited access as a democratic principle from which community colleges should not waver. The presidents made it clear that access to community colleges is assured by design—low-cost, open admissions. Disadvantaged students need not compete in the "sob story sweepstakes" that some have characterized selective admissions processes. However, they acknowledged, they could do more in "marketing and outreach to groups who do not know that community colleges are financially and academically accessible and convincing those who don't think that college is for them that the opportunity is available." Moreover, they suggested, their responsibility can go further than just to affirm or effect access, to asking whether they are providing "access to an education rather than access to enrollment." Admitting that community colleges are "easy entry, but also easy exit," they discussed mechanisms to "heighten retention, and even completion of single courses."

In reflecting on their organizations' options in responding to pressures for expanding remedial courses, the presidents identified access, educational value, and resources as primary concerns. As a case in point, a president identified how his community college set a limit on the number of times students can enroll in the same remedial course. It was the faculty that initiated this policy at his college, in the name of both limiting the time invested and better serving their students. As he recalled,

> We knew of people in our lowest tier of remedial work, semester after semester after semester, and they don't get anywhere. . . . The faculty—not the administration, not the board—the faculty came to the conclusion that there had to be a limit. That we could only invest a certain amount of time and that was it. . . . There was a need to not simply react to all of the social pressure to keep these folks around forever, but to say "No, we're an educational institution." When we are absolutely convinced we cannot produce educational gains, it is time for something else.

So at this president's college, the faculty asserted that access must be more sharply defined, perhaps even delimited by a mix of resource and educational considerations. If they were simply driven by resources, the matter would be clear, said another president who characterized the motive:

> Everybody should have a chance. And, if they can't make it, too bad, it is not my problem. I already got my full-time-equivalent paid by the state. And if I can keep them until the drop-out time, I still get the money.

Yet she quickly added that a revolving door was unsuitable beyond a point, educationally speaking:

> This door was revolving. At what point is that bad? It's bad to bring people in under the pretense of liberalism and then not provide the support mechanisms or the proper advice. . . . We should be able to say to some students "This is not the place for you."

The presidents indicated that community colleges can and should do more to foster dialogue about how students are served educationally, yet they noted strong political pressures on their colleges to expand remedial enrollments. They referred to major obstacles that reside in the politics of race and class in contemporary society and infuse wider debates about where and how remedial education should take place. Noting that remedial courses enroll large numbers of students who are members of minority and lower income groups, the presidents observed these dynamics on their campuses. As a case in point, they cited the City University of

New York's 1998 policy shift to allow remedial education only in the community colleges, which political leaders used as a lever to advance a conservative agenda (Gumport and Bastedo 2001). In their view, remedial education suffers a "negative spillover" from the public's dissatisfaction with K-12 education, for "the public doesn't want to pay twice for this." In spite of controversy in this arena, some presidents recognized their potential to do more than simply offer as many sections of basic skills that resources will allow. They could monitor what students get for those resources and identify alternatives if educational needs cannot be met at their college.

Their accounts suggest a range of accepted practices and rationales in the arena of remedial education. Capping enrollment on remedial courses or limiting the number of times a student can reenroll in the same course can be cast as good for the college and good for the students. While some presidents report that these are basically sound operating principles, others state that they must assert educational values in a context of heightened economic and political pressures. I attribute this capacity to a mix of logics in use, allowing for different priorities to be legitimately invoked. This flexibility, however, fosters ambiguity, which increases the likelihood that remedial education will remain a contested arena. When the presidents say they seek to move beyond the demand-response scenario, they signal the capacity to respond selectively, and more specifically, they underscore their college's primary responsibility as an educational institution in a political or economic context that threatens to compromise this identity. It is worth noting that what it means to be an educational institution is itself open to alternative interpretations. The presidents' accounts refer either to serving students' learning needs, whatever they may be, or to privileging the transfer function over instruction in basic skills. Practically speaking, either function has had traction in the environment during the 1990s, making it unclear which would be the most prudent course for their organization.

In addition to remedial education, a second major domain where presidents said they seek to transcend the presumed demand-response scenario is in the arena of workforce training. The presidents' accounts indicate the prominence of economic priorities and values within an industry logic, but they also show the potential (even their responsibility, according to some) to assert the educational purposes and values that align with a social institution logic.

Several presidents spoke of the pressure to meet the training needs of specific companies. One president perceived a direct match between what her college could offer and what the companies need. She observed how companies find that training in-house is "pretty expensive for them to do," whereupon they "turn to community colleges."

> They are doing it for two reasons. They want the training and they also want the customer base. For example, Cisco is going all through the country approaching community colleges to start teaching academies. The purpose is to train technicians to be Cisco certified. . . . From a Cisco point of view, it is great because you are going to hand over your training to somebody else. It is going to cost them a lab, which isn't very expensive. The community colleges will train, and they are reimbursed by the state to do the training. . . . Then there is this huge pool of employees that Cisco customers can hire.

Such company-sponsored training also enables students to acquire an identity and a purpose in addition to competency in a specific skills set.

While it is clear from this account why such an arrangement is economically advantageous for the company and boosts enrollments for the community college, the presidents were quick to point out that not all of the community college interests are necessarily served. To illustrate this point, one president explained how a proposed agreement contained an exclusivity clause, prompting her college to consider whether it is appropriate to exclude other companies from competitive access to the resources of a public institution. In another example, a president identified

---

[P]residents stated that they were mindful of managing the downside of providing training for companies.

---

how a company mandated a specific facility for the training program. From her perspective, this triggered a conflict in that classrooms are paid for by the state: "The practicality of it is, are we going to dedicate a classroom that is going to be locked up twenty-four hours a day with [that company's] equipment and that is its only use?" She then brought up a related practical consideration:

> Then let us say the company has a downturn. A few years ago this happened, and this lab all of a sudden went empty. It taught us a lesson. You don't want to get so tight, and dedicate your space so much that you don't have flexibility.

While a president has the option not to sign the agreement if the terms are deemed unacceptable, there is tremendous pressure not to walk away, especially if neighboring colleges are doing it. As one president clarified, "Well, there is a tension. . . . To use Cisco again as an example, if all of our neighboring colleges are going to do Cisco, then I better do Cisco too. So there is that push." The overriding question for the organization to determine is when it is an opportunity that simply cannot be missed, either because of financial benefit or pressure to conform to the practices of successful peers, or when its terms cross over the line of what is considered educationally appropriate.

Overall, the presidents stated they were mindful of managing the downside of providing training for companies, including monitoring the possibility that their involvement could become too large, especially for community colleges close to big industrial areas. Referring to short-term training activities as their "shadow college," some presidents invoked the danger that this function might move in from the periphery to become central to the college's identity. Yet others urged keeping it in perspective, noting that it is possible to "accentuate certain programs without detracting from the overall educational mission." As one president stated,

> When we talk about training, we need to think about things in context. If you talk about a Cisco academy you are talking about 25 students in an institution that may have 15,000. So we are not talking about being overrun by training per se. But . . . I think in the short term, we need them in, we need them trained, we need them out.

Another president offered a different view. Her college had a more extensive array of training activities, and she spoke of the potential for both positive and negative effects. She saw it as an opportunity to "bring greater visibility" to her college and to cultivate new revenue: "I look for organizations to work with that have technology needs, because I want to use this as a way to make connections with those organizations that might lead to donations." She then admitted that devoting energy to serving companies diverted their attention from the curriculum:

> Is there a downside? Yes. The downside goes to how the president and the senior officers have a finite amount of energy. . . . Then it is not available for some of the work that needs to be done on the plain old traditional curriculum. To me, this also goes back to [the question], Whose institution is it?

As the presidents spoke at length about additional parameters they considered relevant in determining how to meet the training needs of specific companies or industry more broadly, their language signaled some divergence in underlying values. Coinciding with an industry logic, their accounts portrayed them as entrepreneurial, willing to risk yet eager for the business, taking the initiative to make inquiries to specific companies and government agencies. Yet their language also makes evident a social institution logic, as they either implicitly or explicitly reshape demands for training or skills into opportunities for education—"contract education," "general education," and "lifelong learning." In so doing, serving the training needs of industry becomes elevated to an educational plane of activity, what colleges are supposed to do.

The presidents described how they persuade employers to seek education, not just training. As one president depicted what she saw as the result of her efforts, the employers initially requested skills but came to see the benefit of exposure to general education:

> The CEOs and personnel directors, they wanted skills at first. . . . We were the social voice saying what you really want is a broader base because what you want is someone who can be more analytical and more trainable, able to redevelop new skills at a later time. And so, a lot of employers don't even talk about these kinds of trainable skills any more. They are talking about—we need people who can work in teams, we need people who can think critically, we need literacy, we need computational skills—and a lot of that translates into a lot of the core for the general education we offer.

Several presidents conveyed similar experiences, and they described what they saw as a twofold imperative for them to push general education: it is good for the students in the short run, and it opens the door to their further education. This point was also raised in the context of discussing how contract education can be beneficial for both parties. As one president said of her college,

> Right now it is a win-win. We don't participate in contract education for the sake of doing it. We are very selective about what we do get engaged in. . . . We almost use contract education as an opportunity for opening the door to "regular" education that students might want to get interested in once they have a taste. . . . [For example,] we come in to a bank that just bought a whole new system of computers and train all of the employees on how to use those computers. We make some money on the side that's going to be used for whatever. But what we really are trying to do is get them hooked on education, to understand that this is a lifelong learning process. So we see it also as a recruitment tool. . . . If it were just the money alone, it would not be as important as the fact that I am doing a service with money.

From her perspective, the potential for long-run educational value ("doing a service") was more important than the immediate economic gain, although both were clearly salient.

I explored with the presidents whether there was a line they would not cross if industry had a training need that they did not want to meet. One answered, "There's no line per se. But there is a line in the minds of the community. I think it's incumbent upon the leadership of the college to . . . to know what seems appropriate for that community's college." I probed further about the specific context of her college and asked for an example. She remarked that

> Cosmetology would be a good example. That would be an area where, frankly, community colleges are authorized to offer such a program, but it would be something that I don't think we'd even entertain. One, because there's been no request or demand. And secondly, that's probably not consistent with the image we have developed based on our other curricular offerings. . . . When we're talking about career programs, they tend to be more of . . . the white-collar end of the programs.

She concluded, "We manage for the balance and the demand." Obviously, not all community colleges have this balance or the leeway to develop it. Yet this example does show that local communities are an additional layer filtering the pressures and expectations for what community colleges can legitimately pursue. Overall, the presidents' portrayal of what is feasible and appropriate in meeting workforce training needs reflects a vocabulary of motives and parameters that on one hand aligns with an industry logic but on the other hand also permits the community colleges to enact educational and community values corresponding to a social institution logic.

Two additional examples from the interview data underscore this point. One is prioritizing resources for student services (e.g., advising, counseling) and child care ("it is number 1," "an overwhelming need"). According to one president, "I realize those things lose money, but they are important to the very heart of what we are about." While such activities themselves do not add revenue, they enable students to remain enrolled. So the commitment of resources to these services may be seen as coinciding with industry logic imperatives to improve customer service and boost enrollments, or it may be seen as extending education to students who would not otherwise seek it. While the first interpretation secures the college's place as a responsible business, the second transforms the practical need for child care into a morally compelling right intertwined with educational opportunity. A second example illustrates the legitimacy of more than one value set, as well. One president described how they created a program in fine and performing arts in spite of the fact that the music and drama departments were "literally dying" and "could easily have been eliminated." They cultivated the demand by contracting with performing arts organizations that already had a built-in audience, inviting them to

---

Presidents spoke most forcefully of attempting to move beyond the demand-response scenario in contexts where educational values and democratic purposes seemed at risk.

---

rehearse under her college's auspices in a class, and "the enrollments surged from there." From her perspective, the creative challenge in developing academic programs was to find suitable intersections of economic and educational interests. In retrospect, other factors also came into play: reshaping this program enabled the college to claim some curricular distinctiveness among nearby colleges, while it also catered to the high-culture tastes of the relatively affluent surrounding community.

The data analysis has illuminated how community colleges are embedded in an institutional environment with two distinct logics in use. It is noteworthy that presidents spoke most forcefully of attempting to move beyond the demand-response scenario in contexts where educational values and democratic purposes seemed at risk. One president asserted their responsibility to promote and preserve educational values in her state, where "the legislature is on our case about workforce training, but we don't hear them complaining about our falling short on the transfer function." She then conveyed concern over the consequences of such expanded services for the identity of the community college:

> The external pressure for training, for continuing education, for contract education, for remedial education. . . . They are wonderful entities and we need to provide those services.

> But I see [them] as having grown enormously. I see pressure for academic expectations
> has gotten smaller. . . . I think the joy of the community colleges is its access investment,
> and its service responsiveness, and its really being democracy's colleges. The question is
> how we are being democracy's colleges, and how that is perceived by people in community
> colleges and to some extent by the public.

In raising the question of "how we are being democracy's colleges," she called on the presidents to consider the possibility that the community colleges' historical role as democracy's colleges is threatened and that it either has already been or will be altered. In so doing, she also thereby implied a measure of self-determination for the colleges to reshape the pressures on them. This notion finds legitimacy in two different beliefs: in the strategic capacity of organizational actors to redirect the enterprise and in the idea that some autonomy for public colleges is necessary for them to enact their fundamental responsibility to society.

The larger conceptual point is that two conditions enable these presidents to articulate their organizations' potential to move beyond the demand-response scenario. First, the existence of more than one logic allows for the possibility of an alternative value set, when and where the presidents deem necessary and/or appropriate. And second, they explicitly align themselves with educational values in contexts they perceive as threatening to diverge from education or to derail their legacy of providing access and enabling transfer.

Conclusion

I have proposed that the wide range of accepted practices and values as manifested in contemporary community colleges can be accounted for in part by multiple institutional logics. At least in the short run, the coexistence of two logics has enabled community colleges to legitimately engage in a variety of activities while positioning themselves as responding to changing demands and even at times as seeking to alter the terms of demands. The formidability of the industry logic's imperatives, and its extended structural embeddedness, points to uncertainty over its cumulative impact, most notably, whether community colleges will continue to assert educational values in contexts where economic and political factors are presented as determinative grounds for reshaping organizational priorities and practices. Since community colleges occupy a significant space between high schools and four-year colleges and universities, their trajectory is of utmost importance. How these issues are framed, how presidents perceive pressures, and what their colleges do are all significant for the future of community colleges, just as they are for public higher education, for three reasons.

First, as is the case for all public colleges and universities, external forces continue to redefine whom community colleges serve and how. As a president noted, "Our institution is in some ways the aggregate of decisions made by [other] people." It is worth noting from the focus group data that presidents assert their obligation to scrutinize demands in the name of serving the long-term public interest. Yet the public interest is neither unified nor clearly defined. In fact, several actors position themselves as speaking on behalf of the public interest, while other interests may be at work. When policy makers speak, it is not clear whether they are speaking for national, state, or local interests or for their political or individual interests. When employers speak, it is not clear whether they are speaking for their company, their industry, their employees, or their own professional interests. When college presidents speak, it is not clear whether they are speaking on behalf of the public interest, their sector's interest, their organization's interest, or their own managerial interests. The role of divergent interests in the sustainability of logics warrants further exploration.

Determining what serves the public interest is further complicated by the fact that the public itself may have a conception of public higher education that leaders of colleges and universities find wanting. One community college president in the focus groups lamented that higher education is not unique in its susceptibility to societal currents:

> We have fast food, fast information, and everything is immediate. That is the world we live in, and that gets translated to social institutions. I am thinking of relating the struggle in our colleges with the struggle that many churches are going through.

Another president echoed this concern, forecasting that the public might look to colleges to serve a circumscribed credentialing role instead of "really making a difference in the person's life."

> How about this "any time, anywhere, in the car, in the radio" kind of education? Then people will just come in and you know, if they take a test and they already know it . . . or even they maybe had a life experience and they already know this, expect us to just credential them.

This is yet another reason why the presidents assert that being demand driven is insufficient.

Ultimately, state legislatures are a primary site where such expectations and interests are articulated. In strictly instrumental terms, the state may see community colleges as essentially service providers; as such, their programs and activities should directly correspond to the changing demands of those who fund them. Failure to demonstrate they are doing so would be imprudent, especially in an accountability climate that prizes measurable contributions to both economic development and postsecondary participation. Not responding to demands—even if only symbolically—risks not only a loss of resources but also a loss of public trust. In fact, their legacy of responsiveness can be viewed as exempting community colleges from the criticism often levied on the rest of higher education as complacent, arrogant, and resistant to change. However, to conceptualize community colleges as solely service providers would render them similar to other agencies and organizations the state contracts with to procure services, such as hospitals or prisons. While there is nothing inherently wrong with their being seen as service providers, imposing a procurement orientation on community colleges would constitute a historical shift if expectations for short-term training and basic skills were to eclipse their role of providing entry-level higher education. Moreover, if community colleges are seen as service providers, campus leaders' currency as educators is devalued, and state legislatures are even less likely to seek their input. In this sense, what community colleges do and become also has consequences for college presidents, who already tend to express discomfort if they are seen solely as CEOs; thus, organizational identity and professional identity are inextricably linked.[15]

The second reason why the trajectory for community colleges is significant resides in the observation that they have been well positioned to enact an industry logic and accrue legitimacy from it. Evidence suggests that a preponderance of employers and elected officials are satisfied with community colleges' preparation of the workforce. In fact, it is not uncommon for local employers to participate in setting the curriculum, serving on an advisory board for a department or a program. Students seem satisfied as well. The value accruing to students is apparent especially for those who acquire skills in high-demand fields, such as information technology, not only because of projected earnings but also because they gain the expertise to build and repair software and hardware on which many professionals and organizations centrally depend. In addition, structurally speaking, several obstacles that are prominent in other segments of public higher education have less salience for community colleges, including a large proportion of tenured faculty, alumni who may embody a logic that dominated in an earlier era, or a long-standing academic structure with its own self-reinforcing momentum to preserve existing knowledge areas. The absence or muting of such conditions within community colleges makes for less structurally embedded conflict when economic imperatives come to the fore.

Nevertheless, even those community colleges with severe resource constraints persevere in articulating a social institution logic and demonstrating that they are educational institutions. Practically speaking, it would be worth studying how community colleges are able to do so, especially in a context of pervasive accountability demands from external groups with different expectations. By re-infusing educational purposes into contexts that put a premium on all things economic, community colleges may demonstrate the possibility of restructuring for the market while still promoting educational values and fortifying commitments to academic ideals for which there is currently little demand. With experience reconciling such competing pressures, community colleges may offer exemplary practices for other segments of higher education rather than being perceived by the academic community as a bottom rung of the prestige ladder.

Finally, monitoring where community colleges are headed is vitally important because of the high stakes for society. Community colleges constitute a significant national investment, both symbolically and in real terms. Enrolling some 36 percent of the country's postsecondary students, community colleges are chartered to improve the life chances of many by providing higher education to all who seek it, offer an array of training activities, and make available a range of lifelong learning opportunities and facilities for their communities. Beyond that, community colleges serve as a major arena of social activity in which fundamental American beliefs are visibly pursued, ranging from equal opportunity and civil rights to economic and technological progress. Since their institutional purposes are anchored in prevailing interpretations of these beliefs, changes in community colleges could indicate significant shifts in how these beliefs are defined as well as how higher education is expected to enact them.

Notes

1. Unlike four-year colleges and universities, community colleges were for the most part grouped together within a single category in the Carnegie Classification of Institutions of Higher Education from its development in 1971 through 2000. (One exception is a separate category introduced in 1994 for Tribal Colleges, most of which are two-year colleges and some of which are considered community colleges.) Recognizing the heterogeneity of two-year colleges along several dimensions, the Carnegie Foundation for the Advancement of Teaching has placed a high priority on differentiating them in future classifications. The 2000 edition of the classification introduced a new hybrid category, "Baccalaureate/Associate's Colleges," leaving the associate's college category for all exclusively subbaccalaureate colleges and those where bachelor's degrees account for less than 10 percent of undergraduate awards (McCormick 2001, 16). Other efforts to develop a classification scheme for community colleges have been under way (Katsinas 1996; Institute for Research on Higher Education 1998; Phipps, Shedd, and Merisotis 2001).

2. Community colleges granted 308,531 associate's degrees in 1980; degree production increased 38 percent, to 425,846 in 1998. Prebaccalaureate certificate production increased more dramatically from 77,898 in 1980 to 158,384 in 1998, or 103 percent. The data show increases in liberal arts fields for those decades—the share of total for liberal arts degrees increased from 10.3 percent to 17.5 percent—and for liberal arts certificates from 2.2 percent to 6.1 percent of total. The trend is equally strong in terms of volume: liberal arts degrees increased by 133.5 percent during this period compared to only 10.5 percent in non–liberal arts degrees; liberal arts certificates increased by 448.5 percent compared to 74.8 percent for non–liberal arts certificates (National Center for Education Statistics 1980, 1998).

3. Scott (2001) characterized a shift within this scholarly tradition. Early neoinstitutionalists (e.g., Meyer and Rowan 1977; DiMaggio and Powell 1983) viewed institutional effects as constraints on organizational structure and behavior, operating for the most part in opposition to technical and efficiency concerns. Later theorists turned their attention to institutional processes (including change) and conceptualized institutional factors as shaping and interacting with interest-based action, thereby framing rational decision making. In part as a corrective to analyses that characterized organizations as overly passive, recent work has examined the potential for their strategic responses to institutional pressures (e.g., Oliver 1991; Goodstein 1994), albeit within the binding constraint of institutional environments and isomorphic processes (Powell 1991).

4. In my larger research project, I use historical case study data to examine the specific conditions in which one or more logics came into use as well as the conditions in which coexisting logics are harmonious or in conflict and how a particular logic is supported or weakened. This article draws on focus group data that do not locate presidents' accounts within their particular organizational-environmental conditions. So my analytical aim is more modest, to demonstrate the general pattern of logics in use and to establish that these additional dynamics warrant study.

5. *Occupational education* was initially the generic term covering the more specific categories of vocational, semiprofessional, and technical programs. After the 1950s, *career education* replaced *occupational education* as the generic term (Eaton 1994). By the 1990s, *workforce training* was commonly used. These shifts in terminology signal that more extensive changes occurred. Scholars have employed different approaches to analyze those changes. For example, Clark (1960) characterized how external conditions shaped the development of the formal organizational structure and the internal elaboration of "cooling out practices," while Brint and Karabel (1991) emphasized the capacity of organizational leaders to promote change, arguing they became proponents of occupational training within unfavorable market conditions and in anticipation of the preferences of state officials and business leaders.

6. National data show that the founding of colleges and burgeoning enrollments were more dramatic during the 1960s and 1970s than during the final two decades of the century. According to the American Association of Community Colleges, 646 new community colleges were created during the 1960s and 1970s. That composes 56 percent of the 1,155 colleges listed at the beginning of 2000. During the 1980s and 1990s, only 97 new community colleges were founded (48 in the 1980s, 49 in the 1990s), which is 4 percent of the 2000 total. Similarly, two-year college enrollments increased much more rapidly during the 1960s and 1970s than in the 1980s and 1990s. National Center for Education Statistics data show that from 1965 to 1980, enrollment in two-year colleges increased 286 percent, from 1,172,952 to 4,526,287. The National Center for Education Statistics projected two-year enrollment of 5,847,000 for 2000, only 29 percent more than 1980 enrollment. Small annual percentage increases in enrollment were evident between 1985 and 1992 and after 1998 and are projected beyond 2000 (National Center for Education Statistics 2000). Whether state funding will correspond with these increases and thus ease financial pressure remains to be seen. It is equally plausible that the funding will not keep pace and community colleges will be pressured to serve more students with less funding.

7. Relative to other segments, community colleges' state funding per full-time-equivalent student has been about one-third that of public Research I universities, one-half that of other public research and doctorate-granting universities, and two-thirds that of state comprehensive colleges and universities. Between 1975 and 1995, state funding per full-time-equivalent student declined for community colleges by 6 percent, while it increased for Research I universities by 6 percent and for other doctorate-granting universities by 4 percent. Between 1985 and 1995, the decline in state funding per full-time-equivalent student for community colleges was even more pronounced: 10 percent. This is somewhat mitigated by the fact that community colleges are supported to a greater degree by local funding, yet even it declined 15 percent during this period (Gumport and Jennings 1999).

8. National data on degree production and certificates are available through 1998, so they do not capture the growth of these fields in the past four years.

9. See Adelman (2000) for a comprehensive review of the massive certification enterprise, which has gained momentum since 1997. However, he found that the major providers to date are not community colleges and about half of all certification is provided by entities outside the United States.

10. One solution is to boost enrollment wherever possible. This is not in itself a simple solution, for increased enrollments require programmatic and structural adjustments and may entail new pressures. In California, for example, enrollment projections give cause for concern: 538,000 new students are expected to enroll between 1994-1995 and 2005-2006, and community colleges are expected to absorb about 75 percent of the total (Hayward, Breneman, and Estrada 1998). Campus leaders are looking at how to build their capacity to handle the projected influx: whether state support will keep pace or the state will seek productivity gains (e.g., increased student credit hours per faculty full-time-equivalent) and whether revenue-generating and fund-raising efforts from nonstate sources will help yield sufficient resources to meet their goals.

11. A sustained line of concern among researchers is the transfer rate of community college students to four-year colleges. Longitudinal comparison is made difficult by the absence of consensus in defining the appropriate denominator (Bradburn and Hurst 2000). In 1989, the national transfer rate was estimated to have been 22 percent of those who first enrolled in a community college and transferred to a four-year college within five years, although there was tremendous variation from one college to the next, ranging from 3 percent to 42 percent. In terms of degree completion rates, fewer than one-fourth of individuals who began in a community college in 1989 had earned an associate's degree (17.5 percent) or a certificate (5 percent) five years later, and 6.4 percent had earned a bachelor's degree (Nettles and Millett 2000).

12. The ability of presidents to perceive and respond to changing environmental pressures has been a visible concern among higher education researchers (e.g., Cohen and March 1974; Birnbaum 1989; Neumann 1989). Some insights can also be found in memoirs, but these have tended to be authored by presidents of the highly selective campuses in American higher education, both private (e.g., Kennedy 1997) and public (e.g., Duderstadt 2000; Kerr 2001). Little is known about the perspectives of community college presidents. Some basic survey data do exist, as reported in, for example, Eaton (1994) and more recently in Ross and Green (2000).

13. Focus groups are an effective method for obtaining actors' perceptions and are regarded as having high face validity (Krueger 1988; Morgan 1988). The basic principle is that participants' thoughts and beliefs can be explicated through focused conversations with others who are familiar with a common set of issues.

Participants are often assured that their identity and the identity of their organizations will be disguised, and I followed that principle in this study. My focus groups included presidents and chancellors from a mix of colleges and universities, with one group consisting solely of community college representatives, several of whom had been community college faculty earlier in their careers. The sessions were audiotaped and fully transcribed, yielding 362 pages of single-spaced verbatim transcript. Transcripts were subsequently checked against the videotapes to ensure accuracy. Prior to coding, a procedure was developed to disguise the identities of participants yet permit analysis by institutional type. Transcripts were coded according to major categories in the conceptual framework and examined for disconfirming evidence that would refute patterns that emerged from the initial coding.

14. I use the term with hesitation. Astin (1998) argues that the remedial concept is misleading for three reasons. Students in these courses tend to have lower scores, which are identified as problematic when they fall below an arbitrary line. Also, the presumption is often that these students have different learning styles and thus need to be segregated for a specific pedagogical treatment. Finally, relatively speaking, higher education settings at all levels of study appear to have students who may be deemed underprepared. Furthermore, as Dougherty (2002, 309) cautioned, the term "remedial education" connotes "repairing the defects of previous education," which does not apply to adults who are looking to "brush up" on math or writing skills.

15. See Brint and Karabel (1991) on the status concerns of community college leaders.

References

Adelman, C. 2000. *A parallel universe: The certification system in information technology*. Washington, DC: U.S. Department of Education.

Astin, A. 1998. Evaluating remedial education is not just a methodological issue. Paper presented to the Conference on Replacing Remediation in Higher Education, Stanford, CA, 26-27 January.

Bailey, T., and I. Averianova. 1998. *Multiple missions of community colleges: Conflicting or complementary?* CCRC brief no. 1. New York: Community College Research Center, Teachers College, Columbia University.

Birnbaum, R. 1989. Responsibility without authority: The impossible job of the college president. In *Higher education: Handbook of theory and research*, edited by John Smart, 31-56. New York: Agathon Press.

Bradburn, E., and D. Hurst. 2000. *Community college transfer rates to 4 year institutions using alternative definitions of transfer*. Report no. 2001197. Washington, DC: National Center for Education Statistics, U.S. Department of Education.

Brint, S., and J. Karabel. 1989. *The diverted dream*. New York: Oxford University Press.

———. 1991. Institutional origins and transformations: The case of American community colleges. In *The new institutionalism in organizational analysis*, edited by Walter Powell and Paul DiMaggio. Chicago: University of Chicago Press.

Cameron, K. 1983. Strategic responses to conditions of decline. *Journal of Higher Education* 54:359-80.

Chaffee, E. E. 1985. The concept of strategy: From business to higher education. In *Higher education: Handbook of theory and research*, edited by John Smart, 133-72. New York: Agathon Press.

Clark, B. R. 1960. *The open door college: A case study*. New York: McGraw-Hill.

———. 1998. *Creating entrepreneurial universities*. Surrey, UK: Pergamon.

Cohen, M. D., and J. G. March. 1974. *Leadership and ambiguity: The American college president*. 2d ed. Boston: Harvard Business School Press.

DiMaggio, P. J., and W. W. Powell. 1983. The iron cage revisited: Institutional isomorphism and collective rationality in organizational fields. *American Sociological Review* 48 (2): 147-60.

Dougherty, K. 2002. The evolving role of the community college. In *Higher education: Handbook of theory and research*, edited by John Smart, 295-348. New York: Agathon Press.

Dougherty, K. J. 1994. *The contradictory college*. Albany: State University of New York Press.

Dougherty, K. J., and M. F. Bakia. 2000. *The new economic development role of the community college*. CCRC brief no. 6. New York: Community College Research Center, Teachers College, Columbia University.

Duderstadt, J. J. 2000. *A university for the 21st century*. Ann Arbor: University of Michigan Press.

Eaton, J. S. 1994. *Strengthening collegiate education in community colleges*. San Francisco: Jossey-Bass.

———. 1995. *Investing in American higher education: An argument for restructuring*. New York: Council for Aid to Education.

Friedland, R., and R. Alford. 1991. Bringing society back in: Symbols, practices and institutional contradictions. In *The new institutionalism in organizational analysis*, edited by Walter Powell and Paul DiMaggio. Chicago: University of Chicago Press.

Goodstein, J. 1994. Institutional pressures and strategic responsiveness: Employer involvement in work-family issues. *Academy of Management Journal* 37 (2): 350-82.

Grubb, W. N. 1999. *Learning and earning in the middle: The economic benefits of sub-baccalaureate education*. CCRC briefs nos. 2 and 3. New York: Community College Research Center, Teachers College, Columbia University.

Grubb, W. N., N. Badway, D. Bell, D. Bragg, and M. Russman. 1997. *Workforce, economic and community development: The changing landscape of the entrepreneurial community college*. Berkeley, CA: NCRVE and Mission Viejo League for Innovation.

Gumport, P. J. 2000. Academic restructuring: Organizational change and institutional imperatives. *Higher Education: The International Journal of Higher Education and Educational Planning* 39:67-91.

———. 2001. Built to serve: The enduring legacy of public higher education. In *In defense of American higher education*, edited by Philip Altbach, Patricia J. Gumport, and D. Bruce Johnstone. Baltimore: Johns Hopkins University Press.

———. 2002. Universities and knowledge: Restructuring the city of intellect. In *The future of the city of intellect: The changing American university*, edited by Steven Brint. Stanford, CA: Stanford University Press.

Gumport, P. J., and M. Bastedo. 2001. Academic stratification and endemic conflict: Remedial education policy at CUNY. *The Review of Higher Education* 24 (4): 333-49.

Gumport, P. J., and J. Jennings. 1999. *Financial challenges in public higher education: A trend analysis*. Technical report no. NCPI-1320 for the U.S. Department of Education. Grant no. R309A60001. Stanford, CA: National Center for Postsecondary Improvement.

Gumport, P. J., and B. Pusser. 1997. Restructuring the academic environment. In *Planning and management for a changing environment: A handbook on redesigning postsecondary institutions*, edited by Marvin Peterson, David Dill, and Lisa Mets. San Francisco: Jossey-Bass.

———. 1999. University restructuring: The role of economic and political contexts. In *Higher education: Handbook of theory and research*, edited by John Smart, 146-200. New York: Agathon Press.

Gumport, P. J., and B. Sporn. 1999. Institutional adaptation: Demands for management reform and university administration. In *Higher education: Handbook of theory and research*, edited by John Smart, 103-45. New York: Agathon Press.

Hayward, G., D. Breneman, and L. Estrada. 1998. *Tidal wave II revisited*. Number 98-4. San Jose, CA: National Center for Public Policy and Higher Education.

Hearn, J. C. 1988. Strategy and resources: Economic issues in strategic planning and management in higher education. In *Higher education: Handbook of theory and research*, edited by John Smart, 212-81. New York: Agathon Press.

Institute for Research on Higher Education. 1998. The user-friendly terrain: Defining the market taxonomy for two-year institutions. *Change* 30 (January/February): 35-38.

———. 2002. A report to stakeholders on the condition and effectiveness of postsecondary education, part 3: The employers. *Change* 34 (January/February): 23-38.

———. 1998. Washington, DC: National Center for Education Statistics, U.S. Department of Education.

Karabel, J. 1972. Community colleges and social stratification. *Harvard Educational Review* 42 (4): 521-62.

Katsinas, S. G. 1996. Preparing leaders for diverse institutional settings. In *Graduate and continuing education for community college leaders*, edited by J. C. Palmer and S. G. Katsinas. San Francisco: Jossey-Bass.

Keller, G. 1983. *Academic strategy: The management revolution in American higher education*. Baltimore: Johns Hopkins University Press.

Kennedy, D. 1997. *Academic duty*. Cambridge, MA: Harvard University Press.

Kerr, C. 2001. *The gold and the blue: A personal memoir of the University of California, 1949-1967*. Berkeley: University of California Press.

Krueger, R. 1988. *Focus groups*. Newbury Park, CA: Sage.

Leslie, D., and E. K. Fretwell. 1996. *Wise moves in hard times*. San Francisco: Jossey-Bass.

Levin, J. 2002. The baccalaureate degree and the evolving identity of the community college. Paper presented at the annual meeting of the Council for the Study of Community Colleges, 20 April, Seattle, WA.

McCormick, A. 2001. The 2000 Carnegie classification: Background and description. In *The Carnegie classification of institutions of higher education, 2000 edition*, 9-31. Menlo Park, CA: Carnegie Foundation for the Advancement of Teaching.

Meyer, J. W., and B. Rowan. 1977. Institutionalized organizations: Formal structure as myth and ceremony. *American Journal of Sociology* 83 (2): 340-63.

Meyer, J. W., and W. R. Scott. 1992. *Organizational environments: Ritual and rationality*. Rev. ed. Newbury Park, CA: Sage.

Morgan, D. 1988. *Focus groups as qualitative research*. Newbury Park, CA: Sage.

National Center for Education Statistics. 1980. *Higher education general information survey*. Washington, DC: Department of Education.

———. 1995. *Integrated postsecondary education data system*. Washington, DC: Department of Education.

———. 1998. *Integrated postsecondary education data system*. Washington, DC: Department of Education.

———. 2000. *Digest of education statistics*. Washington, DC: Department of Education.

———. 2001. *Digest of education statistics*. Washington, DC: Department of Education.

Nettles, M., and C. Millett. 2000. *Student access in community colleges*. New Expeditions Issues Paper Series, no. 1. Washington, DC: Community College Press, American Association of Community Colleges.

Neumann, A. 1989. Strategic leadership: The changing orientations of college presidents. *Journal of Higher Education* 12 (2): 137-51.

Oliver, C. 1991. Strategic responses to institutional processes. *Academy of Management Review* 16 (1): 145-79.

Phipps, R. A., J. M. Shedd, and J. P. Merisotis. 2001. *A classification system for 2-year postsecondary institutions*. Report no. 2001-167. Washington, DC: National Center for Education Statistics, U.S. Department of Education.

Powell, W. 1991. Expanding the scope of institutional analysis. In *The new institutionalism in organizational analysis*, edited by Walter Powell and Paul DiMaggio. Chicago: University of Chicago Press.

Ross, M., and M. F. Green. 2000. *The American college president: 2000 edition*. Washington, DC: American Council on Education.

Ruppert, S. 2001. *Where we go from here: State legislative views on higher education in the new millennium*. Washington, DC: National Education Association.

Scott, W. R. 2001. *Institutions and organizations*. 2d ed. Thousand Oaks, CA: Sage.

Scott, W. R., M. Ruef, P. Mendel, and C. Caronna. 2000. *Institutional change and healthcare organizations*. Chicago: University of Chicago Press.

Townsend, B. 2001. Blurring the lines: Transforming terminal education to transfer education. In *The new vocationalism in community colleges*, edited by D. Bragg, 63-72. San Francisco: Jossey-Bass.

The Uneven Distribution of Employee Training by Community Colleges: Description and Explanation

By
KEVIN J. DOUGHERTY

Community colleges have recently attracted great attention because of their important role in supplying employee training to many business establishments. But despite this major role, there is surprising variability in community colleges' supply of, and employers' demand for, employee training. While a few community colleges supply a lot of employee training, many provide little. Moreover, although large employers and ones in industries such as manufacturing tend to utilize the community college heavily, smaller employers and ones in industries such as retail trade use it much less. This article analyzes the causes of this variability in the demand for and supply of employee training and suggests policy responses. Public policy, while encouraging broader community college and industry partnership in employee training, must also move to counteract the harmful impacts of extensive employee training on other missions of the community college such as transfer preparation, remedial education, and general education.

Keywords: contract training; business community colleges; workforce development

A major theme in recent commentary, research, and policy making on the economy has been the key role of employee training as a source of economic growth and worker well-being. The confluence of an aging workforce, declining job

Kevin J. Dougherty is an associate professor in the Higher Education Program and a senior research associate at the Community College Research Center at Teachers College, Columbia University. This article draws on research he recently completed for Community College Research Center on the community college role in workforce preparation and economic development. He is now leading a Community College Research Center project on the impact of public and private performance accountability systems on community colleges. Dougherty's research on the community college's historical development and impact on students is summarized in The Contradictory College *(1994, State University of New York Press), which won the 1997 Willard Waller Award of the American Sociological Association.*

NOTE: The research reported here was conducted with the support of a grant by the Sloan Foundation to the Community College Research Center at Teachers Col-

DOI: 10.1177/0002716202250211

stability, and continuing industry demands for a more flexible workforce have resulted in considerable emphasis on the importance of the training of workers already in the labor force (Carnevale and Desrochers 2000; Commission on the Skills of the American Workforce 1990; Johnson, Packer, and Associates 1987; Marshall and Tucker 1992).

This emphasis in turn has led to considerable attention to the role of community colleges in providing employers with employee training. Today, about 30 percent of business establishments of more than twenty employees use community colleges as one of their training providers (Frazis et al. 1997, 49, 71; Lynch and Black 1998, 77). To be sure, there are other training providers that employers use even more frequently than community colleges to provide employee training: for example, equipment suppliers or vendors and, less so, private consultants, industry associations, and for-profit schools. Yet community colleges merit attention, particularly from educational policy makers, because they are higher education institutions that provide an unparalleled opportunity for allowing employee training to become an avenue of educational mobility (Dougherty 2001, 2002). They do this by allowing employees to acquire educational credentials such as associate's degrees that are not only economically useful in and of themselves (Grubb 2002) but also increasingly convertible into baccalaureate degrees. For example, at the behest of the major auto manufacturers, many community colleges have established auto technician training programs that lead to an associate's degree (Dougherty and Bakia 1999, 2000). Moreover, some of those community colleges have forged agreements with four-year colleges allowing those acquiring associate's degrees in automotive technology to go on to pursue bachelor's degrees in applied subjects (Derry, 1997). This educational pathway is part of a more general phenomenon of the increasing conversion of formerly subbaccalaureate technical training into higher degrees, including baccalaureate degrees.[1]

Community colleges offer employee training in two main ways. Employees can simply register in the regular courses at community college, with employers picking up the cost of tuition. Or more proactively, employers can contract with community colleges to offer courses that are designed to the specifications of employers. The courses may be customized to the employers' desires regarding course content, course schedule and structure (for example, the course may not be semester long and may be offered only on weekends), location (the training is delivered at the contractor's premises), or student composition (the students are exclusively ones referred by the employer) (Dougherty and Bakia 2000).

lege, Columbia University. I wish to thank Marianne Bakia for her very able assistance in gathering the data on community college provision of contract training. I also wish to thank Gregory Kienzl for help with the statistical analysis. For their excellent comments on earlier versions of this article, I wish to thank Debra Bragg, Joshua Haimson, Michael Horrigan, Jerry Jacobs, Stuart Rosenfeld, Harold Salzman, Kate Shaw, and David Weiman. Finally, I wish to thank the following present and former members of the Community College Research Center for their support at the time the research for this article was being conducted: Thomas Bailey, Lisa Rothman, Jennafer D'Alvia, Margaret Terry Orr, Dolores Perin, and John Wirt.

Despite employers' extensive use of community colleges as providers of employee training, there is surprising variability in employers' demand for, and community colleges' supply of, employee training. Larger business establishments use community colleges for training much more heavily than smaller establishments. And establishments in certain industries utilize it more extensively than those in other industries (Frazis et al. 1997, 1998; Zeiss et al. 1997, 41).[2] This variation in business utilization of the community college is problematic on both economic and social equality grounds. As I will show below, many factors besides differences in skills demands play a role in explaining this uneven utilization. This

---

Community colleges merit attention . . . because they . . . provide an unparalleled opportunity for allowing employee training to become an avenue of educational mobility. . . . They do this by allowing employees to acquire educational credentials such as associate's degrees that are not only economically useful in and of themselves . . . but also increasingly convertible into baccalaureate degrees.

---

influence of nonskill factors argues that smaller employers and employers in certain industries (particularly nonmanufacturing) are receiving less training than would be optimal for purposes of economic growth. In addition, there is a social equality dimension. Smaller employers and ones in less training-intensive industries tend to attract less advantaged workers. To the degree they receive less training, particularly in general skills, these workers have reduced opportunities for occupational mobility within and across firms and therefore reduced opportunities for improving their economic condition (Lynch and Black 1998, 70).

Just as there is variation in employer utilization of the community college, there is also great unevenness in community college supply of employee training. For example, in the area of contract training, while most community colleges provide such training, a few provide a lot, and many provide only a little. Moreover, urban community colleges provide a lot more contract training courses and serve many more employers than do rural colleges (Johnson 1995, 100; Lynch, Palmer, and Grubb 1991).

Unlike the uneven business utilization of the community college, the uneven supply by community colleges of employee training cannot be read simply as a problem. It is a more ambiguous phenomenon. On one hand, weak development of employee training may harm local employers and thus the local economy. It may also deny community colleges such benefits as increased enrollments, new revenues, greater external political support, and information on employer skills needs that allow occupational education programs to better keep up with the changing demands of the labor market (Dougherty and Bakia 2000, 225-32). At the same time, a very vigorous employee training effort may harm the community college. Traditionally, the primary purposes of American education have been as much about cultivating citizenship as serving economic efficiency (Labaree 1997). But as community colleges ardently pursue a strong connection with business and the economy, their interest in the traditional tasks of schools may attenuate, either because of an organizational attitude/cultural change or because of a loss of administrative attention (Dougherty and Bakia 2000, 233-35). There is scattered evidence that involvement in contract training reshapes the attitudes of community college faculty and administrators by leading to an impatience with the notion of education for purposes other than job preparation. In addition, because administrators' time and attention are finite, the more time they devote to expanding contract education, the less attention and energy they may have for such traditional missions as education for citizenship, providing access to the four-year colleges, and serving underprepared students. The transfer program may particularly feel the effects of a loss of administrative attention. It takes great administrative energy and attention to construct and maintain effective college transfer programs (for more on this, see Dougherty and Bakia 2000, 233-35).

Given the importance of employee training for our economic health, the community colleges' sizable role in providing that training and the economic benefits and mobility opportunities afforded by that community college role, it becomes important to unearth the causes of this variability in business demand for, and community college supply of, employee training. Is the lesser utilization of the community college by smaller employers simply due to lesser need or greater availability of alternative suppliers, or instead, is it due to lesser ability to stimulate community colleges to respond to their needs? Similarly, is the low supply of employee training by many community colleges indicative of lesser demand by local employers, or does it stem from impediments to community college responsiveness? If this unevenness in employer utilization and community supply of employee training is not due mostly to variations in employer demand, this raises significant questions about public policy. What can be done to ensure that smaller employers needing training are able to secure that training on an equal footing with larger employers?

At the same time, because of the possible negative impact on community colleges of an extensive involvement in employee training, it also becomes important to think of ways to neutralize harmful side effects. What can be done to ensure that community colleges more equally provide employee training, while at the same time guarding against the potential danger of a weakened emphasis on other missions of the community college such as transfer preparation or general education?

Data Sources

For data on business utilization of the community college for employee training, this article draws on a variety of large surveys of employers conducted by the federal government and others. These surveys ask business establishments differing in size and industry how much formal training they finance and through what means they secure such training. It should be noted that business establishments and business firms are not coincident. An establishment is an economic unit that usually has a single physical location and engages predominantly in one type of economic activity. A business firm, meanwhile, may consist of many establishments. We will focus on establishments because data are much more readily available on them than on firms and because, given the internal heterogeneity of many firms, the establishment is often the locus for training.

For data on community college provision of employee training, the article draws on two sources. The first is a number of surveys of community colleges asking them whether they provide contract training to employers and how deep that involvement has been. The second source is a series of interviews, conducted by the Community College Research Center, of both employers and community college officials concerning the provision of contract training. The employers were concentrated in five industries varying in skill intensity and average establishment size: auto manufacturing, auto repair, construction, apparel making, and banking. The community college officials were located at more than twenty community colleges in four states: California, Texas, Florida, and New York (Dougherty and Bakia 1999, 2000).

Employers' Uneven Utilization of Community Colleges

Demand by employers for formal training of their employees is quite uneven across industries and size of business establishments. Larger business establishments and ones in manufacturing and health care disproportionately draw on the community college for employee training. Conversely, smaller establishments and those in wholesale and retail trade and, less so, construction underutilize the community college relative to their share either of establishments or of employment (Frazis et al. 1997, 1998; Zeiss et al. 1997, 41). Let us explore in greater detail the effect of these two factors: establishment size and industrial sector.

Variation by establishment size

The larger the employer, the more likely it is to draw on the community college for formal training (Frazis et al. 1997, 71; Zeiss et al. 1997, 41).[3] In a 1995 survey of 1,062 establishments with more than 50 employees, the U.S. Bureau of Labor Statistics found that 57 percent of establishments with more than 500 employees drew on community colleges for formal training in the past twelve months, while the comparable percentages were 35 percent for establishments with 100 to 499 employees and 27 percent for establishments with 50 to 99 employees (Frazis et al. 1997, 49, 71). Meanwhile, a study specifically of contract training found a similar pattern. In a 1995 survey of 2,473 businesses that contracted for training with 104 community colleges, the National Workforce Development Study found that 55 percent of those employers had more than 100 employees (Zeiss et al. 1997, 41). Yet only 2.2 percent of all U.S. business establishments in 1994 had that many employees (U.S. Census Bureau 1997, 544), indicating that large employers are overrepresented among those contracting with community colleges for training.[4]

Unfortunately, the Bureau of Labor Statistics and the National Workforce Development Study do not analyze the causes of this variation by establishment size in utilization of community college workforce training. However, by pulling together a variety of pieces of evidence, we can provide an explanation. And what emerges is that employer skills demands are only one of several factors determining why larger employers more often utilize the community college. As pointed out above, the fact that smaller employers are significantly less likely to use community colleges and that nonskill factors play an important role in determining this lower utilization raises important questions of economic efficiency and social equity.

Large employers' greater provision of formal training to employees

A number of studies find that the larger the firm or establishment, the more likely it is to provide formal as versus informal training[5] to its employees (Baron, Black, and Loewenstein 1987; Bartel 1989; Bishop 1997, 27-28; Frazis, Gittleman, and Joyce 2000; Knoke and Kalleberg 1994; Lynch and Black 1998).[6] And if a business establishment provides more formal training, it is more likely to utilize a community college. This association between employer size, propensity to provide formal training, and use of community colleges can be seen in Table 1.

In its 1995 Survey of Employer Provided Training, the Bureau of Labor Statistics found that larger establishments are more likely to have formal training programs than are smaller ones, even with controls for such other characteristics as industrial sector, employee characteristics, union presence, growth rate, turnover rate, number of fringe benefits provided, and number of high-performance workplace practices used (Frazis, Gittleman, and Joyce 2000, 453). This finding was replicated in other studies. Using the Educational Quality of the Workforce National Employer Survey, Lynch and Black (1998, 69) found that larger establish-

TABLE 1

VARIATIONS BY ESTABLISHMENT SIZE IN PROVISION OF FORMAL TRAINING AND UTILIZATION OF COMMUNITY COLLEGES

Establishment Size: Number of Employees (1994)	Community College Utilization: Percentage of Establishments Utilizing Community Colleges for Formal Training (1995)	Extent of Formal Training (1): Percentage of Establishments that Provided Formal Training in the Past Twelve Months (1995)	Extent of Formal Training (2): Percentage of Employees Who Received Formal Training in the Past Twelve Months (1995)	Intensity of Formal Training: Hours of Formal Training per Employee, May-October 1995 (employer survey)
500 or more	57.0	98.1	71.0	12.0
100-499	35.2	94.4	73.0	12.1
50-99	26.5	90.8	61.1	5.7

SOURCE: Frazis et al. (1997, 54-55, 71).

ments were significantly more likely to provide employee training even with controls for employee characteristics (social composition, occupational distribution, average education, and unionization) and business establishment usage of certain workplace and organizational practices (benchmarking, total quality management, job rotation, self-managed teams, and number of organizational levels) (Lynch and Black 1998, 69).

The tendency of large establishments to more often provide formal training may be traced in turn to six factors: capital intensity, more formalized job classifications and descriptions and more extensive internal labor markets, more use of high-performance work practices, larger human resources departments, greater ability to pay for formal training, and greater ability to bear the risk of losing trained employees.

Capital intensity. It has been argued that larger employers provide more formal training because they tend to have more physical capital and need to upgrade it more often. As a result, they have a greater need to train and retrain their employees on how to use the firm's equipment (Frazis, Herz, and Horrigan 1995, 12).

Occupational structure. Larger employers tend to have more formalized occupational structures, with more formal job classifications and definitions of job tasks as well as clearer and more extensive internal labor markets by which workers can rise from one position to another. These factors are in turn associated with greater incidence and intensity (measured by percentage of employees trained and per capita expenditures) of formal training (Knoke and Kalleberg 1994, 541-43). An indication of how internal structure mediates the impact of establishment size on the incidence of formal training is Knoke and Kalleberg's (1994, 542) finding that controlling for measures of job formalization and the presence of internal labor markets reduces by half the impact of establishment size on incidence of formal training.

Use of high performance work practices. Several studies find that the use of high-performance work practices—such as job rotation, quality circles, employee involvement in decisions on technology, self-managed teams, and total quality management—are associated with a higher incidence and intensity of formal employee training (Frazis, Gittleman, and Joyce 2000, 452, 455, 459; Lynch and Black 1998, 73; Osterman 1995, 140). Moreover, Frazis, Gittleman, and Joyce (2000, 456, 459) found that degree of utilization of high-performance work practices substantially mediates the impact of employer establishment size on intensity of training provision.

Size of human resources departments. The greater propensity of larger employers to engage in formal training may also be traceable to the larger size of their human resources departments (Salzman, Moss, and Tilly 1998, 8, 17). Institutional theory in sociology suggests that human resources staff will push for more training to further their organizational/professional objectives. Moreover, the presence of a larger staff is indicative of a firm's commitment to a notion of the worker as organization citizen, which leads to a view of training as a "membership right" (Scott and Meyer 1994). Evidence in favor of this argument is Osterman's (1995) finding that a strong human resources department—marked by its involvement in strategic decisions—has a statistically significant impact on the proportion of employees receiving formal off-the-job training (Osterman 1995, 140).

There is surprising variability in employers' demand for, and community colleges' supply of, employee training. . . . This variation in business utilization of the community college is problematic on both economic and social equality grounds.

Capacity to bear the costs of training. In many cases, larger employers encounter lower per-trainee costs of training because they can spread the costs of training programs (designing a curriculum and securing a trainer, training site, and instructional materials) over a larger number of trainees, so that their per-worker training costs will be lower for the same kind of training demanded by a small establishment (Frazis, Herz, and Horrigan 1995, 12; Grindel, 1997; Lynch and Black 1998, 65-66). But even if their training costs are no lower, large employers typically can better afford to pay the costs of training, whether directly in the form of payments to training vendors or indirectly in the form of lost work time (Doucette 1993, 15, 17; Knoke and Kalleberg 1994, 543; Zeiss et al. 1997, 78, 80).

In addition, larger employers are better able to leverage state subsidies. A study of state programs subsidizing employer-focused job training found that 39 percent of their funds went to establishments with more than 250 employees, yet they represent only about 1 percent of all establishments (Regional Technology Strategies 1999, 10; U.S. Census Bureau 1998, 549). Larger employers have an advantage in getting state subsidies for a number of reasons. They are more aware of these subsidies and have superior intellectual and political resources to put together winning applications for state aid. Moreover, the state workforce aid programs often utilize funding criteria that advantage larger employers. Sometimes, state programs explicitly take size of firm into account. But more often, size is implicitly taken into account in the form of requirements such as the requirement that training projects involve a certain minimum number of jobs (Regional Technology Strategies 1999, 98-158).[7]

Capacity to bear the cost of losing trained employees. Economists often argue that larger employers more often provide formal training because they are better able to bear the risk that trained employees—especially if trained in programs that are formally structured and thus have greater external currency—may become more attractive to outside employers and leave. Larger employers are better able to run this risk because they have more resources to retain workers. They can pay better and are better able to tie training to promotion through internal training markets (see above). Moreover, if a recently trained employee does leave, they have a larger supply of coworkers to take his or her place (Frazis, Herz, and Horrigan 1995, 12; Lynch and Black 1998, 69; Rosenfeld 1999). An analysis of the Educational Quality of the Workforce National Employer Survey data set provides evidence to back up this argument. Looking at training in four different areas (computers, teamwork, basic education, and sales and customer service), Lynch and Black (1998, 72-74) found that small business establishments were much less likely than large ones to provide training that was highly transportable to another firm (the first three in the list above) but only slightly less likely to provide training that was more firm specific and thus less transportable to other employers (sales and customer service). But it is not just a greater tendency to provide formal training that leads large employers to draw more heavily on community colleges than do small employers. Even if large and small employers were equal in their provision of formal training, large employers are more likely to draw on community colleges because they are more aware of them and because community colleges are more interested in serving larger employers.

Large employers' greater awareness of community colleges

According to our interviews with community college contract training directors, large employers are more aware than are small ones that community colleges can provide employee training and that state funds are available to pay for that training. Small employers, on the other hand, are harder to interest in training because they are more caught up with day-to-day survival and are more suspicious of government-provided programs (Williams, 1997). As the economic development director of a Midwestern community college noted,

> When you're dealing with the small to mid-sized companies, a lot of them don't even know the community college is here, let alone that there's other support services through the college. Or if you mention that we're funded from a government agency, wow, they don't want anything to do with it, because they don't want the red tape. It's an educational process, especially with the smaller and mid-size companies. They're not always open to outside support and help. . . . It's tough working with that small to mid-sized company, but they're the ones who really need the help, but they don't even know it.

One reason that large employers are more aware of community colleges is that they have more human resources staff to scan for and evaluate external training vendors. Moreover, large employers more often interact with local economic development groups, which often involve community colleges among their members. Having worked with community colleges as part of these groups, large employers find it natural to turn to those colleges when they later discover a need to train their employees (Dalton, 1998; Pickar, 1998; Wood, 1998). A dean for contract training at a community college noted,

> Because we work so closely with the EDC [Economic Development Commission] at mid-Florida and the Chambers of Commerce, and our county government . . . we're part of that group. Because we work so well together, there's a lot of cross-selling that goes on between those entities and the companies so that they have a much more favorable impression of the college than you may have in some other areas.

But it is not just employer demand that determines the greater tendency of community colleges to work with larger employers. Factors specific to the community college also play a role.

Community colleges' greater interest in large employers

Although community colleges do try to reach employers of all sizes, it is also clear that they prefer working with larger employers. According to contract training directors at community colleges, larger employers are easier to work with because they are better able to afford contract training and a community college does not have to pull together several different employers to provide a big enough enrollment base for a training program (Armstrong, 1997; Grindel, 1997). As the director of contract training at a community college noted,

> Our experience has been that it's really the larger businesses that are going to be involved in contract ed. If you're dealing with a smaller company, one of the real problems is trying to put together a class for them in terms of designing, et cetera, in terms of their needs. The costs are going to get pretty severe if you're only training three or four or five people, and so one of the things that we work at is putting together consortia of small businesses so that we can do a contract kind of education and training for the consortia that then makes it possible for the individual companies to afford it.

A second advantage of working with large employers is that it provides community colleges with greater potential economic and political payoffs in the future, whether in the form of subsequent training contracts or help in lobbying local and state government bodies for more funds (Dougherty and Bakia 2000, 222-23). A contract training director for a Michigan community college spoke to the second point:

> There have been companies who have gone to the state and to the [Michigan] Jobs Commission to say what a good job college X has done. . . . There are companies that are very willing to be a champion for the college, support our millage proposals, bond proposals, whatever.

Variations by industry in usage of community colleges

Business usage of community colleges as training providers varies markedly not only by the size of employers but also by the industry they are located in. The 1995 Bureau of Labor Statistics Survey of Employer Provided Training found that, on average, 31 percent of establishments with fifty or more employees utilize community colleges for formal training. However, certain industries are much more likely to enlist community colleges: finance, insurance, and real estate (47 percent of establishments in that industry sector) and durable and nondurable manufacturing (47 percent and 41 percent, respectively). Meanwhile, other industries drew on community colleges at a much lower rate: retail trade (9 percent of establishments), wholesale trade (24 percent), construction (25 percent), and transportation, communications, and public utilities (27 percent) (Frazis et al. 1997, 71). This variation by industry in utilization of community colleges can be seen in Table 2.

The Bureau of Labor Statistics findings are echoed by the National Workforce Development Survey of employers who are known to contract with 104 community colleges in twenty-seven states. The same industries emerge as above-average and below-average users of the contract training services of the community college (Zeiss et al. 1997, 41).[8]

Four factors may explain this variation by industry in business utilization of community colleges: the average size of employers, capacity to attract state subsidies for workforce training, community college interest in serving that industry, and availability of alternative suppliers.

Establishment size

Part of the reason that some industries utilize the community college more than others is that they are more heavily populated by large employers (see Table 2). The correlation between percentage of establishments in an industry with more than 100 employees and percentage of establishments using community colleges is .462. As analyzed above, large employers are more likely to utilize community colleges for several reasons: they provide more formal training to their employees, they are more aware of community colleges, and community colleges find them more desirable clients.

Yet while the correlation above clearly shows the impact of industry differences in establishment size on the utilization of community colleges, the fact that the correlation is not even higher indicates that other factors are also significantly shaping the utilization of community colleges.

Industrial targeting of state aid for workforce training

Some industries are also more likely to utilize the community college because state subsidies for workforce training, which are strongly routed through community colleges,[9] tend to favor certain industries over others. A 1999 study of state

TABLE 2

VARIATIONS ACROSS INDUSTRIES IN UTILIZATION OF COMMUNITY COLLEGES, ESTABLISHMENT SIZE, AND FORMAL TRAINING

Industry	Community College Utilization: Percentage of Establishments Utilizing Community Colleges for Formal Training (1995)	Establishment Size: Percentage of Establishments with 100 or More Employees (1994)	Extent of Formal Training (1): Percentage of Establishments Providing Formal Training in the Past Twelve Months (1995)	Extent of Formal Training (2): Percentage of Employees Receiving Formal Training in the Past Twelve Months (1995)	Intensity of Formal Training: Hours of Formal Training per Employee over Six Months (employer survey) (1995)
All industries	31.3	2.2	92.5	69.8	10.7
Manufacturing: durable goods	47.1	7.6	88.1	78.3	11.7
Finance, insurance, real estate	47.0	1.4	95.6	87.4	16.6
Services	42.1	2.1	93.5	70.7	11.0
Manufacturing: nondurable goods	41.3	10.5	95.2	85.4	11.9
Mining	28.0	4.0	96.7	94.7	14.4
Transportation, communications, public utilities	27.1	3.3	96.5	81.4	18.3
Construction	25.1	0.7	94.7	71.2	5.0
Trade: wholesale	24.1	1.5	98.4	68.1	8.4
Trade: retail	9.4	1.7	88.7	48.8	3.7

SOURCE: Frazis et al. (1997, 1998).

funding for employer-focused job training found that 70 percent of total funding does go to manufacturing firms and twenty-eight states target aid to specific industries (Regional Technology Strategies 1999, 9). This industrial targeting often involves naming specific industries such as biotechnology or the manufacturing sector in general (Regional Technology Strategies 1999).[10] But the industry targeting also occurs through the use of general criteria—such as the criteria that the industry must produce many high-wage jobs, have growth potential, be technologically intensive, be export oriented, be new to the state, or be likely to leave the state—that may not designate specific industries but do tend to favor industries such as manufacturing and disqualify industries such as construction and retail trade (Regional Technology Strategies 1999, 121, 140, 143, 148; Tornholm, 1998). The director of a Midwestern state program funding community college contract training described how it was targeted:

> Apparel would not be eligible. Banking would not be eligible. We're trying to focus on base economy. We're looking at manufacturing world headquarters, research and development. The apparel industry in [our state] is almost all retail. Banking is what we would call service sector kinds of things. . . . There's just a huge amount of manufacturing going on in [our state,] and that does bring in dollars to our base economy, and we are limited in the dollars we have available, and our demand for grants is more than twice as much as the money we have available. So as we try to focus on where you get the biggest bang with multipliers for your dollars it tends to be primarily manufacturing.

As the statement above indicates, an industry's ability to leverage public subsidies is a product in good part of state government's assessment of the industry's importance to the community, especially its tax base. In addition, states tend to be much less generous to industries that are place bound and thus cannot easily leave the state: most notably, retail trade. And of course, simple political power—which is often hard to distinguish from economic importance—also plays a role in securing large state subsidies for a particular industry. The belief that a certain industry is key to a state's future—as is the case of the auto industry in Michigan or pharmaceuticals in New Jersey—may be testimony as much to its accumulated political power as to a dispassionate assessment of its likely future contribution to the state's economy.

Community college interest

Another factor behind the relatively low usage of community colleges by a certain industry may be that the community colleges are less interested in supplying training to that industry versus others. For example, human resources officials in construction firms, particularly in industrial construction, frequently complained that community colleges are insufficiently interested in providing them with training (Ehlers, 1997; Ray, 1997). A top executive of a large construction firm argued that community colleges seem to have a real hang-up with construction because they don't see it as a stable industry. In other words, people don't go for twenty years to the same location to go to work. They move from one location to another, so they have a little problem in dealing with that. . . . They don't look at it as, wait a minute, that workforce is going to move within the same state, not necessarily across country. The other side of that too . . . construction contracting . . . is the largest employer in the United States. We have more people working in construction contracting than you have in any other single industry. When you think about that, you've got to wonder why the community college systems aren't more receptive to helping develop that workforce.

The extent of such community college unresponsiveness is not clear and may well be exaggerated by industry sources. However, it is noteworthy that the construction industry has made a major effort to expand an alternative training supplier: courses offered by the employers' associations using curricula developed by the industry-supported National Center for Construction Education and Research (Ehlers, 1997; Heffner, 1998; Ray, 1997). As an executive for a major construction firm stated,

Because of the failing of the community colleges, what's happening is the professional organizations that are associated with the industry [the Associated Builders and Contractors and the Associated General Contractors of America] . . . are filling that void and . . . are providing training. They know the industry, they know the kind of schedules we operate on, they know what the skills are that we need, they can tap directly into these contractor organizations, and so what's happening is the role of the community college in the construction industry is being taken over by these professional chapters.

Alternative suppliers of training

As the statement above indicates, an industry's utilization of the community college may be relatively low if it has a full array of alternative suppliers. In general, industries can draw not just on community colleges but also on their own training staffs, postsecondary vocational schools (public and private), private consultants, equipment vendors, trade and professional associations, and labor/management joint apprenticeship programs (Frazis et al. 1997, 71; Jacobs 1992, 27, 33; Lynch and Black 1998, 77).

In the case of the construction industry specifically, its relatively low usage of community colleges may be attributable in part to the fact that the industry has well-developed alternative sources of training besides community colleges. In the 1995 Bureau of Labor Statistics survey of employee training, 58 percent of construction establishments utilized training provided by union, trade, and professional organizations, more than double the average for all industries (24 percent) (Frazis et al. 1997, 71). As we saw in the previous section, employer associations such as the Associated General Contractors and the Associated Builders and Contractors run their own programs, sometimes using their own facilities and sometimes renting space from community colleges, but providing their own instructors (Ehlers, 1997; Heffner, 1998; Ray, 1997).

In addition, there are labor/management apprenticeship programs run by unions. Although the craft unions are no longer as strong as before, they still run extensive joint training programs in conjunction with the firms they have organized (which band together in industry associations of union-organized firms). These union/management programs—which offer apprenticeship and in-service training—often are quite large and structured, with formal curricula and their own training facilities and specialized instructors (Lawson, 1998; Sillars, 1999; Somers, 1999).[11] For example, the training director of a carpentry joint apprenticeship training committee stated,

> We have commercially purchased textbooks. We have instructors that lecture. Our program in and of itself is about 60 percent classroom lecture and written paperwork, test type situations just like a college would be, and it's just as tough as a college. . . . We've got a very disciplined program that requires just as much as a college.

In contrast to construction, the finance, insurance, and real estate sector is a heavy user of community colleges, with 47 percent of establishments paying community colleges to provide employee training, well above the 31 percent average for establishments in all industries (Frazis et al. 1997, 71). However, this figure could well have been much higher if the financial sector were not to have ready access to training provided by trade and professional organizations. More than one-third (37 percent) of finance, insurance, and real estate establishments utilize "trade, professional, or union organizations" (really only the first two) as training providers, well above the 24 percent average for establishments in all industries (Frazis et al. 1997, 71).[12] For example, the banking industry draws heavily on the American Institute of Banking, founded in 1901, which offers courses—addressed both to bank managers and lower-level employees—that cover all facets of banking (American Institute of Banking 1998). Although regional American Institute of Banking chapters do work with community colleges on occasion (Laguna, 1998), they also directly compete with them (Owen, 1998). For example, a regional director for the American Institute of Banking described some of his contract education offerings, which were done entirely apart from the community colleges:

> One of the larger banks in [our state] [came] to me yesterday . . . saying . . . would I be able to put their [writing] program together for them, and this would be offered across the state with my instructors. . . . So we do in-house training quite often. I've done proposals for computer training for two different banks in this state that I'm waiting to hear back on.

For-profits as challengers to community colleges. Before leaving the issue of business utilization of community colleges, it would be worthwhile to discuss the impact of the rapid growth of for-profit institutions on business demand for community colleges. For-profit institutions have definitely entered the market for employee training, including contract training, with the for-profit share of two-year institutions rising from 19 percent in 1989 to 28 percent in 1999 (Bailey, Badway, and Gumport 2001; Kelly 2001).

Yet it is not clear whether for-profit institutions pose as great a competitive threat to community colleges as some fear (Zeiss 1998). For example, it is important to keep in mind that the for-profit share of enrollments among two-year institutions actually fell from 4.1 percent in 1993 to 3.9 percent in 1998 (Bailey, Badway, and Gumport 2001). This failure to rapidly grow in enrollments may reflect the fact that community colleges continue to enjoy some significant advantages over for-profit colleges.

One involves pricing. Because of state and local aid, community colleges are not entirely dependent on tuition revenues and can charge less money than for-profit schools (Bailey, Badway, and Gumport 2001; Dalton, 1998). As the director of continuing education at a community college put it,

> A national training school has a facility near us, and they're doing quite a bit of training . . . but their training is more expensive than what we would normally charge, again because we are a community college and we receive both state funding and we have a local tax base.

Moreover, community college credentials tend to be more prestigious than those of vocational schools or noneducational training providers, in part because they tend to be more creditable toward a baccalaureate degree (Cantor 1992, 13-14; Choulochas, 1998; Light, 1998).[13] As one of the originators of the automotive service education programs for one of the major auto companies noted,

> We wanted it [the automotive technician program] to get to a college degree, that's why we did not favor proprietary schools: because you spend big money to get a piece of paper that may or may not have a great deal of value in the real world. We wanted these young people to have an opportunity to get an educational experience as well as a technical training experience, the result of which would be two things. One, that we'd have a very well-educated and competent technician. But at the same time, we'd have someone who had the foundation for growth both within the dealers' organization and at the same time within the community.

Community colleges also benefit from the perception that they are not fly-by-night operations; they are here to stay. On the other hand, proprietary schools—fairly or not—are seen as less stable and reliable (McDougal, 1998; Pickar, 1998).[14] As a training executive for one of the major car makers put it,

> The regulation of some of those vocational colleges is . . . I'm not sure it's as good as it could be. So I'd want to be very concerned that this vocational college that all of a sudden springs up and says, "I'm going to provide you this or that," that indeed they are. I guess I'm talking about reputation and track record. Do they really have the resources both from a teaching standpoint and from an equipment and facilities standpoint to give you good training, or are they just saying they're going to and it ends up being something less than that?

As we have seen, employee training by community colleges is unevenly distributed across employers differing in size and industry, and that unevenness of distribution is due not just to differences in skill demands but also to other factors such as state aid criteria, employer awareness of community colleges, and community college interest in employers. The conclusion to this article will take up the policy implications of this finding.

Variations in Community College Supply

Virtually all community colleges provide employee training. In fact, the vast majority provide contract training that is specifically customized in some fashion to the desires of employers.[15] However, the magnitude of supply is very uneven across community colleges. Focusing on contract training, two national surveys in 1989 and 1994 found that the number of students enrolled at a given college ranged between lows of 3 or 10 and highs of 27,000 or 55,000 (Johnson 1995, 100; Lynch, Palmer, and Grubb 1991, 17). These figures are collected in Table 3.

A major axis of this uneven distribution of employee training is degree of urbanization. A 1989 national survey of community colleges found that the median urban community college offered twice as many courses and serviced 48 percent more employers than did the median rural college, with suburban community colleges falling in between (Lynch, Palmer, and Grubb 1991, Table A-2).

To the degree that community college contract training can be a useful stimulus to economic growth, this unevenness in its supply is of concern and suggests the need for further analysis and perhaps a policy response. However, as we will note below, deeper community college involvement in employee training also carries the danger of significant negative side effects. Hence, our response to the uneven supply of employee training by community colleges cannot be simply one of pushing colleges to become more involved.

On further examination, several factors appear to account for why community colleges differ so much in the size of their contract training programs: the volume of employer demand, the degree of administrative leadership, and the amount of fiscal and human resources available to community colleges to develop and market curricula, equip training facilities, and staff courses.

Employer demand

Clearly, the size of a community college's contract training program will vary in good part due to the volume of local demand by employers. This in turn will depend on the number and size of local employers, the magnitude of their training needs, their capacity to bear the costs of training, their awareness of the community college, and the availability of alternative training suppliers to the community college (Bragg 1990, 17). Several of these factors have already been reviewed above, so we will focus just on the number and size of local employers.

Typically, rural community colleges have fewer employers (although some of those employers can be large, as in the case of branch plants in the rural South) and consequently smaller contract training programs. To be sure, urban community colleges typically do confront more competing suppliers than do rural colleges. But

TABLE 3

EXTENT OF CONTRACT TRAINING ACROSS COMMUNITY COLLEGES

	Doucette (1993, 4)	Lynch, Palmer, and Grubb (1991, 17-19)	Johnson (1995, 88, 90, 100)
Date of survey	Fall 1992	Fall 1989	Fall 1993
Response rate (%)	69	72	47
Percentage of two-year colleges offering			
Employee training	96		
Contract training specifically		94	89
Median enrollments in contract			
training		919	1,125
Mean enrollments in contract			
training		1,867	2,733
Range of enrollments (lowest			
college to highest college) in			
contract training		10 to 27,000	3 to 55,000

on the other hand, urban colleges usually are surrounded by more employers who might demand contract training.

Leadership by the community college administration

Even if a community college has a high volume of employer demand, it may be led by top administrators who are not greatly interested in pursuing employee training (Doucette 1993, 15; Grubb et al. 1997, 19-20; Harrison, 1997; Johnson 1995, 138, 159-61; Tornholm, 1998, 8-9; Williams, 1997, 5). Presidents and other top officials can greatly facilitate a community college's employee training program by defining it as central to a college's mission, removing structural and policy barriers (often based on traditional academic practices), and securing the funds necessary to market the program and develop new courses (Bragg et al. 1991, 135; Johnson 1995, 138; Zeiss et al. 1997, 61, 64-66). For example, the development of an advanced technology center at Rock Valley Community College (Rockford, Illinois) in the mid-1980s was attributed by internal and external observers to the strong interest of the president, who conceived the idea, rounded up business support, and got a bond issue passed to pay for the center (Jacobs 1995; Williams, 1997, 5). And in the case of Columbus State Community College (Columbus, Ohio), the active support of the president allowed the contract training director to, in his words, "request special procedures from other college departments (admissions, registrar's office, personnel, business office, data processing) to accommodate the non-traditional flow of registration, fee collection, and hiring instructors required for corporate training" (cited in Johnson 1995, 160-61).

Administrative leadership may be absent or only weakly present because a president may view contract training as an unnecessary function or a distraction from more fundamental missions such as college access or transfer preparation (Armstrong, 1997; Irwin, 1998; McNeil, 1998). For example, the president of a community college with a strong commitment to academic and transfer education stated,

> In the early nineties, before I first came to this college, we had been doing some, but not much, [community services and contract education]. [Due to a state budget crisis,] we were cutting millions of dollars out of our budget, like everyone was. . . . We couldn't spend our money on everything. So we eliminated our contract education program, and we eliminated our community services program. The community services program wasn't making any money; neither was our contract education program. They were just costing not only money, but they were—it was, again, there was a need to focus on things you do well. . . . The reason we haven't reestablished any focus on contract ed is because being a three-college district, [another] college decided that they really wanted to go into this in a big way. So they approached us . . . and said, "Would you mind if we took a leadership role in developing partnerships with business and industry and providing the kinds of things that they need from a community college system?" I thought that was a really good idea.

Community college leaders who see contract training as clashing with other missions have some justification for their belief. There is evidence that active involvement in contract training may sap the commitment, attention, time, and energy community college administrators need to promote traditional missions of the community college such as baccalaureate preparation, remedial education, and general education (Dougherty and Bakia 2000, 233-35). For instance, there is evidence that involvement in contract training moves community college faculty and administrators away from a commitment to the traditional values of education toward a narrower allegiance to a conception of education as training. In a national survey in 1993-1994, contract training directors frequently stated the importance of running their operations in a businesslike, nontraditionally academic, way: "We run our customized training as a business, not as an educational entity. We are very close to our customers. . . . You cannot afford to run contract training like a traditional college" (cited in Johnson 1995, 154). This vocationalized attitude not only will influence contract training administrators and faculty themselves but also may spread to their more academic colleagues. Moreover, a growing emphasis on contract training may undercut traditional community college missions by diverting administrators' time, attention, and energy. The more they devote to expanding contract education, the less they may have for maintaining and advancing traditional missions such as providing access to the four-year colleges, serving underprepared students, and providing a general education (Dougherty and Bakia 2000, 233-35).

A lack of administrative support for employee training may also stem from a fear of faculty opposition to overly applied training and too much entanglement with business. For example, in a 1992 survey of workforce training directors at community colleges, 13 percent rated faculty opposition or lack of support for contract training as a major problem, and 50 percent rated it as a minor problem (and 37 percent as not a problem) (Doucette 1993, 15).

Finally, weak administrative support for employee training can simply be due more to inattention than to opposition. We found this in the case of a community college located in a major metropolitan area. Despite the wealth of contract training opportunities available, its contract training operation was neither large nor well organized. The main explanation seemed to be a lack of administrative leadership, due to the highly politicized nature of education policy in that city, which has resulted in high turnover among top administrators and the appointment of people of mediocre competence.

Fiscal resources

A major complaint of contract training officers is that they do not have enough funds to properly operate their units (Bragg 1990, 17-18; Doucette 1993, 15, 22; Zeiss et al. 1997, 61, 78). A 1992 national survey of workforce training directors at

---

Employee training by community colleges is an ambiguous phenomenon. Too little training may harm local economies and deny community colleges students and revenues. Too much training may greatly weaken baccalaureate transfer preparation and remedial education.

---

community colleges found that 35 percent agreed that "inadequate operating budget of training unit" was a major obstacle. They felt that their budgets were insufficient to develop the right curricula, properly equip their training facilities, and hire enough outside experts to teach specialized courses that the regular faculty cannot cover (Doucette 1993, 15, 22). As a director of workforce training at an Illinois community college put it, "Financial limitations make it an on-going struggle for the community college to keep up with current technology. Equipment purchases and staff development and training are the first areas to be cut when budgets are tight" (cited in Bragg 1990, 18).

Human resources

Effective contract training programs need staffers able to develop courses responsive to business demands, market those courses to business, provide instruction, and manage the courses in a way business finds acceptable (Johnson 1995, 132, 139-41, 149, 161, 170; Zeiss et al. 1997, 67-68). For example, in a national survey of community colleges engaged in contract training, a major explanation given by contract trainers for why certain community colleges are seen as leaders in contract training is that they have "a quality staff, with appropriate skills for marketing contract training" or they "operat[e] the unit as a business, with specialists like grant writers on staff to help finance the entire operation" (cited in Johnson 1995, 139-40). Yet many community colleges, particularly small rural colleges, find it difficult to attract or retain the staff and faculty necessary to mount effective contract training programs (Bragg 1990, 17-18; Bragg et al. 1991, 13; Deegan and Drisko 1985, 16; Doucette 1993, 15; Grubb et al. 1997, 20; Jacobs, 1997, 16; Johnson 1995, 132-33, 140-41, 149, 161, 170; Palmer 1990, 35-36, 44; Zeiss et al. 1997, 61, 67-68). For example, in a 1992 national survey, 22 percent of workforce training directors at community colleges agreed that "lack of experienced trainers or expertise" was a major obstacle to providing workforce training (Doucette 1993, 15).[16]

Summary and Conclusions

Despite its broad prevalence, employee training by community colleges is quite unevenly distributed. Business utilization of the community college for such purposes varies greatly by establishment size and industry. And while most community colleges offer employee training, some offer a lot and many only a little.

Business' variable utilization of community colleges

Business usage of the community college for employee training is unevenly distributed across employers differing in size and industry. Larger employers more often use community colleges for employee training than do smaller ones. This disproportionate usage is best explained by differences between large and small business establishments in the magnitude of their provision of formal training to employees and in their willingness to use community colleges to provide that training. Larger establishments provide more formal training because they are more capital intensive, have more complex job structures and internal labor markets, make greater use of high-performance work practices, have larger and more active human resources departments, and have a greater capacity to bear the costs of formal training, including the risk of losing employees who have undergone that training. Beyond their greater provision of formal training, larger establishments are also more likely to utilize community colleges to provide that formal training because they are more aware of community colleges and community colleges see them as more attractive customers.

Business utilization of community colleges for employee training also varies greatly by industry. Employers in health care, manufacturing, transportation, communications, utilities, and finance and insurance draw on community colleges much more than do employers in wholesale and retail trade, apparel making, and construction. Apparently explaining this variation in usage are interindustry differences in the average size of business establishments (and therefore provision of formal training), the tendency of state subsidies for employee training to target certain industries, greater community college interest in serving certain industries rather than others, and interindustry differences in the availability of training providers others than community colleges.

While for-profit institutions have definitely entered the market for employee training, it is not clear that for-profit institutions pose as great a competitive threat to community colleges as some fear. The advantages community colleges enjoy over proprietary schools (cheaper cost, greater capacity to facilitate movement toward a baccalaureate degree, and better reputation), when coupled with the still very small enrollments of the for-profit sector, argue for some sobriety in judging claims that the for-profit colleges will cut deeply into employer demand for community college training of their employees.

The fact that the differences in firm usage of the community colleges for employee training are not simply outgrowths of differences in skill demands but rather are shaped as well by other factors raises the question of whether public policy should intervene to ensure a less uneven usage of the community college. The role of nonskill factors argues that smaller establishments and ones in certain industries (particularly nonmanufacturing) are receiving less training than is optimal for economic growth. In addition, there is a social equality dimension. Smaller employers and ones in less training-intensive industries tend to attract less advantaged workers. To the degree they receive less training, particularly in general skills, they have fewer opportunities for occupational and economic mobility (Lynch and Black 1998, 70).

Government cannot easily erase some of the advantages enjoyed by larger private employers or certain industries, whether deeper pockets, larger human resources departments, or more appeal to community colleges. However, government agencies can make their own subsidies of employee training more size and even industry neutral by such means as earmarking a certain portion for smaller employers or certain industries or giving community colleges bonuses for aggressive efforts to service smaller employers and neglected industries.

This tilt in favor of smaller employers may help correct for the possibility that state funds may be unnecessarily subsidizing employee training by larger employers that are well able to finance it themselves. For example, a survey by the Office of Community Colleges of the State University of New York of 169 employers who had contracted with New York State community colleges for training found that only 33 percent said that no training would have occurred in the absence of the state-subsidized training. Another 34 percent said they would have trained with their own staff, 26 percent stated they would have purchased training elsewhere, and 7 percent gave other answers (Winter and Fadale 1990, 5).

Community colleges' variable supply of employee training

Community college supply of employee training is as uneven as business demand. While most community colleges offer contract training, some offer a lot and many only a little. This great variation among community colleges may be due to differences among them in magnitude of local employer demand, degree of leadership by community college administrators, and amount of fiscal and human resources to develop curricula, equip facilities, market programs, and hire appropriate instructors. Even with a high volume of local employer demand, a community college may not offer much in the way of contract training if it is led by top administrators who do not favor a strong role in employee training. Presidents may oppose such training because they view it as a distraction from more fundamental missions such as college access or transfer preparation, they fear faculty opposition to overly applied training and too much entanglement with business, or they simply are distracted by other organizational concerns. Even with strong administrative leadership, a community college may not be able to pursue a strong role in contract training if it lacks the necessary fiscal and human resources. Many contract training officers complain about budgets that are too low to do a good job in developing curricula and marketing them to business, equipping facilities, and hiring capable instructors.

The weak development of employee training in certain community colleges is not necessarily a problem requiring policy intervention. On one hand, weak development of employee training may harm local employers and thus the local economy. It may also deny community colleges such benefits as increased enrollments, new revenues, greater external political support, and better information on the changing demands of the labor market. On the other hand, a vigorous employee training effort may harm the community college, reducing the attention, time, and energy available to foster traditional missions of the community college such as baccalaureate transfer preparation or remedial/developmental education.

If community colleges are to protect their traditional avocational functions even as they deepen their involvement in employee training, it is important to provide specific incentives for pursuing equality of college access, transfer education, general education, and so forth. This could be done through a state accountability system that bestows funds or acclaim on community colleges that actively pursue not only expanded employee training but also greater college access for disadvantaged populations, a rich general education, effective transfer education, and so forth. (See Dougherty, Kim, and Hong 2002 for more on state accountability systems.)

APPENDIX

COMMUNITY COLLEGE SHARE OF STATE AID FOR EMPLOYEE TRAINING: STATES WHERE SHARE IS 30 PERCENT OR HIGHER

State	Program	Funding (1998) (in millions of dollars)	Community College Share (%)
Colorado	Colorado FIRST Customized Job Training Program	5.6	80
	Existing Industry Job Training Program	2.1	80
Idaho	Workforce Development Training Fund	3.6	75
Illinois	Prairie State 2000 Authority	3.6	40
Kentucky	Bluegrass State Skills Corporation	3.1	35
Louisiana	Quick Start Training Program	1	100
Massachusetts	Employed Worker Collaborative	1.5	40
Michigan	Economic Development Job Training	31	70 (required)
Minnesota	Minnesota Job Skills Partnership	7.4	70
Mississippi	Industrial Training Program	5.5	100
Missouri	DESE Customized Training Program	5	50
North Carolina	Focused Industrial Training	3.7	100
	New and Expanding Industry Program	10.1	Majority
	Occupational Continuing Education	10.5	100
South Carolina	Special Schools	7.9	Most
Texas	Skills Development Fund	13	100 (required)
Washington	Washington State Job Skills Program	0.6	75
Wisconsin	Customized Labor Training Program	4.2	40
	Workforce Education Funding	0.5	100

SOURCE: Bosworth (1999), Regional Technology Strategies (1999, 98-158).

Notes

1. In some cases, states are encouraging community colleges and four-year colleges to establish mechanisms for transferring vocational credits and degrees at community colleges toward baccalaureate programs at four-year colleges (Horine 1998; Pitter 1999; Rifkin 2000; Washington State Board for Community and Technical Colleges 1997, 10). In other cases, community colleges have been exploring the option, and sometimes securing state approval, to themselves provide four-year degrees in applied subjects (Cook 2000; Healy 1998; MacDonald 1999; Schmidt 1999). For more on this, see Dougherty (2002).

2. There is evidence that employer-provided or -financed training also appears to be more common in business establishments that offer extensive employee benefits, are committed to innovative workplace practices, and have below average employee turnover. Interestingly, unionization is only weakly related to employer provision of formal employee training. If there is any relationship, it is that unionized establishments provide less formal employee training, seemingly because their workers are more experienced and require less training (Frazis et al. 1997, 1998; Frazis, Gittleman, and Joyce 2000).

3. Although size of an establishment is positively related to whether it uses the community college for formal employee training, size is negatively related to the proportion of an employer's formal training that is delivered by community colleges. The larger the business establishment, the greater the tendency to call on

community colleges for formal training but also the greater the proportion of formal training delivered by in-house trainers (Frazis et al. 1997, 72-74).

4. The response rate in this survey was 53 percent. The community colleges themselves decided which employers should be sent surveys. The average number of employers responding per community college was 24, with a range between 3 and 145 (Zeiss et al. 1997, 40).

5. The Bureau of Labor Statistics defines formal training as "training that is planned in advance and that has a structured format and defined curriculum" (Frazis et al. 1997).

6. Several analyses also find that establishment size has no relationship, or even a negative relationship, to measures of intensity of employee training such as the percentage of employees being formally trained or the number of hours they are being trained (Knoke and Kalleberg 1994; Lynch and Black 1998; Osterman 1995, 140). However, this seeming absence of an impact of employer size on training intensity may stem from the fact that these studies may be examining the impact of size after having controlled for the very processes that channel its effect. Frazis et al. (1997) and Frazis, Gittleman, and Joyce (2000) found that size has a significant impact on number of training hours employers provide before variables for extensiveness of benefits and of use of high-performance work practices are controlled, suggesting that the latter play a major role in mediating the effect of size on extent of formal training (Frazis et al. 1997, 55; Frazis, Gittleman, and Joyce 2000, 456, 459). And it so happens that the analyses reported by Lynch and Black (1998) and Osterman (1995) include as controls variables measuring high-performance work practices.

7. For descriptions of specific state programs that take firm size into account—explicitly or implicitly—in awarding funds, see the state case studies in Regional Technology Strategies (1999).

8. The latter survey does turn up one heavy user of community colleges that is not discussed by the Bureau of Labor Statistics survey: the health care industry.

9. Across forty-three state programs (with several states having more than one program), community colleges received 34 percent of the training funds allocated by those programs in 1998 (Bosworth 1999; Regional Technology Strategies 1999, 98-158). In fact, in Michigan, Texas, and Mississippi, the aid programs are required to funnel most or all of their training funds through the community colleges. For example, the Texas Skills Development Fund was set up to fund employment training solely at community colleges (Hall, 1998; Michigan Jobs Commission 1998; Regional Technology Strategies 1999, 93-96, 128, 130, 151). See the appendix for a list of states in which community colleges receive more than 30 percent of state aid for employee training.

10. For descriptions of state programs that target particular industries, see the case studies in Regional Technology Strategies (1999).

11. Some joint apprenticeship training committees in construction do contract with community colleges to provide the classroom training component for apprenticeship programs (Light, 1998; Tesinsky, 1997). But much more commonly, joint apprenticeship training committees ask community colleges to do no more than simply grant college credit for joint apprenticeship training committees–provided training (Armstrong, 1997, 1998; Benson, 1998; Israel, 1998). Given all this, the main customers in the construction industry for contract apprenticeship training and retraining by community colleges are not joint apprenticeship programs but rather nonunionized employers (Grindel, 1997; Heffner, 1998; Horton, 1998; Tesinsky, 1997)

12. The banking industry may be an even heavier user of professional associations for training than is the case with the rest of the finance, insurance, and real estate sector. In an analysis of the AACC/NETWORK National Community College Workforce Development Database in December 1998, only six programs at community colleges definitely involved contract training for the banking industry.

13. This advantage may erode as for-profit schools increasingly provide baccalaureate degrees. Between 1992-1993 and 1997-1998, for-profits increased their share of four-year enrollments from 1.1 percent to 1.9 percent (Bailey, Badway, and Gumport 2001, 65).

14. This perception of instability may be changing with the expansion of for-profit chains such as ITT Educational Services, Corinthian Colleges, DeVry, and the Apollo group (which runs the University of Phoenix) (Kelly 2001).

15. See Dougherty and Bakia (2000) for an extensive analysis of the various forms contract training takes, the factors leading employers to demand it and community colleges to supply it, and the impact of contract training on the community college.

16. Similarly, among the 277 respondents to Deegan and Drisko's 1983 survey of community colleges regarding contract training, 35 percent said that lack of qualified instructors was a major source of problems in providing contract training (Deegan and Drisko 1985, 16).

References

American Institute of Banking. 1998. *Course and product catalog*. Washington, DC: American Institute of Banking.

Armstrong, George M. 1997, 1998. Interviews by Marianne Bakia and Kevin Dougherty with Coordinator, Technical and Professional Training, Continuing Education Division, Hudson Valley Community College. Troy, New York.

Ashley, Dan. 1997. Interview by Kevin Dougherty with department chair, automotive training center, Hudson Valley Community College, Troy, New York.

Bailey, Thomas, Norena Badway, and Patricia J. Gumport. 2001. *For profit higher education and community colleges*. Stanford, CA: National Center for Postsecondary Improvement, Stanford University.

Baron, John, Dan Black, and Mark Loewenstein. 1987. Employer size: The implications for search, capital investment, starting wages, and wage growth. *Journal of Labor Economics* 5:76-89.

Bartel, Ann. 1989. Formal employee training programs and their impact on labor productivity: Evidence from a human resource survey. NBER working paper no. 3026, National Bureau of Economic Research, Cambridge, MA.

Bishop, John H. 1997. What we know about employer-provided training: A review of the literature. *Research in Labor Economics* 16:19-87.

Bosworth, B. 1999. Unpublished tabulations from the 1998 survey of state-funded, employer-focused job training programs. Belmont, MA: Regional Technology Strategies.

Bragg, Debra D. 1990. *Building world-market competitors: Technology transfer and the Illinois community college system*. Springfield: Illinois Council of Public Community College Presidents.

Bragg, Debra D., Russell Hamm, Daniel J. Lavista, and Herbert G. Lyon. 1991. The evolving role of community colleges in technology transfer. *Journal of Studies in Technical Careers* 13 (spring): 125-44.

Bragg, Debra D., Russell Hamm, Daniel J. Lavista, Herbert G. Lyon, and James Jacobs. 1991. *A conceptual framework for evaluating community college customized training programs*. MDS-175. Berkeley, CA: National Center for Research in Vocational Education.

Cantor, Jeffrey A. 1992. Apprenticeship 2000: A model for community college collaboration with business and industry. Results of a national study involving three industries. Paper presented at the annual meeting of the Eastern Educational Research Association, Hilton Head, SC.

Carnevale, Anthony P., and Donna M. Desrochers. 2000. Employer training: The high road, the low road, and the muddy middle path. In *Back to shared prosperity*, edited by Ray Marshall, 300-307. Armonk, NY: M. E. Sharpe.

Choulochas, John. 1998. Interview by Kevin Dougherty with the former National Manager, College Programs, General Motors Automotive Service Education Program (ASEP). Seattle, Washington.

Commission on the Skills of the American Workforce. 1990. *America's choice: High skills or low wages!* Rochester, NY: National Center on Education and the Economy.

Cook, Amy. 2000. *Community college baccalaureate degrees: A delivery model for the future?* Policy paper. Denver, CO: Education Commission of the States, Center for Community College Policy.

Dalton, Marie. 1998. Interview by Kevin Dougherty with Dean of Continuing Education, San Jacinto Community College. Pasadena, TX.

Deegan, William L., and Ronald Drisko. 1985. Contract training: Progress and policy issues. *Community College Journal* 55 (March): 14-17.

Derry, William. 1997. Interview by Kevin Dougherty with Automotive Technology Coordinator, Broward County Community College, Hollywood, FL.

Doucette, Don. 1993. *Community college workforce training programs for employees of business, industry, labor, and government: A status report*. Mission Viejo, CA: League for Innovation in the Community College.

Dougherty, Kevin J. 2001. State policies and the community college's role in workforce preparation. In *Community colleges: Policy in the future context*, edited by Barbara Townsend and Susan Twombly, 129-78. Stamford, CT: Ablex.

———. 2002. The evolving role of community college: Policy issues and research questions. In *Higher education: Handbook of theory and research*, vol. 17, edited by John Smart and William Tierney, 295-348. New York: Algora Press.

Dougherty, Kevin J., and Marianne Bakia. 1999. *The new economic development role of the community college*. New York: Community College Research Center, Teachers College, Columbia University.

———. 2000. Community colleges and contract training: Content, origins, and impact. *Teachers College Record* 102 (February): 197-243.

Dougherty, Kevin J., Jennifer E. Kim, and Esther Hong. 2002. *Performance accountability and community colleges: Forms, impacts, and problems. Final report*. New York: Community College Research Center, TeachersCollege, Columbia University.

Ehlers, Leroy. 1998. Interview by Marianne Bakia with Manager, Craft Training, East Region, Fluor-Daniels Construction, Greenville, NC.

Frazis, Harley J., Maury Gittleman, Michael Horrigan, and Mary Joyce. 1997. Formal and informal training: Evidence from a matched employee-employer survey. *Advances in the Study of Entrepreneurship, Innovation, and Economic Growth* 9:47-82.

———. 1998. Results from the 1995 survey of employer-provided training. *Monthly Labor Review* (June): 3-13.

Frazis, Harley J., Maury Gittleman, and Mary Joyce. 2000. Correlates of training: An analysis using both employer and employee characteristics. *Industrial and Labor Relations Review* 53 (April): 443-62.

Frazis, Harley J., Diane E. Herz, and Michael W. Horrigan. 1995. Employer-provided training: Results from a new survey. *Monthly Labor Review* (May): 3-17.

Grindel, John. 1997. Interview by Marianne Bakia with Interim Division Dean, Technology and Engineering, Cerritos Community College. Norwalk, CA.

Grubb, W. Norton. 2002. Learning and earning in the middle: National studies of pre-baccalaureate education. *Economics of Education Review* 21 (4): 299-321.

Grubb, W. Norton, Norena Badway, Denise Bell, Debra Bragg, and Maxine Russman. 1997. *Workforce, economic, and community development: The changing landscape of the "entrepreneurial" community college*. Berkeley: National Center for Research in Vocational Education, University of California.

Hall, Richard. 1998. Interview by Kevin Dougherty with Director, Business Services, Texas Workforce Development Commission. Austin, TX.

Harrison, David. 1997. Interview by Kevin Dougherty with Director, Advanced Integrated Manufacturing Center, Sinclair Community College, Dayton, OH.

Healy, Peter. 1998. Arizona considers landmark plan to allow community colleges to offer baccalaureate degrees. *Chronicle of Higher Education*, 16 January, A30.

Heffner, John A. 1998. Interview by Marianne Bakia with Executive Director, Training and Educational Services, Association of General Contractors of America, Washington, DC.

Horine, Don. 1998. Associate degrees to start going further: Some will transfer to all Florida universities. *Palm Beach Post*, 26 July, 14A.

Horton, Steve. 1998. Interview by Marianne Bakia with Associate Dean, Evening and Technical Education, San Jacinto Community College, Central Campus, Pasadena, TX.

Irwin, James. 1998. Interview by Kevin Dougherty with the Director, Training Center Operations, General Motors, Detroit, MI.

Israel, Phyllis. 1998. Interview by Marianne Bakia with Coordinator, Safety and Health and Apprenticeship Training, Building and Construction Trades Department, AFL-CIO. Washington DC.

Jacobs, James. 1992. *Customized training in Michigan: A necessary priority for community colleges*. Warren, MI: Macomb Community College, Center for Community Studies.

———. 1995. Rock Valley College (Illinois): A community college commitment to manufacturing. In *New technologies and new skills*, edited by Stuart A. Rosenfeld, 97-105. Chapel Hill, NC: Regional Technology Strategies.

Jacobs, James. 1997. Interview by Kevin Dougherty and Marianne Bakia with Associate Vice President for Community and Employer Services, Macomb Community College. Warren, Michigan.

Johnson, Steven Lee. 1995. Organizational structure and the performance of contract training operations in American community colleges. UMI no. 9617260. Ph.D. diss., University of Texas, Austin.

Johnson, William B., Arnold H. Packer, and Associates. 1987. *Workforce 2000.* Indianapolis, IN: Hudson Institute.

Kelly, Kathleen. 2001. *Meeting needs and making profits: The rise of for-profit degree-granting institutions.* Denver, CO: Education Commission of the States.

Knoke, David, and Arne L. Kalleberg. 1994. Job training in U.S. organizations. *American Sociological Review* 59 (August): 537-46.

Labaree, David F. 1997. *How to succeed in school without really learning: The credentials race in American education.* New Haven, CT: Yale University Press.

Laguna, Connie. 1998. Interview by Kevin Dougherty with Executive Director, South Florida Chapter, American Institute of Banking. Miami, FL.

Lawson, David. 1998. Interview by Marianne Bakia with Training Director, North Texas Joint Apprenticeship Training Committee, United Brotherhood of Carpenters. Arlington, Texas.

Light, Dudley. 1998. Interview by Marianne Bakia with National Training Director, United Brotherhood of Carpenters. Washington, DC.

Lynch, Lisa M., and Sandra E. Black. 1998. Beyond the incidence of employer-provided training. *Industrial and Labor Relations Review* 52 (October): 64-81.

Lynch, Robert, James C. Palmer, and W. Norton Grubb. 1991. *Community college involvement in contract training and other economic development activities.* MDS-379. Berkeley, CA: National Center for Research in Vocational Education.

MacDonald, Mary. 1999. FCCJ sees hope on degree; Legislation key to 4-year program. *Florida Times-Union* (Jacksonville), 29 April, A-1.

Marshall, Ray, and Marc Tucker. 1992. *Thinking for a living.* New York: Basic Books.

McDougal, Terry. 1998. Interview by Kevin Dougherty with Assistant Director for Labor Relations, GM Operations; co-chair, GM/UAW national Joint Apprenticeship Committee. Detroit, MI.

McNeil, Robert. 1998. Interview by Marianne Bakia with Dean, Business and Economic Development, Los Angeles Trade-Technical College. Los Angeles, CA.

Michigan Jobs Commission. 1998. *Economic development job training program.* Lansing, MI: Michigan Jobs Commission.

Osterman, Paul. 1995. Skill, training, and work organization in American establishments. *Industrial Relations* 34 (April): 125-46.

Owen, Thomas. 1998. Interview by Marianne Bakia with Director, Western New York region, American Institute of Banking. Buffalo, NY.

Palmer, James C. 1990. *How do community colleges serve business and industry? A review of issues discussed in the literature.* Washington, DC: American Association of Community Colleges.

Pickar, Gloria. 1998. Interview by Kevin Dougherty with Dean, Economic and Community Development, Seminole Community College, Sanford, FL.

Pitter, Gita Wijesinghe. 1999. Ladders to success: Enhancing transfer from technical associate in science degrees to baccalaureates. Paper presented to the annual forum of the Association for Institutional Research.

Pope, Al. 1998. Interview by Kevin Dougherty with Government Resources Executive, Chrysler Corporation. Detroit, MI.

Ray, Richard. 1997. Interview by Marianne Bakia with Education Director, Workforce Development and School to Work, National Center for Construction Education and Training. Gainesville, FL.

Regional Technology Strategies. 1999. *A comprehensive look at state-funded, employer-focused job training programs.* Washington, DC: National Governors' Association.

Rifkin, Tronie. 2000. *Improving articulation policy to increase transfer.* Policy paper. Denver, CO: Education Commission of the States, Center for Community College Policy.

Rosenfeld, Stuart A., ed. 1999. *New technologies and new skills: Two-year colleges at the vanguard of modernization.* Chapel Hill, NC: Regional Technology Strategies.

Salzman, Harold, Philip Moss, and Chris Tilly. 1998. *The new corporate landscape and workforce skills*. Stanford, CA: National Center for Postsecondary Improvement, Stanford University.

Schmidt, Peter. 1999. Florida's 2-year colleges allowed to offer B.A.'s. *Chronicle of Higher Education*, 2 July, A29.

Scott, W. Richard, and John W. Meyer. 1994. The rise of training programs in firms and agencies. In *Institutional environments and organizations: Structural complexity and individualism*, edited by W. Richard Scott and John W. Meyer. Thousand Oaks, CA: Sage.

Sillars, Stuart. 1999. Interview by Kevin Dougherty with Training Director, Tri-Cities Joint Apprenticeship Training Committee, International Brotherhood of Electrical Workers. Albany, NY.

Somers, John. 1999. Interview by Kevin Dougherty with Assistant Business Manager, International Brotherhood of Electrical Workers local, Fort Lauderdale, FL.

Tesinsky, Suzanne. 1997, 1998. Interviews by Marianne Bakia and Kevin Dougherty with Director, Workforce Development, Seminole Community College, Sanford, FL.

Tornholm, Barbara. 1998. Interview by Kevin Dougherty with Director, Economic Development Job Training, Michigan Jobs Commission. Lansing, MI.

U.S. Census Bureau. 1997. *Statistical abstract of the United States, 1997*. Washington, DC: Government Printing Office.

———. 1998. *County business patterns*. Washington, DC: Government Printing Office.

Washington State Board for Community and Technical Colleges. 1997. *1997-98 articulation and transfer in the state of Washington*. Olympia: Washington State Board for Community and Technical Colleges.

Williams, Donald. 1997. Interview by Kevin Dougherty with Dean, Vocational and Technical Education, Rock Valley Community College, Rockford, IL.

Winter, Gene M., and LaVerna M. Fadale. 1990. Impact of economic development programs in SUNY community colleges: A study of contract courses. *Community Services Catalyst* 20 (2): 3-7.

Wood, Bob. 1997. Interview by Marianne Bakia with Dean, Contract Education and Economic Development, Chabot College. Hayward, CA.

Zeiss, Tony. 1998. Realities of competition. *Community College Journal* (June/July): 8-13.

Zeiss, Tony, John W. Quinley, Phyllis A. Barber, Richard G. Anthony Jr., Patricia Donohue, Sherrie L. Kantor, James F. McKenney, Andrew L. Meyer, Elizabeth Thornton, Robert J. Visdos, Phil Ward, and Jack N. Wismer. 1997. *Developing the world's best labor force*. Washington, DC: Community College Press.

From Access to Outcome Equity: Revitalizing the Democratic Mission of the Community College

By
ALICIA C. DOWD

By expanding higher education's enrollment capacity, community colleges are understood by many to play an important democratizing role in the American postsecondary system. As public institutions, they also face demands for accountability, productivity, and efficiency, which in recent years have led to a greater market orientation. This article analyzes the ideology of efficiency and its effects on the acclaimed democratizing mission of the public two-year sector. It argues that open access in the traditional sense of nonselective, low-cost enrollment has been eroded by the stratification of educational opportunity and by declining college affordability. Technical and economic efficiency are discussed as concepts having meaning and application distinct from the ideology of efficiency and that are not inherently at odds with equity goals. Performance accountability is explored as a mechanism to collect and examine detailed student outcome data and balance efficiency concerns with a focus on equity.

Keywords: college; efficiency; equity; accountability; access

The two-year public sector is the primary point of entry into higher education for low-income students, African Americans, Latinos, immigrants, and working adults (Bragg 2001, 95-96; Nora n.d., Enrollment Patterns). By expanding higher education's enrollment capacity, community colleges are understood by many to play an important democratizing role in the

Alicia C. Dowd is an assistant professor in the higher education administration doctoral program in the Graduate College of Education at the University of Massachusetts, Boston. She teaches research methods, the political economy of education, and higher education finance. Dowd's research focuses on understanding the factors that determine student access and outcomes among those enrolled in community colleges and public four-year colleges. She holds a Ph.D. in educational administration from Cornell University.

NOTE: The author would like to thank David Breneman, Kevin Dougherty, Amaury Nora, the editors, and participants in the fall 2001 Community Colleges in the New Century conference at the University of Massachusetts, Boston, for helpful comments and insightful discussion on earlier drafts of this article.

DOI: 10.1177/0095399702250214

American postsecondary system. With open admissions policies and diverse student bodies, community colleges "in an idealized sense, represent higher education's commitment to democracy" (Rhoads and Valadez 1996, 7). However, critics have argued that community colleges serve mainly to stratify higher education and to shield four-year institutions from new populations of students seeking upward mobility through attainment of a baccalaureate degree (Brint and Karabel 1989). In the 1990s, the ideal of the community college as an agent of democracy was undermined by cuts in public funding and privatization of the public sector (Dougherty 2002a, 303-4, 335; Levin 2001).

As Serban (Burke and Serban 1998) has observed, "The state higher education budget, implicitly or explicitly, sets forth the state's major policy preferences for higher education" (p. 23). In the 1990s, state policy makers sought to emulate the "resurgence of productivity and performance in American business" by providing incentives for colleges and universities to focus on outcomes (Burke and Serban 1998, 1). Through the language and funding stipulations of performance funding, performance budgeting, and outcomes assessment, state governments signaled their preferences for colleges to act more like businesses. These tools were consistent with broader policies intended to encourage colleges to adopt a market orientation and to become more accountable for their expenditures of taxpayers' dollars (Levin 2001, 100). As a result, community colleges have become more responsive to the needs of the business sector (Dougherty 2002a, 303-4; Dougherty and Bakia 2000, 234-36; Levin 2001, xix-xx, 6, 17-18).

Against the din of calls for efficiency, productivity, and accountability, concern for the vitality of the community college's democratizing role is barely evident in the policy agenda (Dougherty 2002a, 339-40; Levin 2001, 112; Rhoads and Valadez 1996, vii). Furthermore, although the ideal of the democratizing effect of community colleges relies on open access, there are signs that access in the traditional sense of nonselective, low-cost enrollment has been eroded and is ineffective in providing equality of educational opportunity. Higher net tuition charges inhibit the enrollment of low-income students (Empty promises 2002), while those students who do enroll in community colleges experience low levels of academic success relative to their peers who begin their studies in four-year colleges (Dougherty 1994, 2002a).

This article analyzes the privatization of community colleges and its effects on the democratizing mission of the public two-year sector. After reviewing the historical role of community colleges in providing educational opportunity in the first section, I summarize the debate contrasting the community colleges' ascribed democratizing role with its stratifying effects in the Educational Stratification and the Reproduction of Inequality section. I adopt Labaree's (1997) conceptualization of three historic and conflicting goals of education in the United States—democratic equality, social efficiency, and social mobility—to characterize that debate. Looking closely at the community college's new market orientation in the Privatization, Capitalist Ideology, and a New Market Mission section, I analyze growing curricular diversification in the community college as a sign of increased stratification of educational opportunity. I argue that privatization and programmatic stratification threaten to undermine democratic equality goals, as epitomized by open admissions. The declining affordability of community colleges is demonstrated in the Declining Affordability section, showing that access has also been eroded by changes in public higher education finance. In the final section, performance accountability systems are discussed, along with proposals to make them more compatible with the acclaimed community college role as a democratizing agent.

Community Colleges and Educational Opportunity

Community colleges are often called the "people's college" (Labaree 1997, 203; Rendon n.d., Introduction, paragraph 1) or "democracy's college" (Brint and Karabel 1989, 205; Shaw, Valadez, and Rhoads 1999, 2). These terms reflect the community colleges' central role in creating educational opportunities and expanding higher education enrollments. Although two-year public colleges have existed since the beginning of the nineteenth century, when they were known as junior colleges, they were established at an "explosive" pace in the 1960s (Dougherty 1994, 118), such that their "degree-credit enrollment quadrupled in fifteen years, rising from 1.0 million to 4.3 million between 1965 and 1980" (Labaree 1997, 190). During that period, they doubled their share of higher education enrollments to account for 36 percent of all students (Labaree 1997, 191). As the total population of undergraduates increased between 1970 and 1998, students at community colleges accounted for nearly two-thirds of enrollment growth. By 1998, more than 5.2 million students, 43 percent of all undergraduates, were enrolled in community colleges (Kipp, Price, and Wohlford 2002).

Low tuition charges and open admissions were the key policies by which community colleges expanded access. Rhoads and Valadez (1996, 36) and Levin (2001, 6) have referred to open admissions as the "fundamental" attribute of the community college identity. Rhoads and Valadez observed,

> Many of America's poor seek a pathway to a better life through the community college. They believe that higher education will provide the way for them, and the "open door" is seen as an opportunity to achieve their version of the American dream. (P. 217)

The language of universal education that fueled the creation of public schools (Labaree 1997, 21) also contributed to the growth of community colleges. In 1947, President Truman's Commission on Higher Education argued, "The time has come to make education through the fourteenth grade available in the same way that high school education is now available" (cited in Labaree 1997, 205). In 1970, the Carnegie Commission on Higher Education "made the community college the centerpiece of its calls for universal access to higher education" (Dougherty 1994, 4) as it promoted the expansion of higher education. It is clear that equal, open access is a key tenet associated with the community college's acclaimed role as "democracy's college."

Education was expanded not only by the founding of additional colleges but by an enlargement of the community college mission. The "comprehensive mission" of community colleges includes four primary components: academic preparation for transfer to four-year institutions, vocational education, general education, and noncredit community outreach (Breneman and Nelson 1981, 19; Labaree 1997, 196). Provision of the first two years of undergraduate education was the primary function of junior colleges in their early years (Dougherty 1994, 191). Vocational training was offered throughout the colleges' history but played a relatively minor role (Labaree 1997, 202) until the mid-1980s when it began to dominate other aspects of the comprehensive mission (Levin 2001, xix-xx; Rosenfeld 1999, 11). Approximately three-fifths of today's students are enrolled in vocational programs (Dougherty 2002a, 301). Labaree (1997) describes general education as having two quite different meanings, the one with an emphasis on providing training in morality and civic responsibility for "effective workers and good citizens" and the other "unalloyed with vocationalism," promoting civic virtue to "protect the republic from markets rather than simply to train docile workers" (pp. 203-4). Noncredit and community outreach programs were added as a primary component of the community college role during the period of expansion in the 1960s. During this time, the term "community" college became more popular, reflecting the shifting balance away from the dominant transfer function (Breneman and Nelson 1981, 22). Outreach programs, like some forms of general education, promote the development of "social, political, and personal competencies" (Labaree 1997, 203) but do not lead to associate's degrees.

These components of the comprehensive mission are at times "contradictory" (Dougherty 1994) and "mutually incompatible" (Labaree 1997, 191). These contradictions may in fact completely undermine the democratizing role of the community college and vacate its claim as the "people's college." In the next section (Educational Stratification and the Reproduction of Inequality), Labaree's (1997) conceptualization of the competing goals of education in the United States is discussed and applied as a framework for analyzing the comprehensive community college mission. Based on this analysis, in the Privatization, Capitalist Ideology, and a New Market Mission section, two threats to the community colleges' democratizing role are presented. The first is the privatization of community colleges, in which efficiency serves as a key theme sounding a capitalist ideology. The second is increased differentiation of educational and entrepreneurial activities, which have proliferated as a market mission has encroached on the colleges' comprehensive mission. Curricular and programmatic differentiation is viewed through a historical lens of growing educational stratification, signaling the erosion of open admissions policies.

Educational Stratification and the Reproduction of Inequality

Labaree (1997) described the U.S. educational system as the product of historic tensions among these three primary goals of schooling, which he called "democratic equality," "social efficiency," and "social mobility." He located the creation of community colleges in a broader struggle among educational constituents for resources necessary to obtain the economic and social returns to schooling. In Labaree's framework, democratic equality goals are evident in calls for equal access to schooling and full participation through education in political and civic life. Social efficiency goals are evident in concerns about workforce preparation, economic development, and the effective use of taxpayers' dollars. Social mobility goals seek to preserve the American dream of the just rewards due talented and hardworking individuals who attain social and economic status through success in the educational system. The social mobility agenda relies heavily on a meritocratic ideology to distribute credentials of varying quality and value. Market mechanisms are favored as the means to provide a great diversity of educational programs and degrees. The role of the student as consumer, rather than as citizen or productive worker, is preeminent.

These three goals are evident in the community college's comprehensive mission. The transfer and community outreach functions of community colleges are most clearly associated with the democratic equality principles of open access, equal opportunity, and civic participation. General education, in its forms stressing citizenship training and community development rather than worker socialization (Labaree 1997, 204), are also viewed as promoting a democratic society. Social efficiency and social mobility goals often, but not always, take shape in opposition to democratic equality and create pressures for stratified educational systems.

Labaree (1997, 37-39) portrayed the diversity of educational forms and credentials found in the American educational system, including the great multiplicity of roles assigned to community colleges, as taking shape in the tensions between two opposing political coalitions. The first coalition combines democratic equality and social mobility goals to forward a progressive educational agenda, emphasizing access, opportunity, and individual attainment.

> The two issues that constitute the area of overlap between democratic equality and social mobility goals—educational opportunity and individual achievement—define the core of a consensus that has driven progressive educational politics in this country for the past century and a half. Organizations representing the working class, ethnic minorities, and women have all seen this educational agenda as a means for becoming participants in the political process and for gaining access to the more attractive social positions. (P. 37)

For their part, the middle and upper classes join this coalition as a means to develop supposedly meritocratic educational institutions, which instead serve to protect and reproduce class interests by legitimating social position as educational achievement. The key to controlling the value of educational credentials lies in creating ever-increasing levels of educational stratification. Access is then restricted to scarce, valuable credentials based on meritocratic structures, such as grading and testing, while the value of degrees available to the masses falls. Labaree (1997, chapter 4) pointed to the declining value of the once-scarce high school diploma to illustrate this process of educational expansion and market differentiation.

A counterweight to the progressive agenda is provided by proponents of social efficiency, who are interested in the efficient use of taxpayers' dollars and effective development of human capital to meet the needs of the economy. This "complex coalition" includes policy makers, employers and business leaders, educational administrators, taxpayers, and working-class students interested in the short-term economic returns of vocational education (Labaree 1997, 38-39). Like programs developed under social mobility goals, socially efficient programs accept and reproduce social inequality. From the social efficiency vantage point, the economy needs workers at all levels of the occupational hierarchy; if one's class of birth is a determinant of one's life chances, this is not of particular concern, as it is in the democratic equality agenda.

Labaree's (1997) conceptualization of credentialism and social stratification draws on the work of scholars who preceded him, particularly, in regard to the two-year public sector, Brint and Karabel (1989), who argued that the primary role of the junior and community colleges was to perform a "sorting function." They wrote, "Wherever they developed, the public junior colleges faced two contradictory tasks: the democratic one of bringing new populations into higher education and the exclusionary one of channeling them away from the four-year institutions that they hoped to attend" (p. 208). Scholars of community colleges have long debated claims of this type and the potential mechanisms by which a sorting function might be carried out (Brint and Karabel 1989; Clark 1960, 1980; Cohen 1990; Dougherty 1994). In Labaree's view, social mobility goals pursued through competitive educational systems and market-oriented program development are insidiously dominant today. His view provides a useful framework for understanding current changes in community college systems, where social efficiency and social mobility goals dominate the vision of democratic equality that was so much a part of the founding rhetoric of the public two-year sector.

Privatization, Capitalist Ideology, and a New Market Mission

The history of the community college reflects the tensions between democratic and capitalist goals (Labaree 1997, 218). As discussed above, democratic goals are embodied in the theme of open access. Capitalist goals, I will argue here, drawing on recent analyses of higher education policy, are embodied in the theme of efficiency. To the extent policy goals are expressed as self-evident, natural, or of unquestioned value, they operate as part of a political and cultural belief system and can be understood to function as an ideology, which the Oxford English Dictionary defines as

> a systematic scheme of ideas, usually relating to politics or society, or to the conduct of a class or group, and regarded as justifying actions, especially one that is held implicitly or adopted as a whole and maintained regardless of the course of events.

Recent research demonstrates that a capitalist ideology has been forcefully reshaping the community college and its mission.

Levin (2001) has conducted a case study of community colleges in the United States and Canada, including three U.S. colleges in Washington, California, and Hawaii. His analysis includes interviews with college administrators and the review of state and federal documents outlining policies affecting community colleges. Federal documents, he concluded, "were almost singly focused on work-force training" (Levin 2001, 103). This focus was embedded in overriding concerns about economic development, national competitiveness, and the desire to increase productivity and efficiency.

Concern for the vitality of the community college's democratizing role is barely evident in the policy agenda.

These themes were also sounded loudly in state policy documents. Social issues received little attention. Service to the growing populations of ethnic minorities, who would soon be in the majority in California, was framed in terms of underemployment, workforce dislocation, and skills training (Levin 2001, 99-107). Community colleges were "directed and coerced to serve the needs of capital through supplying business and industry with a trained workforce" (p. 111). Efficiency was a central theme, as institutions were expected to reduce costs in the face of declining government revenues. Social issues were subsumed under economic issues. Although "access for all was maintained as a primary value . . . for all three U.S. states, expanding and even maintaining access, according to government policy, required 'doing more with less.' " Levin concluded, "Government policy in the 1990s clearly favored the interests of business, industry, and capital. The state's attention to issues of equity, access, and an informed citizenry—issues that could be held up as critical to the community college movement—was marginal" (p. 112). Although the concept of access, the cornerstone of the democratizing mission of the community college, was articulated, it was harnessed to the goals of workforce development and divorced from the promise of upward mobility from which it derives its power. The unquestioned preeminence of economic goals indicates that capitalist values are functioning as ideology in these educational policy documents.

In a review of the evolution of vocational education in community colleges, Rosenfeld (1999) demonstrated that this ideological stance is relatively new. He observed,

> Economic development was *not allowed* to be included among possible goals at the time
> the 1981 Vocational Education Study was released. Nevertheless, by the time the Carl
> Perkins Vocational Education Act of 1984 was drafted, economic development gained the
> legitimacy it sought and was mentioned in the legislation's "Purpose." (P. 11, emphasis
> added)

Prior to 1984, economic development was not cemented as a core value of vocational education. This change in values is significant as a shift in focus from students' personal, academic, and employment needs to the needs of regional and local economies.

The increase in contract training programs at community colleges coincides with this shift in focus from students to industries. Dougherty and Bakia (2000) emphasized the significance of this new clientele: "unlike traditional occupational education, contract training involves an outside party (such as a firm or government agency), rather than the individual student, as the primary client, and from this simple fact flow all sorts of consequences" (p. 199). These consequences include the contractor's involvement in determining course content, pedagogy, and enrollment. Contract training programs are found in more than 90 percent of community colleges, where they account for approximately 17 percent of credit and noncredit enrollments (Dougherty and Bakia 2000, 201). Revenues from contract training programs are quite small, estimated at 1 percent of the median operating budgets of colleges that offer such training (Dougherty and Bakia 2000, 226). However, college administrators view these programs as offering an important service to the community, where the community is defined in terms of business interests. Dougherty and Bakia (2000) described the ideological dimensions of this view:

> The community college orientation to meeting the needs of the "community" is not
> unproblematic. It is a value that is shaped by the fact of business's ideological hegemony
> within this society. Community colleges tend to define community in a way that makes
> employers the central constituents of the "community." There is little or no consideration
> of the possibility that on occasion the interests of the community and of employers might
> actually be opposed. (Pp. 220-21)

The pervasiveness of a capitalist ideology is indicated by changes in the college culture, such as when college administrators espouse business principles and view educational programs as a business (Dougherty and Bakia 2000, 233-35). Levin (2001) found pervasive evidence of such a cultural shift at the institutions he studied: "a pattern was established beginning in the 1980s and institutionalized in the 1990s toward a more corporate and businesslike approach to education." This new culture was evident in a "changing managerial ideology at colleges, with emphasis upon education and training as commodities . . . actions to align the institution with the marketplace, and the drive in operations for economic efficiency" (p. xix). The comprehensive mission of the community college was expanded even further. A market mission became dominant as colleges sought new market niches and customers. The colleges became entrepreneurial "multi-institutions" and developed "colleges within colleges" (Levin 2001, 17, 55) as the traditional curriculum was retained and new programs were added.

The notions of productivity, operational efficiency, and "doing more with less" that Levin (2001) discussed reflect a narrow meaning of efficiency, which is called "production" or "technical" efficiency, while the emphasis on market-oriented outcomes demonstrates the ideological context in which efficiency is a dominant theme today. Production efficiency is defined as obtaining the same quality of output for fewer inputs or a higher number or quality of output for the same level of inputs (DesJardins 2002, 190; Monk 1990, 8-9). These improvements are gained by reducing waste in the production process or by adopting new technologies.

However, economists also define a broader meaning of efficiency for evaluating the impact of public investments on social welfare. An investment is efficient at the point where the value of the additional benefit obtained equals the cost of additional dollars invested;[1] society is investing neither too much nor too little in the program to obtain the desired outcomes. It is difficult to estimate this type of efficiency of social welfare investments in higher education because the full range of quantitative and qualitative outcomes is hard, if not impossible, to measure (Breneman and Nelson 1981, 39-44; DesJardins 2002, 201-2, 209). The value of benefits from investments in higher education and other publicly funded programs is determined through the political process.

The emphasis in today's community college on workforce training and entrepreneurial activities reflects a contemporary political agenda and ideology. The call for production efficiency is a dominant theme of this agenda, but it is important to realize that society could pursue production efficiencies in higher education—and should, in the interest of reducing the burden on taxpayers and releasing funds for other social programs—while placing a different valuation on the potential outputs of public investments in college. For example, the political agenda could shift to place great emphasis on community building through higher education rather than emphasizing workforce preparation. These goals could also be pursued with a concomitant desire to realize production efficiencies, in other words, to effectively foster strong communities while using the lowest level of public resources possible. Efficiency is often viewed as antithetical to equity goals, but this is not necessarily the case (Breneman and Nelson 1981, 43; DesJardins 2002, 176, 198). When I discuss performance measurement below, I will return to this point to recommend that equity advocates retain a focus on production efficiency, while arguing that higher education should increase its concern for the distribution of outcomes.

Programmatic diversification and stratification of educational opportunity. As the colleges have entered new markets, they have become "not only the traditional community colleges, with comprehensive curricula and open access, but also training centers, charter schools, private high schools, language institutes, music conservatories, applied research centers, and businesses" (Levin 2001, xix). Some of these activities, such as contract training, reflect an intensified orientation to the business sector. Other activities, such as the creation of honors programs (Selingo 2002), new structures for remediation (Shults 2001), and dual enrollment agreements with secondary schools (Barnes 2001; State funding 2000, 33-37), reflect an increasing stratification of offerings to the traditional customers of the college: students and taxpayers. Colleges are as apt to create new participation structures for state-sponsored markets as private markets. To the extent these new programs have admissions requirements, which some do, they erode the community college's traditional and fundamental characteristic of open access through open admissions. In addition, those programs that restrict participation to control market perceptions of program quality may well erode the promise of equal opportunity through open admissions by undermining the economic value of open admission degrees.

Labaree's (1997, 26-34) conceptualization of the social mobility goal of education explains the coincidence of a market mission and increasing program differentiation, as well as the consequences of such an orientation for the value of an open enrollment diploma. As educational consumers, parents and students want educational stratification, including academic standards, grading, and hierarchical program levels, because a pyramidal system is necessary to create relative competitive advantage. Through stratification of program levels, individuals of higher class origin gain access to greater educational resources and credentials with greater exchange value in economic and social markets. In this respect, the social mobility goal is distinct from both the democratic and social efficiency goals in that it treats education as a private good, rather than as a public good. "From the social mobility perspective, the chance to gain advantage is the system's most salient feature" (Labaree 1997, 28). The true value of the teaching and learning environment is of secondary concern.

In Labaree's (1997) distinction between social mobility and social efficiency goals, the social efficiency coalition creates a demand for economically valuable learning produced through effective schooling. Education has a true "use value"; it is intrinsically valuable for the production of informed citizens and skilled workers. In contrast, the forces of social mobility "treat education as a form of exchange value" (Labaree 1997, 31).

> Educational credentials come to take on a life of their own. Their value derives not from the useful knowledge they symbolize but from the kind of job for which they can be exchanged. And the latter exchange value is determined by the same forces as that of any other commodity, through the fluctuation of supply and demand in the marketplace—the scarcity of that credential relative to the demand for that credential among employers. (P. 31)

Given that the exchange value of a credential is determined by supply and demand, those students in programs that have selective admissions can expect a higher return on their educational investment. Those in open enrollment programs can expect a lower exchange value.

The social mobility and democratic equality agendas overlap in that both seek greater resources for educational institutions, while the social efficiency coalition of taxpayers and fiscally conservative policy makers aims to reduce costs, promote efficiency, and develop human capital with true use value for the economy. As discussed above, the social efficiency agenda is evident today as the community colleges emphasize workforce training and economic development. The social mobility agenda is evident through the stratification of program offerings and a renewed emphasis—in the community colleges and throughout the educational system—on academic standards. Program stratification is an outgrowth of the new market orientation as colleges respond to all their diverse constituents—the state, businesses, students—as consumers. This consumer orientation is radically opposed to a public orientation, in which access is conceptualized as universal rather than pyramidal.

The structure of new dual enrollment, honors, and remedial programs illustrates the threat to open access posed by program stratification. New York State provides "school-based college level learning," a dual enrollment program through which colleges enroll high school students (Barnes 2001). Offering community college courses to high school students does extend access, but in nonuniform ways. Barnes (2001) reported, "Students respond along with parents to the possibilities to earn college credit and save money" (p. 3). He argued that school-based learning is less "elitist" than advanced placement classes because college credits can be earned without passing an examination, as is required for advanced placement credit. However, the value of the program in creating college access depends on which students actually enroll in the college courses. If academically motivated students take advantage of this benefit while poor students are still struggling to meet mandated core curriculum requirements, the program may simply serve to bring additional benefits to families of college-bound students. Also, since students must pay tuition for these credits (State funding 2000, 36), those from higher-income families are more likely to enroll. This benefit for a select group of high school students is relatively expensive because both the school district and the college count the credits taken in their funding formulas, so the taxpayer is "paying twice for one-time instruction" (Barnes 2001, 5).

Similarly, a news article reporting the creation of honors colleges at community colleges indicated that students in the honors programs would benefit from smaller classes and have the opportunity to work on special projects (Selingo 2002). In this way, the bright students in the honors programs garner greater resources and, not surprisingly, appear to experience greater academic success. At one college, the transfer rate to four-year colleges was 98 percent, more than double the transfer rates of average community college students, as is discussed below.

While "school-based learning" courses may dilute program quality (Barnes 2001, 2) as they extend resources to college-bound students, policy issues surrounding remedial education indicate a desire on the part of policy makers to limit spending on students requiring developmental instruction and to protect collegiate academic standards. This is evident in the trend to restrict remedial instruction to the two-year sector (Dougherty 2002a, 310). The American Association of Community Colleges reported that only 11 percent of colleges responding to a national survey offered degree credit for remedial education. The majority of colleges (76 percent) offered credits, called "institutional credits," that allowed students to count the courses toward financial aid eligibility but not toward graduation. In addition, policies are in place to limit the number of remedial courses taken and concurrent enrollment in degree programs (Shults 2001, 6-8).

While some programmatic initiatives may increase access to higher education, others are likely to reduce the exchange value of an associate's degree. Community college credits have monetary value for high school students who can potentially exchange them later for more valuable private or four-year college credits. Honors program students receive a boost in the value of their degree through bureaucratic structures and real resources that are intended to set them apart from regularly enrolled community college students. Similarly, remedial courses and enrollment structures are designed to place average students one step above remedial students. From a social efficiency perspective, the value and effect of these new structures depend on whether they create teaching and learning environments in which students learn valuable skills to become productive workers. Students too hope to benefit economically from these skills. From a social mobility perspective, the programs create hierarchical credentials for which educational consumers must compete through meritocratic processes. Vocationalism, which potentially brings students labor market returns for learned skills and gives them the prospect of upward mobility, is a lesser threat to democratic equality than privatization, which redirects resources to more powerful educational consumers. However, both privatization and stratification undermine the community college's potential to enact a democratic agenda.

Declining Affordability

The ascribed role of community colleges in creating a more just and democratic society is central to the manner in which community colleges have traditionally been financed, which is with high levels of public subsidy and low levels of direct costs to individual students. Low tuition rates combined with open admissions policies have been the cornerstones of equality of access and opportunity (Breneman and Nelson 1981, 100-103). As discussed above, stratification of program offerings threatens to undermine open admissions. The other cornerstone of access, low tuition, is also being eroded. Tuition rates have increased as a proportion of real income and are not so low today as to be negligible. Average community college tuition and fees in 2001 was $1,705 (McKeown-Moak 2001, 8). In inflation-adjusted dollars, they have more than doubled since 1968 (Kipp, Price, and Wohlford 2002, 8). Furthermore, today, the tuition rate is generally not an indicator of a student's true costs. A significant number of community college students rely on grants and loans to pay for college. As in other sectors of higher education, students must discern the "net price" (tuition and fees minus grant aid) when determining their true costs and gauge the investment value of student loans. While there is great variation in community college tuition and financial aid by state and some states have maintained affordability for low-income students (Kipp, Price, and Wohlford 2002), most systems today cannot point to low tuition rates as a beacon of open door access.

Consistent with the tenets of affordability and access, community colleges have been insulated for many years from the enormous price hikes occurring in other sectors of higher education. In inflation-adjusted dollars, average annual costs in the public two-year sector (including tuition, fees, and expenses) increased 9 percent between 1980 and 1990. This increase was modest compared to price increases of 57 percent for private universities, 30 percent for public universities, and 34 percent for public four-year colleges during the same period (Mumper 1996, 25). While community colleges are certainly still the most affordable college

---

Efficiency is often viewed as antithetical to equity goals, but this is not necessarily the case.

---

option, the total price of attendance, including tuition, fees, books, transportation, and personal expenses, is estimated today at $9,100 (Berkner et al. 2002, 4). (The problem of rising community college prices is compounded by the decline in real income in the lowest income brackets.) Even the relatively small price increases in the two-year sector have had a serious impact on low-income families as college costs now consume a larger proportion of earnings (Mumper 1996, 54). By 2000, low-income families spent 12 percent of their income to pay tuition at public two-year colleges. The comparable figure in 1980 was 6 percent. Only the income of the wealthiest Americans has kept pace with tuition increases (Losing ground 2002, 5). The effect of tuition increases on the poorest Americans is of particular concern because nearly half of students with family incomes less than $10,000 attend community colleges (compared with just 9 percent of students from the highest income families) (Access denied 2001, 10). These are also precisely the students whom the community colleges are intended to serve through their democratizing mission, providing higher education for all regardless of their economic circumstances.

Rising tuition signals the end of the era when low tuition was the "full, posted price" serving as one of the "pillars" of access (Kipp, Price, and Wohlford 2002, 7), but it does not in itself signal the end of affordability. In fact, even as tuition prices increased over time, community colleges became more affordable through the 1970s and 1980s with the creation of the federal Pell grant program. Through financial aid availability, the net price of two-year colleges actually decreased. However, these gains unraveled in the early 1990s. By 1992, the net price was higher than it had been in two decades, and many more community college students, like those in other sectors, were now expected to borrow to finance their education (Mumper 1996, 67-68). A recent study of public college affordability conducted by the Lumina Foundation concluded, based on a comprehensive state-by-state analysis, that community colleges are generally affordable only when students take loans. Financially dependent students from middle-income families were the only ones likely to find community colleges consistently affordable in most states in the absence of borrowing (Kipp, Price, and Wohlford 2002, 22, 26).

Thirty-eight percent of all undergraduates in community colleges received financial aid in 1999-2000, with 33 percent receiving grants and 7 percent receiving loans (Berkner et al. 2002, 9). The numbers were much higher among the 20 percent of community college students who attended full-time, full year. Fifty percent of full-time students received grants, and 17 percent received loans, which averaged $3,900 (Berkner et al. 2002, 12). These numbers represent a sizable increase over the 9 percent of full-time community college students who borrowed an average of $2,000 in 1989-1990 (Berkner 2000, Table 4.4). Borrowing decisions also depend on student status as financially dependent or independent of parents and on enrollment choices. Among independent students enrolled in community colleges in 1995-1996, approximately one-quarter took out a federal loan during their higher education, about twice as many as dependent students (Berkner 2000, Table 4.6). Part-time students, many of whom were not eligible for federal subsidized loans, borrowed to finance their education with much lower frequency (5 percent) in 1999-2000 (Berkner et al. 2002, 22). Students who chose to enroll on a part-time basis may have been discouraged from full-time attendance by the prospect of taking loans, which clearly now sum to nontrivial amounts among those who do borrow, and decided instead to work to finance their education. Possibly in response to higher costs, part-time enrollments have risen at community colleges, from 48 percent of enrollments in 1970 to 64 percent in 1998 (Kipp, Price, and Wohlford 2002, 7).

The increased incidence of borrowing demonstrates that grant aid is not sufficient to defray increases in community college tuition. In fact, the average net price in 1999-2000 was more than $900 for full-time, full-year students and about $500 for part-time, part-year students (Berkner et al. 2002, Table 4.10). Among community college students in the lowest-income quartile in a study of federal student aid data, 92 percent were identified as needing federal aid, but only 63 percent of those with need received aid, including grants and loans. The remaining unmet need for this group to pay the total costs of attending college is estimated at an average of $3,800 among the 85 percent of students who had remaining need. Forty-two percent of middle-income students were also identified as having federal need, but only 58 percent of those with need received aid. Thirty-six percent of students in this group were estimated to have remaining unmet need averaging just more than $3,000 (Berkner et al. 2002, 482, Tables 4.3A, 4.3B, Tables 4.4A, 4.4B, Table 4.5).

As the statistics above show, the amount of unmet financial need—defined as the total cost of attendance minus the expected family contribution minus all types of aid—can be sizable for community college students. It is also a significant barrier to enrollment in the four-year or two-year sector for many students (Access denied 2001, v, 10, 25). A recent report of the federal Advisory Committee on Student Financial Assistance titled *Empty Promises* (2002) stressed the following findings: academically qualified low-income high school graduates with high unmet need attend four-year colleges at much lower rates than their academic peers with low unmet need (52 percent vs. 83 percent); 21 percent attend community colleges (compared to 12 percent); and 22 percent do not enroll in any college at all (compared to just 4 percent). These disparities suggest that qualified students cannot obtain adequate financial aid to attend the college of their choice and signals the "failure of federal, state, and institutional student aid policy to jointly ensure access to postsecondary education" (Empty promises 2002, Figure 11, p. 25).

High unmet need also forces students to choose enrollment patterns that are not optimal for degree completion and academic success. Low-income students are more likely to study part-time. Nearly 30 percent work more than thirty-five hours per week (Access denied 2001, 10). The authors of *Empty Promises* (2002) concluded,

> A generation ago, many students were able to achieve access to higher education by working their way through college. Unfortunately, it is simply not possible today to work enough to cover college expenses without taking a heavy toll on student academic performance. (P. 11)

As students choose part-time enrollment and long hours working off campus, the chances of their persistence and degree attainment declines very significantly (Access denied 2001, 10). Researchers who analyzed federal college student persistence data spanning the academic years 1996 to 1998 found that borrowing combined with less than fifteen hours of work per week constitutes the best college financing strategy for low-income students. They concluded,

> Students at two-year and less than two-year institutions who borrowed and worked part time also were far less likely to drop out than other students at these institutions. Only nine percent of these students had dropped out by 1998, compared with 45% of all low-income students who began at two-year or less-than-two-year institutions.

Among low-income students, the financing strategy of combining relatively limited work hours and borrowing was also associated with enrollment in the four-year sector and full-time, full-year enrollment (King 2002, 25), both of which are factors associated with degree attainment. Thus, borrowing appears to be a key component of academic success. Students who believe that community college attendance comes at a low cost—consistent with the open access tradition—may be grossly underestimating their total costs and undermining their chances of success.

In the future, the prospects for further increases in tuition and net price— further erosion of the important "low tuition" cornerstone of open access—are great. As forty-six states faced budget gaps in the 2002 and 2003 fiscal years (State budget 2002), higher education was particularly vulnerable to spending cuts. In many states, tuition increased sharply (Morgan 2002) and with little integrated planning between tuition and financial aid policies (Longanecker 2002). With worries about college affordability for middle-income students dominating the headlines in the 1990s, financial aid policies shifted toward merit aid at the state level and tax credits at the federal level, both of which disproportionately favor wealthier students and their families. While the Pell grant program received periodic incremental increases, its purchasing power has declined significantly (Access denied 2001). Movement has been away from grant aid toward loan availability, and this trend is unlikely to be reversed in a worsening economic situation. In addition, higher education faces stiff competition in the quest for state dollars from other high-priority budget items such as primary and secondary schooling, health care, and prisons (Ehrenberg 2000, 2-5).

Larger proportions of high school graduates will continue on to college than in the past, expanding public college enrollments. This growth will increase the total subsidy necessary for public colleges if spending per student does not decrease (Kane 1999, 3-6). The new cohort of students will include a large number of students of color, many of whom will be from low-income families and have high levels of financial need. These demographic changes will "greatly increase the gross amount of financial aid required to guarantee access" (Access denied 2001, 5-6), so it is likely that the amount of public funds expended per student will, in fact, decrease, and students themselves will be expected to finance a larger proportion of their college expenses. As tuition charges have increased in recent decades, students have already come to pay a larger share of the costs of higher education, while the share of community college revenues for basic operations coming from state and local general funds has declined. The Institute for Higher Education Policy reported that the average state share fell from 70 percent in 1980 to 50 percent in 1996 (Merisotis and Wolanin 2000). This shift in burden from the state to students supports the characterization of community colleges as an increasingly privatized sector of higher education.

As community college tuition rates have increased in real terms during the past thirty years, financial aid programs have at times functioned effectively to maintain college affordability for low-income students. Today, with rising tuition and the declining value of need-based aid, there is evidence that low-income status is a significant barrier to college enrollment, even at community colleges, despite their open access tradition. The three primary barriers to enrollment are understood by policy analysts to be lack of financial aid, lack of information about available aid, and lack of college preparedness. Analysts debate the relative importance of these barriers, with Kane (1999), for example, urging policy responses addressing information barriers and the Advisory Committee on Student Financial Assistance (Access denied 2001; Empty promises 2002) urgently emphasizing lack of aid and minimizing difficulties associated with lack of information. Cameron and Heckman (2001) reject both lack of aid and lack of information as the primary barriers, focusing instead on failures of academic readiness and the early educational experiences of children from poor families. This policy debate is ongoing, but the era in which low tuition sent a clear signal of college affordability is coming to a close. Larger numbers of community college students are receiving grants and taking loans. Tuition rates no longer represent the direct costs of enrollment for many students, primarily low-income and independent students, who must be savvy about aid systems to determine their net costs.

Community college students (much more so than four-year students) are price sensitive; as tuition increases, enrollments decline. Empirical evidence demonstrates that as community college prices increase, some students will instead choose the four-year sector, and others will not enroll at all, with low-income students more likely to be priced out of higher education. Increases in tuition are not completely offset by the net price reductions effected by grant aid (Cameron and Heckman 2001, 488-91; Heller 1997, 648-50; 1999, 78-83; Hilmer 1998, 342-45; Kane and Rouse 1999, 78-81). Such tuition responses are not observed in the aggregate of recent community college enrollments, which have increased even as tuition and net costs have risen, because other factors, such as increasing four-year college tuition, declining labor market returns for high school graduates, and greater incidence of part-time enrollment, have had countervailing positive effects on enrollment.

A potential policy response to rising tuitions is for states to abandon commitments to low tuition and adopt integrated "high tuition, high aid" policies (Breneman and Nelson 1981, 103; Griswold and Marine 1996). This strategy eliminates the subsidies provided by low tuition to students who can afford the full cost of college or who determine it is a good investment and will enroll even as prices increase. In this respect, it is considered economically efficient because public funds are not misdirected toward outcomes that would occur even in their absence. The resources saved are then redirected to those whose enrollment decisions are affected by financial constraints, thereby increasing access to college. Critics have objected to this approach on the grounds that low-income students rely on the signal of low tuition to understand they can afford college. Since this signal is already compromised, it may be time to seriously revisit high-tuition, high-aid policies as an opportunity to increase the efficiency and equity of higher education finance. College information and advising systems are already badly needed to help students determine their net costs and potential investment returns. Under a policy of high tuition and high aid, additional resources would become available to provide needed financial aid and to finance extensive information, counseling, and articulation systems. The reform of legislative practices and the political will to integrate tuition-setting and financial aid policies presents the greater challenge (Griswold and Marine 1996; Heller 1999; Longanecker 2002).

Performance Accountability as an Instrument of Democratic Equality

During the expansion of the community college system during the 1950s and 1960s, states adopted per-student formula funding policies to allocate resources among institutions. The distribution of state funds was enrollment driven. In addition, many state formulas included adjustments to the per-student allocation to compensate for differences in the preparedness and socioeconomic status of the student body across institutions in a state. In this way, the estimation of a student's fair share of resources compensated for socioeconomic disadvantage. As Burke and Serban (1998) noted, "the desire for equity was a prime factor in the development of funding formulas" (p. 16).

In the past two decades, the rhetorical emphasis of legislative debates and policies pertaining to higher education financing has shifted from equity to efficiency concerns, and financing systems reflect this change. Formula funding has been modified as legislatures have begun to place an increased emphasis on the quality, productivity, and accountability of community colleges. The new financing approaches were termed "performance funding" and "performance budgeting." Recent reports show that with mixed success, states are still exploring the efficacy of these strategies (Albright 1998; Burke et al. 2000; Burke and Serban 1998; Dougherty 2002b; Gaither, Nedwek, and Neal 1994; McKeown-Moak 2000; Schmidt 2002). While the percentage of funds allocated through performance funding is very small—estimated at an average of 3 percent of state higher education spending (Burke et al. 2000, 2; Schmidt 2002)—the shift away from funding based strictly on input levels (numbers of students) to outcomes indicates a new emphasis on accountability. Although the monetary incentives have not been large, campus administrators have responded to them (Dougherty 2002b, 10-14), sometimes in consideration of the additional dollars that flowed to campuses and other times in aversion to the negative publicity generated by poor reviews (Burke et al. 2000, 11; Schmidt 2002). As policy makers "enunciated their priorities" through the development of indicators, college administrators became aware of and focused on those priorities (Dougherty 2002b, 10-11).

Burke and Serban (1998, Table 4.1, p. 53) reported the most common indicators of success for two-year colleges in states that have adopted performance funding. These include retention and graduation rates, job placement, graduation credits and time to degree, licensure test scores, workforce training and development, and two- to four-year transfers. Categorizing common indicators, the authors found a heavy emphasis on efficiency and quality and a few indicators that reflected equity and institutional choice concerns. Indicators for equity measures such as affordable tuition and fees, minority student access and graduation rates, and developmental education services were observed infrequently in either the two- or four-year sector (Burke and Serban 1998, appendix A). Surveys conducted more recently show that the performance measurement trend has gained momentum in the past few years, with more states developing some type of accountability system and utilizing similar measures (Burke et al., 2000; State funding 2000), although new programs are even less likely to include equity measures of student participation and attainment by race than indicators developed in the late 1980s and early 1990s (Burke and Modarresi 2000). In 2000, nearly three-quarters of the states in some way linked campus funding to campus performance (Burke et al. 2000, 1).

The trend toward performance accountability has continued despite "campus resistance" (Burke et al. 2000, 13). A recent news report observed, "Most state legislatures have embraced the practice of linking tax-dollar support for public colleges to performance, even though a large share of public-college officials remain convinced that doing so is a bad idea." College officials have "denounced" the plans as "unworkable, unwise, and unfair" (Schmidt 2002). The design of more recent accountability systems appears to take these objections into account. They are "more flexible, collaborative, and diverse," abandoning mandates for extensive lists of performance indicators in favor of more limited objectives that take diversity of campus missions into account. The campuses themselves have been more involved in designing and selecting the indicators (Burke et al. 2000, 12-13).

This changing dynamic of accountability offers an important opportunity for community college leaders, civic activists, and academic researchers to engage in a political dialogue about the role of the public two-year sector. Those who believe in its democratizing role must argue for the design of performance indicators that include a focus on that role. Current accountability efforts emphasize production efficiency to the neglect of a broader political conversation about economic efficiency. Standards that focus narrowly on production efficiencies through increased outputs, without significant attention to the nature and distribution of those outputs, risk losing sight of the purpose of public investment in public colleges. A full valuation of the economic efficiency of public investments in community colleges must consider the colleges' role in reducing social and economic inequality and strengthening democratic processes. These outcomes must be valued alongside economic development. Although competing political ideologies often place equity and efficiency goals in conflict, they are not necessarily at odds. Equitable programs can be economically efficient in the sense of achieving desired goals more successfully than the next best policy alternative. And they can minimize waste (operate with technical efficiency) while pursuing their objectives. However, inequitable social programs are economically inefficient (when equity is a valued goal), and no improvements in technical efficiency can change that.

Higher education will attract growing numbers of students and place a larger burden on society's resources. Colleges and universities should certainly operate as efficiently as possible, keeping in mind that administrative processes are more amenable to waste reduction than are human development and learning (Bailey 1994). Organizations that function efficiently have greater resources to pursue their objectives, no matter how these objectives are defined. The effort to interject equity goals into accountability programs depends on separating opposition to the overriding capitalist ideology in which efficiency has gained prominence, much to the neglect of principles of democratic equality, from the technical notion of efficiency. Equity goals can be pursued with technical efficiency in administration, program development, pedagogy, and other functions. The appeal to taxpayer support inherent in good management need not be ceded entirely. Efficiency can and should be a watchword of public colleges that value democratic equality as well as those steeped in capitalism.

What would it entail to interject principles of democratic equality, or "equity," a term often used synonymously with notions of justice, fairness, and equality (DesJardins 2002, 177), into performance accountability systems? Answers to this question are explored in this section. First, a definition of outcome equity is provided, with statistics presented to demonstrate that the United States is far from achieving outcome equity in higher education. It is still a matter of active debate whether investment in the public two-year sector instead of in other policy alternatives has had a positive effect on educational and social inequities. Performance accountability systems provide a way to address this issue by measuring outcomes comprehensively by race, gender, and income; over long periods of time; and across different levels of public education. These data systems, which are discussed below, may be analyzed to provide further estimates of community college effects on student outcomes.

Inequitable social programs are economically inefficient (when equity is a valued goal), and no improvements in technical efficiency can change that.

An equitable educational system was to be achieved through equal opportunity to participate in college. But the cornerstones of low tuition and open admissions at "democracy's college" are being eroded by rising tuition rates and programmatic stratification. Nevertheless, "open access and educational opportunity remain *a mantra* for community college administrators" (Valadez 2002, 36, emphasis added). It is time to move beyond the mantra of access and benchmark success by equal outcomes. A continued, singular emphasis by equity advocates on access and equal opportunity, particularly one that opposes efficiency and performance accountability in all its aspects, is a lost opportunity to focus public and legislative attention on unequal outcomes.

Outcome equity. Levin (1994) provided the following definition of educational equity that articulates a standard based on equal outcomes not for individuals but for members of different social groups:

> in all human populations there will be some variance in talents and attainments, even when all members are provided with exceptional opportunities to develop their talents. What that variance will be is certainly open to debate. More questionable, though, are the differences in educational attainments among populations born into different social, economic, and racial circumstances due to inadequate opportunities for human development. A reasonable criterion is that we have obtained educational equity when representatives of different racial, gender, and socioeconomic origins have about the same probabilities of reaching different educational outcomes. (P. 168)

Despite the hope of the decades in which community colleges and federal financial aid programs were founded to remove financial status as a barrier to higher education, income remains a determinant of educational attainment. The era of affirmative action similarly has not eliminated the social and economic disadvantages suffered by people of color. Higher education is far from achieving outcome equity, which, it should be emphasized, calls not for equal outcomes for all students but for equal outcomes on average for different socioeconomic groups.

Those who receive a baccalaureate degree earn almost twice as much as high school graduates and nearly 1.4 times the earnings of associate's degree recipients (Mumper 1996, 6-7). Yet, as the Committee on Student Financial Assistance reported (Access denied 2001), among college-qualified high school graduates,

> only 6% of students with the lowest socioeconomic status (SES) earn a bachelor's degree compared to 40% with the highest SES. Disproportionately represented among low-income students, both black and Hispanic students earn bachelor's degrees at a substantially lower rate than white students,

17 percent and 18 percent among black and Hispanic students, respectively, compared to 27 percent among white students (p. 4, Figure 3). As discussed in the previous section, low-income students are much more likely to not attend college at all, to enroll in the less remunerative two-year sector, and to lower their chances of academic success by enrolling part-time. Those who do attain an associate's degree will earn an average of 1.4 times more than a high school graduate (Mumper 1996, 6-7), but a distressingly low proportion of community college students attain the degree, roughly one in five (Kane and Rouse 1999, 68; Nettles and Millett n.d., Enrollment Challenges). Although the transfer function is central to the community colleges' democratizing role, only 16 percent of community college starters attain a bachelor's degree. This number contrasts sharply with the nearly 60 percent of four-year college starters who obtain a bachelor's (Kane and Rouse 1999, 68). With attrition rates of 44 percent, community college students leave college without a degree more than twice as often as students starting in four-year colleges (Dougherty 2002a, 317). These averages conceal much larger attrition rates for minority students, which Nora (n.d., Persistence Rates) reported at 60 percent (with extreme values as high as 80 percent).

Whether the creation of community colleges has enhanced the educational attainment of low-income and underrepresented groups is a matter of active debate among economists and educational researchers. It is not possible to observe the outcomes that may have been achieved by creating additional four-year campuses rather than community colleges or by providing public subsidies for corporate training programs and union apprenticeships rather than for vocational education at public colleges. Using multivariate statistical techniques, economists estimate the democratizing effect of community colleges—the additional years of higher education completed by those who would have completed none in the absence of a community college—versus the diversion effect—the number of bachelor's degrees never received due to the high attrition and low transfer rates of community college students. Evidence of a diversion effect supports charges that community colleges play a "cooling out" function (Clark 1960), dampening students' educational ambitions and channeling lower-class students into low-paying jobs without opportunity for advancement. The effect is to provide workers to the economy in socially efficient ways while maintaining social stratification (Labaree 1997).

Based on his review of multivariate analyses that control for student characteristics, Dougherty (1994, 67) concluded that community colleges do increase overall college-going rates among high school graduates but diminish baccalaureate degree completion. Controlling for background, aspirations, and ability, studies have estimated "students entering the community college receive 11-19% fewer bachelor's degrees than similar students entering four-year colleges" (Dougherty 1994, 53). Thus, the gap in bachelor's degree attainment is considerable, and the "democratizing effect" of increased higher education participation appears to be undercut by the "diversion effect" of reduced bachelor's degree attainment (Dougherty 2002a, 316). However, in recent research, Rouse (1998) and Leigh and Gill (in press) concluded that the democratizing effect outweighs the diversion effect. Early studies of the effects of community colleges on educational outcomes are now subject to criticism for failing to adequately control for differences in the characteristics of students who "self-select" into further education and those who exit (Cameron and Heckman 2001, 465; Grubb 1999b, 2; Kane and Rouse 1999, 71; Rouse 1994, 602).

New data and estimation techniques have evolved through the 1990s, but the new generation of studies has not yet amassed convincing evidence for the democratization effect. Based on estimates of the higher earnings and employment status of community college students relative to high school graduates, Grubb (1999b) concluded that "critics of community colleges are incorrect in their wholesale condemnation of these institutions" (p. 7). However, estimates of the positive returns to community college study do not address the potential loss of greater earnings and employment status due to the hypothesized diversion from bachelor's degree attainment. Further study is needed to empirically evaluate community colleges as agents of social stratification or mobility. However, it is clear, based on the descriptive statistics above, that college participation and degree attainment in the United States is stratified by race and income. Colleges must play a greater role in addressing these persistent educational inequities.

Equity-inclusive performance accountability. The design of equity-inclusive performance accountability can be achieved by mandating extended analyses of current indicators to look at outcomes by race, gender, and income. With a productive efficiency rationale, the focus has been on improving the rates at which colleges move students through the system and into the workforce, as indicated by retention, graduation, transfer, and job placement. The system is indifferent to the distribution of these outcomes among different socioeconomic groups. Creating equity-inclusive systems depends on redefining the valued outcomes to eliminate this indifference. Such a change would indicate that the distribution of outcomes matters.

College participation rates as determined by enrollment, persistence, graduation, and transfer statistics are already among the most common indicators of performance for two-year colleges. Job placement, licensure test scores, and earnings are also common indicators (Burke and Serban 1998, Table 4.1). By analyzing these outcomes by socioeconomic and racial groups, these efficiency indicators can also serve as equity measures. Equitable outcomes would be indicated by positive answers to the following questions:

1. Do members of different socioeconomic and racial groups in the state enroll in public two-year and four-year colleges at the same rate, or have differences in the enrollment rates declined this year?
2. Do members of different socioeconomic and racial groups living in communities served by this (an individual) college enroll, persist, attain associate's degrees, transfer, and attain bachelor's degrees at the same rate, or are the differences in these rates declining?
3. When academic and vocational programs are categorized by the economic value of the degrees issued, are the rates of completion by members of different socioeconomic and racial groups served by the state and by each college the same, or are differences in rates declining?

In response to the data demands of the accountability movement, rich longitudinal data systems now exist in many states to analyze these equity questions (Grubb 1999a; Sanchez, Laanan, and Wiseley 1999). Approximately twenty states link unemployment insurance data with higher education data to observe the workforce participation of college participants and graduates (Grubb 1999a). Florida is considered a leader in the development of such systems. The state's Postsecondary Progression study analyzes data compiled from the Department of Education, the Community College System, the State University System, the Division of Colleges and Universities, the Office of Student Financial Assistance, and the Department of Labor and Employment Security (Postsecondary progression 2002). This lengthy list demonstrates the high level of bureaucratic collaboration required to develop such an extensive database. Missouri is also now developing an ambitious longitudinal database to track the progress of individual students from high school through college and employment (Wittstruck, Watson, and Monroe 2002).

However, these systems were not born of equity concerns, and equity analyses are liable to neglect even where the data exists to accomplish them. Exceptions exist, such as in California where Sanchez, Laanan, and Wiseley (1999) analyzed postcollege earnings using a linked unemployment insurance and community college system database to report earnings gains by race and ethnicity and by initial socioeconomic status. Sheehan et al. (2002) analyzed the employment and earnings of Ohio public college two- and four-year graduates with a focus on the experiences of low-income students relative to their peers. Reviewing the uses of integrated state data, Grubb (1999a) emphasized that both the technical challenges of developing the databases and the political conflicts have limited analyses to date. However,

> as states move to use these data for accountability and performance-based funding, the problems of overly simple analysis are likely to generate opposition from colleges, who could claim that state figures misstate their local experiences. Thus, political pressures may force states into more sophisticated analyses. (P. 5)

As these pressures mount, college administrators are likely to have the interests of their individual colleges foremost in mind. Therefore, it is imperative that equity advocates in legislative positions, civic organizations, higher educational institutions, and policy institutes realize the potential of these complex data systems and argue for the inclusion and public dissemination of analyses based on socioeconomic status and race.

This proposal for equity-inclusive performance accountability calls for the use of outcome indicators to take an ideological turn away from valuing efficiency as a hallmark of good business practices to valuing efficiency as a means to achieve outcome equity in higher education. It does not address the question of whether performance accountability functions to achieve its current purposes. A case study of the implementation of performance measurement systems provides evidence of mixed results, with some states falling short on important measures of attrition and others improving transfer rates and time to degree (Dougherty 2002b, 20-21). Dougherty (2002b, 17-18) observed that some steps taken by colleges to improve student outcomes were pedagogically valuable, for example improving counseling services, while others served to improve indicators without necessarily helping students learn, for example redefining low-performing credit programs as noncredit and moving them outside the scope of outcome measurement.

In the logic of performance accountability, the articulation of priorities and the link between outcomes and state funds creates incentives for college administrators to achieve desired goals. Accountability systems do not prescribe the methods by which outcomes should be obtained. Colleges themselves are responsible for determining how they will meet the outcome goals. As Dougherty's (2002b) case study demonstrates, the steps taken can be substantive and constructive or simply amount to new ways of counting students, credits, and degrees. Equity-inclusive performance accountability has value in establishing equal outcomes as a goal for higher education. Other efforts to assess administrative and pedagogical practices are also needed to make progress toward that goal. As Nora (n.d.) has indicated, in the future, accountability must focus on the "outcomes of those [students] seeking services, the involvement of students in a new learning paradigm, and their participation in a collaborative learning environment" (Blueprint, paragraph 4). The focus on outcomes is coordinated with pedagogical and administrative reform. To accomplish this goal, he argued, "colleges must design programs that are data driven, based on sound data analyses, and measure conceptually meaningful outcomes" (Blueprint, paragraph 4). Those objectives require an ongoing revision of performance accountability systems.

Higher education scholars have described the positive effect democratic educational communities have on student outcomes (Rendon n.d.; Rhoads and Valadez 1996). Rhoads and Valadez (1996, 217) have conceptualized "education as the practice of democracy" as a foundation for a "philosophical and practical framework from which to structure community college life." Their recommendations for reform include emphases on participatory management, collaborative classroom practices, commitment to multiculturalism, and critical pedagogy that includes issues of social inequality in the curriculum. Rhoads and Valadez also invoked Kincheloe's notion of "good work" to call for a "reconstitution" of vocational education that "challenges dominant conceptions of work and worker identity" (p. 53). They argued for "a broader vision of students, encompassing not only their role as workers but also their role as citizens." It is possible to incorporate this broader vision into performance accountability systems by recognizing efficiency as a mode in which to reach desired outcomes rather than valuing it as an end in itself.

Summary

This article makes a case for using performance accountability systems to measure outcome equity in higher education. By distinguishing technical, or productive, efficiency from an ideology of efficiency, it is possible to oppose efficiency as an end in itself and argue for an emphasis within performance accountability systems on the equitable distribution of higher education outcomes. While community colleges have been called "democracy's college" for their role in providing open access to higher education, access is being undermined today by rising tuition and curricular stratification. Access is an insufficient standard for ensuring democratic equality, as evidenced by persistent inequities in the rates at which low-income students and students of color enroll in college and obtain degrees. Performance accountability systems establish rich longitudinal data sets that should be exploited to shift the rhetorical focus from access and equal opportunity to equal outcomes.

Note

1. More specifically, at the point of efficiency, the "marginal social benefit should equal the marginal social cost of production" (Breneman and Nelson 1981, 41).

References

Access denied: Restoring the nation's commitment to equal educational opportunity. 2001. Washington, DC: Advisory Committee on Student Financial Assistance.

Albright, B. N. 1998. The transition from business as usual to funding for results: State efforts to integrate performance measures in the higher education budgetary process. Denver, CO: State Higher Education Executive Officers.

Bailey, S. K. 1994. Combating the efficiency cultists. Change 26 (May/June): 72.

Barnes, K. J. 2001. A study of SUNY community college sponsorship of school-based college-level learning in high school. Paper presented at the Association for the Study of Higher Education, Richmond, VA, November.

Berkner, L. 2000. *Trends in undergraduate borrowing: Federal student loans in 1989-90, 1992-93, and 1995-96*. Statistical Analysis report no. NCES 2000-151. Washington, DC: National Center for Education Statistics.

Berkner, L., A. Berker, K. Rooney, and P. Katharin. 2002. *Student financing of undergraduate education: 1999-2000*. Statistical Analysis report no. NCES 2002-167. Washington, DC: National Center for Education Statistics.

Bragg, D. D. 2001. Community college access, mission, and outcomes: Considering intriguing intersections and challenges. *Peabody Journal of Education* 76 (1): 93-116.

Breneman, D. W., and S. C. Nelson. 1981. *Financing community colleges: An economic perspective*. Washington, DC: Brookings Institution.

Brint, S., and J. Karabel. 1989. *The diverted dream: Community colleges and the promise of educational opportunity in America, 1900-1985*. New York: Oxford University Press.

Burke, J. C., and S. Modarresi. 2000. To keep or not to keep performance funding. *Journal of Higher Education* 71 (4): 432-53.

Burke, J. C., J. Rosen, H. Minassians, and T. Lessard. 2000. *Performance funding and budgeting: An emerging merger?* Fourth annual survey. Albany: Nelson A. Rockefeller Institute of Government, State University of New York.

Burke, J. C., and A. M. Serban, eds. 1998. *Performance funding for public higher education: Fad or trend?* San Francisco: Jossey-Bass.

Cameron, S. V., and J. J. Heckman. 2001. The dynamics of educational attainment for black, Hispanic, and white males. *Journal of Political Economy* 109 (3): 455-99.

Clark, B. R. 1960. The "cooling out" function in higher education. *American Journal of Sociology* 65:569-76.

———. 1980. The "cooling out" function revisited. In *Questioning the community college role*, Vol. 32, edited by G. Vaughn. San Francisco: Jossey-Bass.

Cohen, A. M. 1990. The case for the community college. *American Journal of Education* 98:426-42.

DesJardins, S. L. 2002. Understanding and using efficiency and equity criteria in the study of higher education policy. In *Higher education: Handbook of theory and research*, edited by J. C. Smart and W. G. Tierney. New York: Agathon.

Dougherty, K. J. 1994. *The contradictory college: The conflicting origins, impacts, and futures of the community college*. Albany: State University of New York Press.

———. 2002a. The evolving role of the community college: Policy issues and research questions. In *Higher education: Handbook of theory and research*, Vol. 18, edited by J. C. Smart and W. G. Tierney, 295-348. New York: Agathon.

———. 2002b. Performance accountability and community colleges: Forms, impacts, and problems. Paper presented at the American Educational Research Association, New Orleans, LA, 1-5 April.

Dougherty, K. J., and M. F. Bakia. 2000. Community colleges and contract training: Content, origins, and impact. *Teachers College Record* 102 (1): 197-243.

Ehrenberg, R. G. 2000. Financial prospects for American higher education in the first decade of the twenty-first century. Paper presented at the ACE annual meeting, Chicago, 20 March.

Empty promises: The myth of college access in America. 2002. Washington, DC: Advisory Committee on Student Financial Assistance.

Gaither, G., B. P. Nedwek, and J. E. Neal. 1994. *Measuring up: The promises and pitfalls of performance indicators in higher education*. Vol. 5. Washington, DC: George Washington University, Graduate School of Education and Human Development.

Griswold, C. P., and G. M. Marine. 1996. Political influences on state policy: Higher-tuition, higher aid, and the real world. *Review of Higher Education* 19 (4): 361-89.

Grubb, N. W. 1999a. *The economic benefits of pre-baccalaureate education: Results from state and local studies*. CCRC brief. New York: Community College Research Center, Teachers College, Columbia University.

————. 1999b. *The economic benefits of sub-baccalaureate education: Results from national studies*. CCRC brief. New York: Community College Research Center, Teachers College, Columbia University.

Heller, D. E. 1997. Student price response in higher education. *Journal of Higher Education* 68 (6): 624-59.

————. 1999. The effects of tuition and state financial aid on public college enrollment. *Review of Higher Education* 23 (1): 65-89.

Hilmer, M. J. 1998. Post-secondary fees and the decision to attend a university or a community college. *Journal of Public Economics* 67:329-48.

Kane, T. J. 1999. *The price of admission: Rethinking how Americans pay for college*. Washington, DC: Brookings Institution.

Kane, T. J., and C. E. Rouse. 1999. The community college: Educating students at the margin between college and work. *Journal of Economic Perspectives* 13 (1): 63-84.

King, J. E. 2002. *Crucial choices: How students' financial decisions affect their academic success*. Washington, DC: American Council on Education.

Kipp, S. M., III, D. V. Price, and J. K. Wohlford. 2002. *Unequal opportunity: Disparities in college access among the 50 states*. New Agenda Series, Vol. 4, No. 3. Indianapolis, IN: Lumina Foundation for Education.

Labaree, D. F. 1997. *How to succeed in school without really learning: The credentials race in American education*. New Haven, CT: Yale University Press.

Leigh, D. E., and A. M. Gill. in press. Do community colleges really divert students from earning bachelor's degrees? *Economics of Education Review*.

Levin, H. L. 1994. The necessary and sufficient conditions for achieving educational equity. In *Equity outcomes in education*, edited by R. Berne and L. O. Picus. Thousand Oaks, CA: Corwin.

Levin, J. S. 2001. *Globalizing the community college: Strategies for change in the twenty-first century*. New York: Palgrave.

Longanecker, D. A. 2002. Ensuring access through integrated financing policy. *Network News* 21:1-3.

Losing ground: A national status report on the affordability of American higher education. 2002. San Jose, CA: National Center for Public Policy and Higher Education.

McKeown-Moak, M. P. 2000. Financing higher education in the new century: The second annual report from the states. Paper presented at the American Education Finance Association, Austin, TX, 9-11 March.

————. 2001. *Financing higher education in the new century: The third annual report from the states*. Denver, CO: State Higher Education Executive Officers.

Merisotis, J. P., and T. R. Wolanin. 2000. *Community college financing: Strategies and challenges. New expeditions: Charting the second century of community colleges*. Issues paper no. 5. No. 1523. Annapolis Junction, MD: American Association of Community Colleges, Association of Community College Trustees.

Monk, D. H. 1990. *Educational finance: An economic approach*. New York: McGraw-Hill.

Morgan, R. 2002. Students at public colleges brace for large tuition increases. *Chronicle of Higher Education*, 22 March, p. A26.

Mumper, M. 1996. *Removing college price barriers: What government has done and why it hasn't worked*. Albany: State University of New York Press.

Nettles, M. T., and C. M. Millett. n.d. Student access in community colleges. Retrieved 1 July 2002 from http://www.aacc.nche.edu/Content/NavigationMenu/ResourceCenter/Projects_Partnerships/Current/NewExpeditions/IssuePapers/Student_Access_in_Community_Colleges.htm.

Nora, A. n.d. Reexamining the community college mission. Retrieved 1 July 2002 from http://www.aacc.nche.edu/Content/NavigationMenu/ResourceCenter/Projects_Partnerships/Current/NewExpeditions/IssuePapers/Fulfilling_the_Promise_of_Access_and_Opportunity.htm.

Postsecondary progression of 1993-94 Florida public high school graduates: 2002 update. 2002. Tallahassee, FL: Council for Education Policy, Research, and Improvement.

Rendon, L. n.d. Fulfilling the promise of access and opportunity: Collaborative community colleges for the 21st century. Retrieved 20 March 2002 from http://www.aacc.nche.edu/Content/NavigationMenu/ResourceCenter/Projects_Partnerships/Current/NewExpeditions/IssuePapers/Fulfilling_the_Promise_.htm.

Rhoads, R. A., and J. R. Valadez. 1996. *Democracy, multiculturalism, and the community college: A critical perspective*. New York: Garland.

Rosenfeld, S. A. 1999. *Linking measures of quality and success at community colleges to individual goals and customer needs*. Paper presented at the Independent Advisory Panel Meeting, National Assessment of Vocational Education, Washington, DC, 6-7 May.

Rouse, C. E. 1994. What to do after high school: The two-year versus four-year college enrollment decision. In *Choices and consequences*, edited by R. G. Ehrenberg. Ithaca, NY: ILR Press.

———. 1998. Do two-year colleges increase overall educational attainment? *Policy Analysis and Management* 17 (4): 595-620.

Sanchez, J. R., F. S. Laanan, and W. C. Wiseley. 1999. Postcollege earnings of former students of California community colleges. *Research in Higher Education* 40 (1): 87-113.

Schmidt, P. 2002. Most states tie aid to performance, despite little proof that it works. *Chronicle of Higher Education*, 22 February, A20.

Selingo, J. 2002. Honors programs boom at community colleges. *Chronicle of Higher Education*, 31 May, A20.

Shaw, K. M., J. R. Valadez, and R. A. Rhoads. 1999. *Community colleges as cultural texts*. Albany: State University of New York Press.

Sheehan, R., A. Lechler, W. Wagner, and D. Heller. 2002. A study of higher education experiences and outcomes: Focus on low-income, dependent students. Paper presented at the NASSGAP/NCHELP Financial Aid Research Conference, Denver, CO, 15 June.

Shults, C. 2001. *Remedial education: Practices and policies in community colleges*. Research brief no. AACC-RB-00-2. Washington, DC: American Association of Community Colleges.

State budget and tax actions 2002: Preliminary report. 2002. Denver, CO: National Conference of State Legislatures.

State funding for community colleges: A fifty state survey. 2000. Denver, CO: Center for Community College Policy, Education Commission of the States.

Valadez, J. R. 2002. Transformation of the community colleges for the 21st century. *Educational Researcher* 31 (2): 33-36.

Wittstruck, J., D. Watson, and R. Monroe. 2002. Linked longitudinal administrative data sets. Paper presented at the NASSGAP/NCHELP Financial Aid Research Conference, Denver, CO, 15 June.

The Social Prerequisites of Success: Can College Structure Reduce the Need for Social Know-How?

By
REGINA DEIL-AMEN
and
JAMES E. ROSENBAUM

A study of fourteen colleges finds that community colleges require certain kinds of social know-how—skills and knowledge less available to disadvantaged students. They present seven obstacles: (1) bureaucratic hurdles, (2) confusing choices, (3) student-initiated guidance, (4) limited counselor availability, (5) poor advice from staff, (6) delayed detection of costly mistakes, and (7) poor handling of conflicting demands. However, we find that a very different kind of college—the private occupational college—takes steps to structure out the need for this social know-how and address the needs of disadvantaged students. We speculate about possible policy implications.

Keywords: community colleges; proprietary; cultural capital; higher education; college students; dropout

In recent decades, community colleges have vastly changed higher education, and they have adapted in amazing ways. In addition to offering two years of a college education at low cost, they offer unprecedented flexibility to meet the diverse needs of nontraditional college students. For working students, community col-

Regina Deil-Amen, Ph.D., is an assistant professor in the Department of Education Policy Studies at Pennsylvania State University. She completed her Ph.D. in sociology at Northwestern University and continues to serve as a consultant for the College to Career study at their Institute for Policy Research. This study explores institutional differences between public and private colleges in how they prepare students for jobs in the subbaccalaureate labor market. Her main fields of interest are higher education access and inequality, institutions, race, and culture.

James E. Rosenbaum, Ph.D. is a professor of sociology, education, and social policy at Northwestern University. His interests include education, work, careers and the life course, and stratification. He has just completed a book in the Rose monograph series on the high school to work transition, and he is now conducting studies of the transition between community colleges and work.

NOTE: The authors wish to thank Steven Brint, Stefanie DeLuca, Kevin Dougherty, John Meyer, and the editors of this volume for comments on earlier versions of this

DOI: 10.1177/0002716202250216

leges offer satellite campuses and convenient class schedules (Saturday, Sunday, and evening classes). For students with poor high school skills, they offer remedial coursework, sometimes even below eighth-grade level. For immigrants, they offer English language training. Community colleges enroll high school students, high school dropouts, older students, working students, and students from diverse backgrounds and with diverse goals.

Despite these amazing accommodations, we find that community colleges still pose hidden obstacles that present difficulties for nontraditional college students. Similar to the four-year colleges on which they are modeled, community colleges require certain kinds of social know-how—skills and knowledge that are more available to middle-class students than to the lower-income students who are a large portion of community colleges. These social know-how requirements constitute a hidden curriculum of social prerequisites necessary for navigating and succeeding in a college environment. The community college staff we interviewed are barely aware that these obstacles present systematic problems for students; they assume that students have the social know-how necessary to succeed. While these requirements may not be difficult for middle-class students who get help from college-educated parents, we find that they pose great difficulties for nontraditional students who lack this know-how and who face additional outside commitments and pressures, the very students these colleges were created to serve.

We find that community colleges present seven obstacles for students with less access to knowledge about college: (1) bureaucratic hurdles, (2) confusing choices, (3) student-initiated guidance, (4) limited counselor availability, (5) poor advice from staff, (6) slow detection of costly mistakes, and (7) poor handling of conflicting demands. Based on case studies in public and private two-year colleges, we find that community colleges implicitly demand social know-how about how to navigate a college environment and its bureaucratic structures. Our research identifies what social know-how students must possess, and it illustrates the deleterious consequences for students who lack this know-how. We suggest that students' social know-how—their knowledge about how to handle enrollment, class registration, and financial aid; to initiate information gathering; to access sound and useful advice; to avoid costly mistakes; and to manage conflicting demands—is likely to affect their ultimate college success.

However, we find that these social know-how requirements are not inevitable. Indeed, we report a study of a very different kind of college—the occupational college—that takes steps to structure out the need for this social know-how. These practices specifically address the needs of disadvantaged students who must face difficult decisions, strong competing pressures, little availability of crucial information, and large risks from even small mistakes. If community colleges are to serve nontraditional students, they must address this emerging issue of social know-how.

article. They are also indebted to the Sloan Foundation, the Spencer Foundation, and the Institute for Policy Research at Northwestern University for financial support. Of course, this article does not necessarily reflect their views.

Background and Previous Research

Community colleges have rightly been praised for democratizing higher education and making it accessible to all people, regardless of economic or educational background. Since 1960, while enrollment in four-year colleges has nearly doubled, enrollment in two-year schools has quintupled (National Center for Educational Statistics 1998, 206). The low tuition and open-access admissions policies of these institutions have reduced the barriers to higher education for disadvantaged populations.

While high schools used to be the last schools attended by most students, colleges have increasingly taken that role. While only 45 percent of high school graduates enrolled in college in 1960, 67 percent enrolled by 1997 (National Center for Educational Statistics 1998), and more than 60 percent of undergraduates participated in subbaccalaureate education (Bailey 2002, 4). Moreover, two-year colleges focus on serving disadvantaged students and on providing occupational preparation (Brint and Karabel 1989).

Much prior research on community colleges has been quantitative, focusing on degree completion (Dougherty 1994). A few ethnographies have examined behaviors, practices, and experiences within community colleges (London 1978; Neumann and Riesman 1980; Richardson, Fisk, and Okum 1983; Weis 1985), but these studies have not systematically explored the institutional mechanisms that affect retention across multiple institutions.[1] While Tinto (1993) provided a model explaining student persistence at four-year colleges, few of Tinto's factors exist at two-year colleges—residential dormitories, extensive extracurricular activities, and so forth.

Private two-year colleges are even more neglected. The best studies are either old (Wilms 1974) or purely quantitative (Apling 1993). However, a recent statistical analysis also described a single for-profit college and suggested practical lessons for community colleges (Bailey, Badway, and Gumport 2001). Our study explores that suggestion in greater detail.

This article also provides a new view of the sociological concept of cultural capital. Bourdieu and Passerson (1977) contended that schools have implicit requirements of certain knowledge and skills (cultural capital) that low socioeconomic status students often lack, and these hard-to-see requirements interfere with their educational attainments. This study examines community college practices that generate these requirements and private college practices that avoid these requirements and seem to remove cultural capital obstacles to students' attainments.

Sample and Data

Our sample includes two types of colleges: seven community colleges and seven private occupational colleges in a large Midwestern city and surrounding suburbs.

Our research uses interviews, analyses of written materials, observations, and surveys in these colleges. Four of the occupational colleges are for-profit, or proprietary, colleges. The other three are nonprofit colleges. All offer accredited two-year degrees.

We focus on accredited programs leading to applied associate's degrees in a variety of business, health, computer, and technical occupational programs. We conducted more than 130 semistructured, one-hour interviews with administrators, administrative staff, program chairs, and deans. We interviewed 80 community college students and 20 occupational college students. Surveys of more than 4,300 students indicate strong similarity in the types of students at the two types of colleges: both enroll large proportions of low-income and racial minority students.[2]

Findings

Community colleges provide a vast array of programs: transfer to four-year colleges, two-year occupational degrees, remedial classes, General Equivalency Diploma preparation, English as a second language, adult basic education, vocational skills, contract training, continuing education, and lifelong learning. These institutions offer something for every segment of the population, and the diversity of students is a testament to their success in making higher education accessible.

However, attrition has long been a serious problem. More than 42 percent of high school graduates leave two-year colleges without a degree (Dougherty 1994). In Illinois, state data indicate that roughly 45 percent of the students who begin in community colleges do not return by the following year (excluding transfers),[3] and the rate is similar in the community colleges we studied (40 percent).[4]

Although more options sometimes leads to better decisions, they can also increase the need for information and may create confusion and mistaken choices. Multiple options make it difficult to coordinate college offerings and to allocate fixed resources. The career dean at one community college stated, "It's a balancing act, and we have these external pressures on us to do 14 million things." A dean of instruction noted that part of the challenge is "knowing exactly what our role is." These multiple missions may limit community colleges' capacity to serve as an avenue of social mobility.

While low-income, relatively young minority students face many cultural barriers (Zwerling and London 1992), choice itself can be another obstacle. Community colleges offer many program options and give students the autonomy to steer their own route through the educational process. This can be liberating for some but overwhelming for others. We find that disadvantaged students with limited time and finances to devote to education are often confused about their choices. They do not know how to get the information they need, and small amounts of confusion can evolve into large problems of wasted time and poor decisions. Students often come from public schools where counseling services are limited, and they lack the know-how they need to make the required choices.

We find that many students are first-generation students whose parents have not attended college. In some of these cases, families may not provide financial or other support. Beatriz, for instance, reported,

> Getting myself into college was not an easy task at all to accomplish. Since I came from a Mexican family of eight, it was almost impossible to think of finishing high school, much less enter college. In my house, school was not really emphasized. Work, on the other hand, was all my parents talked about. . . . Many times, my father would yell at me, telling me I was just wasting my time and money and I was gonna go nowhere.

Other families provide emotional support but not information or financial help. For example, when asked if his parents encourage college, Derrick said, "Basically, it's my decision. They give me a pat on the back and say 'I'm glad you're doing it.'" However, his family cannot provide financial help, so Derrick works two part-time jobs to pay tuition and living expenses. Many students' families cannot provide guidance, information, or savings.

As we note below, we find that these community colleges pose seven obstacles for students with less social know-how, and occupational colleges have devised ways to reduce the need for this social know-how.

Bureaucratic Hurdles

While community colleges' size allows them to offer a broad range of courses and degrees, their complexity demands that students acquire and assess a great deal of information about courses, requirements, and options. Students who lack the social know-how needed to navigate through college are at risk of making serious mistakes that imperil their college careers.

First, bureaucratic hurdles arise from the size and complexity of community colleges. Students find their complicated class schedules and college catalogs difficult and time consuming to understand. At a community college that serves a high poverty area, the academic support center dean notes that many students make mistakes in selecting classes on their own, and they later learn that their degree will take longer than they had anticipated.

> [Students] were constantly saying to us, "Nobody told me. I didn't know." . . . We can claim that . . . everything that they need to know we write down [somewhere]. [laughs] . . . It doesn't work that way. So they were getting frustrated, we were getting frustrated.

The college's reputation was suffering, as prospective students and their parents began asking questions. The dean of career programs noted that students want to know "how long it's going to take me" and say, "I don't wanna take a lot of unnecessary courses. I need to have a time line." He hears parents saying, "This is how much money I got. How much is it going to cost? They got two years, they'd better be at the end of the road."

This was a problem at the other community colleges in our sample as well, where the issue includes transfer. A student at another urban college commented, "One of my friends went [here], and she told me, 'Don't go there because you're going to waste your time. You're going to take classes that you won't need when you transfer.' "

In addition, students face other hurdles: filling out enrollment forms, registering for classes, applying for financial aid, making choices that efficiently accumulate credits toward a degree, and fitting in work and family obligations. Students must figure out how to overcome these obstacles each semester. One student complained about his seven-hour registration ordeal: "I went to registration at 12, and I didn't get out until 7," and he became so frustrated that he did not register the second semester and did not return until four years later.

Information is hard to obtain. Students report having to search all over campus to get information about specific program requirements, to learn which courses lead to their desired goals and meet requirements most quickly. Many students are not aware of the state and federal financial aid options available. Some wrongly assume they would not qualify for aid because they are working full- or part-time or because the tuition is low. Students who apply for financial aid complain about the difficulty of the forms and the lack of assistance at these colleges. Unfortunately, many students faced unpleasant and even hostile encounters with financial aid staff in their attempts to complete the financial aid process. Two weeks after she started, Rosa still had not finished the financial aid process. She said of the financial aid department,

> They're rude. This lady kicked me out. . . . I didn't have . . . my security card. She said, "Ah, just get out of here. Just go. You don't have anything ready. Go." . . . I understand they get frustrated, but they don't have to be rude.

Corrie, who grew up in "the projects" and is now living with friends while she puts herself through school to become an occupational therapist, also faced hostility:

> The financial aid office wasn't what I expected. . . . I've had a bad experience with them. They're just very nonchalant about your funding, and I feel like a lot of them don't care because it's like, "It's not me getting the money, and I don't really care." And I've been yelled at a couple of times in financial aid by my counselor.

Bureaucratic hurdles continue in other domains. Because of problems with community college staff, when Lisette needed more information about transfer, she went directly to the college to which she planned to transfer to get information. Many students had similar problems getting correct information, and some, like Lisette, learned through other students or older siblings to seek information directly from the four-year colleges. Unfortunately, students who lack this know-how often found that poor information extended their time in college.

Confusing Choices

Second, students face a confusing array of hard-to-understand choices because of the wide variety of programs, each having different requirements for their various degrees and certificates. Students may not even have a clear picture of their goals, which makes it harder to get good advice. Indeed, in our interviews, most students who had not chosen a major had not sought counselor advice about their course selections in their first year. In the words of one administrator, this often results in students' "wandering aimlessly through the curriculum, amassing large numbers of hours but not making progress toward a degree." He feels this explains the fact that a third of the college's students failed to complete 75 percent of their courses, which is considered unsatisfactory academic progress and threatens their financial aid eligibility.

Community colleges implicitly demand social know-how about how to navigate a college environment and its bureaucratic structures.

Even after students have chosen a program, choosing classes is still a daunting task. It can be difficult to schedule all the required courses in the correct order while still paying attention to prerequisites and general education courses and synchronizing course schedules with work and family schedules. We encountered many students who were confused about general education requirements and the necessary prerequisites for their major courses. If students do not fulfill a course requirement, they may have to wait an entire year before the course is offered again. These mistakes can be overwhelming setbacks for students with limited resources and constrained timetables, and they can lead to disappointment, frustration, and eventual dropout.

Given the complex course catalogs and class schedules and the lack of structured guidance, these are surprisingly easy mistakes to make. Even sophisticated observers could have difficulty: the authors, both Ph.D.s, spent many hours trying to understand some of the catalogs' labeling systems for classes and degrees, and several interviews were necessary to clarify the information. Not surprisingly, disadvantaged students rarely know what questions to ask. Due to the catalog's lack of clarity and her misunderstanding of how these classes fit into her program requirements, Annette was not aware that the remedial courses she had to take would not count toward her degree:

Why didn't anyone tell me that? . . . They had me registering and everything. . . . This is going to hold me back. . . . So I still have two years to go 'cause none of these classes here even count. So I was a little upset about that because it was really misleading.

Apparently, Annette is not alone in her uncertainty. Our surveys find that many community college students, especially from low-income families, were uncertain of their program and degree requirements and course prerequisites.

The Burden of Student-Initiated Assistance

Third, the burden of student-initiated guidance also raises obstacles, especially for disadvantaged students. Although community colleges make guidance available to students, the colleges require that students initiate the process of seeking out guidance. The consequences of this situation for at-risk students are fourfold. First, students must be aware of what kind of help they need and when they need it. Second, they must be informed about how and where to get this help. Third, they must actually go get it. Fourth, students must seek this information well in advance.

Unfortunately, these conditions do not serve first-generation college students well. Those students whose parents have not attended college cannot easily get advice about how to succeed, what pitfalls to avoid, or how to plan their pathway through college. These students are left to navigate college on their own.

Often, students do not even know that they need help, so they do not take the initiative to seek it out, particularly for long-range planning. Although students know they must ask counselors or faculty to approve their course selections for the next semester, students do not seek information about long-term plans, such as figuring out how to meet their degree requirements efficiently or discussing their educational or career goals. As a result, students are often left without a plan of action, and they make seemingly arbitrary decisions about their classes, the direction of their education, and their career goals.

Even for students who talk to counselors, first-generation students' limited knowledge of college and career paths often make these interactions ineffective. Students often cannot see the pathway for how to get to their occupational goal, and they ask questions and gather information based on wrong assumptions. Putting the burden of initiating advice on inexperienced students leads to poorly directed college strategies, particularly when counseling assistance is focused on selecting classes, not on mapping out long-range plans. Sonia, for instance, is a first-generation college student who comes from a low-income family of eight. In her interview, it was clear that her only source of career advice had been her older brother, who was in his early twenties. She is following the requirements for a math major although she wants to be an accountant or possibly major in computer science. When we asked what career she is considering, Sonia told us accounting. However, in her brief meeting with a counselor, he only asked about her course interests, which led him to suggest only a math major.

Sonia: Well, I was confused. . . . I had to talk to a counselor. . . . He wanted to know what I was going to major in. . . . I told him I liked math, so I'm taking math courses. . . . So that's it.
Regina: Did you try to go through other degrees, like accounting?
Sonia: No.
Regina: Did you tell him that you were interested in those things, too, or just math?
Sonia: Just math. I figured math and accounting were maybe the same. I'd never taken accounting.

In the brief session, Sonia did not think to mention her career interests, so she is pursuing only one option. If it becomes too difficult or uninteresting, she has no plan for considering alternatives, and her courses were not chosen to provide prerequisites for other majors.

Limited Counselor Availability

Fourth, the limited availability of counselors is a serious obstacle to getting good advice. Counselors at community colleges are typically overburdened, responsible for advising students not only about academic planning but also about the transfer process, career exploration, part-time job placement, and personal issues. They are vastly understaffed, with typically 800 students per counselor. According to one counselor, "We don't have a command performance. Obviously, we couldn't have with just 8 of us for over 6,000 students." This 1:750 ratio is actually better than many of the other community colleges in our sample, and it can be compared with high schools where a ratio of 1:400 is common and is widely believed to be inadequate.

In fact, some administrators report that students need to schedule appointments months in advance to see a counselor. Counselors typically schedule thirty minutes for each appointment, and times fill up quickly, especially around registration time when counseling is needed most. One administrator highlighted the need for students to plan far ahead of time: "they're going for preregistration and they go make an appointment, and then it's October, and the counselors say, 'Well, you could come in December sixth.' " Students report being "too busy" to see counselors, but that should not be mistaken for indifference. For instance, Dan tried to see a counselor several times, but each time, he had to schedule one far in advance, and then he either forgot or could not make the appointment.

None of the community colleges involved in the study required students to meet with counselors even once during their schooling. The majority of students we interviewed had not spoken with a counselor because of the difficulties and delays entailed. Although she is conscientious about meeting the various demands on her, Lauren is completing her second semester and yet reports, "I haven't talked directly to counselors."

Even when they meet, inadequate staffing also affects the students' interactions with counselors. If students do not know exactly what they need help with, then the counseling experience can be ineffective and anxiety ridden. Rolanda described her unsuccessful experience:

I talked to one of the counselors, but since there was a lot of people waiting, it was kind of fast. We didn't have much time to talk. Also, when you go to a counselor, many times you don't really know what you're going to talk about. You have an idea, but you don't know what questions to ask. I think counselors should ask more questions of us. They just answer our questions then say, "OK, you can go, since you don't know what to ask." It's hard. There are things we don't know.

As a result of her negative experience, Rolanda has avoided seeking further advice from counselors. Instead, she picks classes on her own from a transfer form that she noticed on the wall outside the counselors' offices.

Poor Advice from Staff

Fifth, poor advice is common. The complexity is so daunting that information proves to be challenging even for counselors and administrators. Students in search of information report that they often got conflicting opinions, which directs them to radically different actions. Many students report being guided into courses that were unneeded and thus a waste of their time and tuition money. Unfortunately, for students with limited resources, the time wasted and mistakes involved in figuring things out on their own can prevent them from completing their educational goals.

Even when students see a counselor, the information is sometimes wrong. Counselors might fail to get sufficient information about program offerings and requirements from departments, and their information is also often out of date. Some department chairs admitted that they had little communication with counselors:

Interviewer: How much direct contact does your department have with the counselors?
Department Chair: Very little. . . . I would say it's pretty much just "hello" in the hallway or something. There's no real . . . contact with them, unless they have some kind of question or something or we find out they're giving out bad info, we'll go down there from time to time to straighten them out or something.

Some administrators complain that counselors often have mistaken notions about their programs. With so many programs to understand and so many other responsibilities, counselors sometimes have difficulty keeping track of all the changes in requirements and curriculum. One department chair reports that students sometimes come to him complaining that the counseling office is giving incorrect information, which appears to make their plans unachievable. This chair will send these students back down to speak with the counselors again; "I tell them, . . . You know, stick to your guns and tell them, 'This is my life.' Or, don't go to them at all. Have me sign the darn registration and I'll do it!"

Other students' transfer plans are delayed due to poor and contradictory counseling from different counselors, who rarely have a long-term relationship with students. For example, Deanna spent four years at community college before she actually transferred, and although she was extremely happy with her teachers and classes, she complained about the counseling system:

> The only thing I had a problem with was the counselors weren't very helpful . . . not at all. . . . You go to them for what classes you need to take. I feel I took a lot of wasted classes. You didn't get much help. Now that I'm in a university, I realize if I would have just had a good counselor I probably would have avoided a lot of this. You had a different one every time you went. I would have graduated in the two years like I should have if I had a better counselor. . . . I feel like [students] just don't get out of there. It's a rut you can get into. . . . Counselors don't tell you what you need to do. People are walking around blindfolded. . . . They don't know what to do.

Although counselors can see students' transcripts, they often lack detailed knowledge about students other than their grades. They also may not understand the program requirements.

Because counselors' advice is often inadequate, many students get advice from worse sources—faculty in other programs unrelated to their own. Although students must have their registration forms signed before they can register, this form can be signed by "any full-time faculty"—not just counselors. Often, this signing takes place during extremely busy and chaotic open registration periods, which are not conducive to careful guidance. Only students who know the value of counseling, who show initiative, and who make plans in advance manage to get counselors' time. Thus, most advising is done by faculty, who have no counseling training and who may not know the requirements for the student's particular program. Within this system, there is no assurance that the individual who signs the form can assess whether students are on track for graduation or whether a course will transfer or even count in the student's major. Anyone can sign their cards, and as a result, students are often entirely responsible for mapping out their own academic progress. For students with little knowledge about the college process, this responsibility can lead to small mistakes, which result in major setbacks.

Like many students we interviewed, Carlos's experience with his urban public high school's guidance counselors was limited to discipline problems. "[In high school] the only time you got to see a counselor was when you were in trouble. It was like that. Like, for cutting or whatever you did." So, when he first began community college, Carlos thought that a good student is one who manages to avoid seeing counselors. He did not seek out any additional help to determine what courses he should take:

> Nobody told me to go see a counselor. No. They just had that open registration. You go talk to anybody. The teachers are like, "What classes do you want? Here, go register. You've got your financial aid? Go take care of it." Things like that.

In hindsight, he realized that getting a counselor's advice would have been important "so you don't waste your time here." He thinks the fact that they leave it up to the student to seek assistance contributed to his initial difficulties:

> Like, for example, they gave me a Biology 101. This was my first semester here . . . when I was first out of high school. I didn't know anything about college. . . . I thought I was getting credit for it, but I wasn't. Now when I dropped it, I got an F because I didn't see a counselor. I didn't even know you were supposed to go see a counselor. . . . Then when I went to go retake the class, the class isn't even offered anymore. Then I find out that you don't even need the class. I saw my GPA. . . . It brought me down.

This bad experience in his first semester led to his decision to drop all his classes and quit altogether. He did not return until several years had passed. Five years later, Carlos, twenty-three years old at the time of our interview, was starting his sixth semester of community college, yet he had accumulated only about two semesters of college credits. Having learned the value of seeking advice the hard way, he now speaks to counselors at four-year colleges for information about transfer:

> Everything I've done was because I went to visit counselors at other schools. They helped me. They're the ones telling me what classes to take and this and that. Here, I don't know what the problem is, but they're not doing their job.

Carlos's lack of exposure to academic or career advising in high school was similar to that of many of the low-income students we interviewed. They lacked cultural capital regarding the value of counseling and therefore faced difficulties seeking this type of assistance in community college.

Delayed Detection of Costly Mistakes

Sixth, students' mistakes are easy to make and hard to detect, and even a few simple mistakes can be devastating. Given the complexity of choices and the inaccessibility of guidance, students often make mistakes. An admissions counselor says that first-generation college students face many difficulties because information about the system is not apparent. "They don't even know what type of degree they're getting. They're not aware of whether the degree they're getting is a terminal degree or not." Ivette, who is in her second full-time semester and aiming for an A.A. degree, responded to the question about when she expects to complete her degree by saying, "I still haven't seen what credits I need for the classes." Although her classes had been mostly remedial and do not count toward her degree, she assumed she could finish a two-year associate's degree within the "promised" two years.

Although their choices are crucial, students often do not understand their situation. The risks of student error are increased because they do not know what they do not know. Many students we interviewed did not know how to distinguish between different types of degrees and different types of credits. Considerable background knowledge is required to make these distinctions, and failure to see crucial distinctions can have serious repercussions. For example, Raymond had trouble distinguishing between credit, noncredit, and remedial classes, and he did not understand the difference between required and optional courses. Because he did not seek counselors' advice at registration, he signed up for a reading class, after finding that a math class he needed was closed. He did not realize that the reading class was remedial, and he was paying for a course that would not count for degree or transfer credit.

Students' mistakes are often not detected for some time. Many students reported that they subsequently discovered that they had wasted time and money in courses that do not contribute toward their educational goals and that they had made less progress than they expected. Denise's problems, for instance, resulted from problematic counselor advice and her own mistakes. In her second year, she realized that she cannot finish this year—a major adjustment given her financial and child care constraints:

> I took it upon myself to be my own counselor. I took five unnecessary classes because I thought I knew everything. . . . The first counselor I had, the one that gave me those wrong classes, . . . wasted my time, so I took it upon my myself and I didn't go see a counselor anymore. She gave me wrong classes, but I messed up more.

Such discoveries are disappointing and may lead students to drop out of college. Although we did not interview dropouts, our respondents described struggles that led them to contemplate dropping out, and they reported that many of their friends did drop out in comparable circumstances.

Community colleges are expected to be all things to all people. They have made concerted efforts to remain flexible, preserve choice, and minimize the constraints on students. However, without good counseling, a multitude of options can lead to poor choices for students without the necessary know-how. For students who are not familiar with the system and do not seek out appropriate help, higher education can pose overwhelming choices. By the time these students have learned how to navigate the system, many may have lost valuable time and tuition dollars or may have given up and dropped out.

Disadvantaged students are especially harmed by the lack of accessible and reliable information. Often, no one in their family or social circle has attended college, so they may not be aware of how colleges work or even what programs are offered. In our interviews, administrators and faculty often spoke about students who lacked clear direction or goals:

> I think when a lot of students come in, they don't know what they want to do. And a lot of them, I think, are like pinballs. They're bouncing from one thing to another, you know, before they find something that they actually like.

Our results help explain why many students who intend to transfer to four-year colleges take courses that do not count for transfer credit at four-year colleges (Dougherty 1994).

In addition, low-income students generally have limited time and money for college and may often have parents pressuring them to take full-time jobs. For such students, the longer they take to choose their program, the greater the chance that they will run out of time or money and be forced to drop out of school with only an array of unrelated courses to show for their efforts. For such students, confusing choices and poor guidance creates frustration and disappointment, which may lead students to give up on the pursuit altogether.

Poor Handling of Conflicting Demands

Seventh, colleges poorly handle conflicting outside demands. Compared with other students, nontraditional students usually face more numerous and more severe conflicts with outside demands. Students report many problems that pull them away from school: parent illness, financial need, child care crises, unanticipated pregnancies, automobile breakdowns, and work obligations. Unlike young, full-time students, nontraditional students often have less flexible outside prior commitments and crises that impinge on their studies, and some lack know-how about how to balance school with other demands.

Administrators, faculty, and staff at these community colleges boasted that the variety of morning, afternoon, evening, and weekend class times allowed students to arrange their school schedule around their outside obligations. However, although this approach clearly adds flexibility, it ironically imposes further problems. Class schedules are driven by student demand rather than planned sequencing, and course schedules change every term, so students cannot anticipate their class schedule from semester to semester. Given the vast array of course options that community colleges offer, administrators cannot create coordinated schedules for students. Students report that the courses they need to take are often scheduled at vastly different times of day, and some are not offered for several semesters. This makes their education extremely difficult to coordinate with outside work and family commitments. Moreover, their course schedules in the spring term are invariably quite different than those in the prior term, so the work and child care arrangements created in one semester fail to work in the next. In addition, some students find that necessary courses are already closed to additional students, conflict with other necessary courses, or are not being offered in the term originally expected. Ironically, community colleges' attempts at flexibility may delay students seeking to finish their degrees.

Moreover, even though these conflicts are common, community colleges do not systematically provide students with advice or assistance to handle these conflicts. This failure to provide know-how that will help students cope with conflicts is not limited to just course selection and degree planning.

Community colleges view work as an unfortunate necessity that competes with school. One program chair described this view: "Well, in the best of all possible worlds, I think a student should not work. But, that is not an option for most of our students. . . . They have to make money." Although community college administrators are proud of their nontraditional student body, their comments about work commitments imply that the traditional student model is the ideal. When asked why students do not succeed, faculty members often suggested that students need to reduce their work hours to solve the problem.

Viewing the problem as external to the college, they do not focus on institutional strategies for improving retention. Rather than helping students incorporate school and work, they merely tolerate work as an economic necessity. These community colleges help students find part-time jobs, but they are often unrelated to students' area of study (cf. Grubb 1996).

The occupational colleges in this study have found ways to transform implicit rules into explicit organizational structures and policies.

Many students are in desperate need of career counseling and advice about how to explore opportunities that will best prepare them for their desired career. For example, one student sought a career in film, but he did not understand how to gain experience in that industry: "I'm going to be starting at Blockbuster Video . . . because I want to . . . make movies, work in film. Blockbuster seems like a pretty good place to get some knowledge." This student was trying to incorporate his need to work while in school with his desire to gain some experience related to his chosen field of study. However, he has received no guidance from the college about how to do that.

In fact, most community college faculty members believe that students should try to minimize work hours. Working is seen as an impediment to success in school. Other than offering classes at different times and minimizing out-of-class group projects, the community colleges do little to help students manage their work and school responsibilities.

The New Private Occupational Colleges

Given students' many problems at community colleges, it is useful to examine alternatives. While most two-year college students are at public colleges, about 4 percent attend private colleges (Bailey, Badway, and Gumport 2001). Like community colleges, the private colleges we studied offer accredited two-year degrees, and we selected colleges that offer similar applied programs such as business, accounting, office technology, computer information systems, electronics, medical assisting, and computer-aided drafting. Each college offers degrees in three or more of these program areas, which are intended to lead directly to related jobs.

Although for-profit colleges acquired bad reputations due to past abuses and even fraud, 1992 federal legislation led to the demise of 1,500 schools and compelled the remaining schools to improve (Apling 1993). We selected occupational colleges that passed the same accreditation standards as community colleges and offer associate's degrees of similar quality to community colleges. As such, they are comparable to community colleges but dissimilar to 94 percent of other business and technical schools, which offer no degree above a certificate (Apling 1993). These private colleges should not be considered a random sample: they are some of the best programs in these fields and may be considered to represent an ideal type.[5]

We focus on the ways these colleges structure out the need for much of the social know-how that the community colleges require. They have developed original structures and processes that appear to reduce barriers to disadvantaged students with limited know-how by helping them navigate the administrative obstacles in college.

Structuring Out the Need for Social Know-How

The occupational colleges in this study have found ways to transform implicit rules into explicit organizational structures and policies. They create programs that students can easily understand, master, and negotiate, even if students know very little about how college works. In fact, many of these occupational colleges have found that they can improve student success by making their curriculum more structured, not less. By structuring students' choices, they have found that they also reduce the likelihood that students will make mistakes in their course choices. These colleges also implement strong guidance and tight advisory relationships with their students, which facilitates completion and successful work entry.

While community colleges have become overburdened with competing priorities and functions, occupational colleges continue to provide a limited number of clearly structured programs that lead disadvantaged students to a two-year degree and a stable job in the primary labor market. They accomplish this by procedures that address the seven above-noted problems in community colleges, as we detail below.

Eliminating Bureaucratic Hurdles

First, occupational colleges minimize bureaucratic hurdles. Enrolling is a simple process handled mainly by a single individual who makes all the arrangements for a student. Every student is then assigned to a single adviser who assists in selecting courses. Information is available in one place, and students do not have to run around the college getting information. Students deal with one staff person, not a bureaucratic tangle of scattered offices. Furthermore, registration each term is a simple matter, and as noted later, course choices are simple and offered in the same time slots over the year, avoiding schedule conflicts. Students choose a package of coordinated courses, rather than selecting from a long menu of individual course choices with fluctuating and conflicting time slots.

Occupational colleges also reduce the bureaucratic hurdles to financial aid. At community colleges, obtaining financial aid is largely up to students, and little help is provided. Heckman (1999) has noted the low take-up rate on federal and state financial aid programs, and he speculated (based on no empirical data) that it was due to students' decisions not to seek aid. Our interviews with community college staff and students indicate that students do not apply because they do not know about it or they cannot figure out the complex forms. In contrast, occupational colleges help students through the application process to get the best aid package possible. Admissions staff physically walk applicants to the financial aid office, where a staff person answers all questions and fills out the financial aid application with each student (and their parents, if desired). Occupational colleges treat financial aid as an integral part of the application process, and college staff members explain and simplify the process. This is rarely done by the community colleges we studied or by those studied by others (Orfield and Paul 1994).

Reducing Confusing Choices

Second, while community college students face a confusing array of hard-to-understand course and program choices with unclear connections to future career trajectories, occupational colleges offer a clear set of course sequences aimed at efficient training for specific career goals.

When students first arrive at community colleges, they are often uncertain about what degree or program to pursue. Community colleges encourage students to explore, yet their model for exploration is based on that of four-year colleges—sample from a wide variety of unrelated courses that are highly general, do not specify clear outcomes, and may count for some programs but not for others. Much like a cafeteria where the customer is supposed to choose from the seven different food groups, students are encouraged to sample from five or more academic disciplines without much regard for future career goals.

This nondirective approach may work well for middle-class students who can count on four years of college, but it presents difficulties for many nontraditional students with a shorter time frame. Exploration at some community colleges is largely confined to liberal arts courses, in which many of these students have done poorly in the past. Confusion also arises from the lack of clarity about the implications and relevance of specific choices to future careers. For students with limited resources who must obtain a marketable degree with a minimum of forgone wages or tuition dollars, this approach is problematic (Wilms 1974). Many disadvantaged students do not understand college offerings, face strong pressures to get through school quickly, and seek an efficient way to improve their occupational qualifications and get better jobs.

Occupational colleges help students to determine from the outset what degree program best coincides with their abilities, interests, and needs. When they enroll, every student is required to sit down with an admissions counselor who will go through all the degree programs and the courses they entail, with an explanation of implications, sequences, requirements, and job outcomes. Students' achievement and goals are assessed. In the words of one student,

> You go through all the programs, and they evaluate you, and you take some tests. They just interview you, what you like, what you don't like. . . . They get a feel for you, and they tell you, you know, "We recommend this one. We think you'd be good at it."

In some cases, students are advised not to attend the college since their occupational goals do not coincide with program offerings. For students unsure of their future goals, this personal attention from a counselor who is familiar with all the degree possibilities can be very helpful.

While this approach lacks the breadth of exploration in community colleges, it does entail exploration. Obviously, for these nontraditional students, many of whom did poorly in high school, the very effort to try out college is a daring and risky exploration, and each college course provides a challenge that could end their effort. In addition, while these occupational programs are far more directive than community colleges, they allow some exploration and some redirection of career trajectory after the first semester or after the first year. Moreover, at some occupational colleges, students who do well in the associate's program are encouraged to transfer to a bachelor's degree program in a related field.[6]

College-Initiated Guidance and Minimizing the Risk of Student Error

Third, in contrast to the burden of student-initiated guidance, occupational colleges have actually structured out the need for students to take the initiative to see a counselor when they need assistance. Instead, the colleges take the initiative by developing systems that provide guidance without students having to ask for it. They automatically assign each student to a specific counselor who monitors his or her academic progress. Students must meet with their advisor each term before registering for courses, and advisors provide assistance that is specific to each student's needs. One administrator explained the typical way that these meetings work. An advisor will sit down with the student and tell him or her,

> Next quarter, you're going to take these classes, you have these options. . . . In this time slot, you can take this class or this class. Now, do you want to take psych., . . . soc., . . . political science, or . . . history? Here is why you are taking these classes. This is required here.

In addition, the occupational colleges have registration guides that tell students exactly what courses to take each term to complete their degree in a timely manner. Although this limits course flexibility, most students appreciate the system because it helps them to complete a degree quickly and prevents them from making mistakes. According to one student,

> I think it's a good idea; a lot of people start taking classes that they don't really need and it throws them off. I think it's good . . . it's simple . . . all you have to do is follow it. There's no, "Oh my god, I didn't know I had to take that class!" There's a lot of classes where you have prerequisites. But if you go in that order, you have no problem.

In our survey of 4,300 students, we asked, "Have you ever taken any course which you later discovered would not count toward your degree?" While 45 percent of the community college students responded, "yes," this had happened to them, only 16 percent of the private occupational college students reported the same.[7]

Investing in Counselors and Eliminating Poor Advice

Fourth, while community colleges offer very few counselors, occupational colleges have invested in counseling services and job placement staff. For example, one of the occupational colleges we studied has four academic advisors and one dean devoted exclusively to counseling 1,300 first-year students, a ratio of 260 students to each staff person. Moreover, this college has five additional advisors for assisting with job placement. This provides a sharp contrast to community colleges, where counselors perform many counseling tasks, including personal, academic, and career counseling, and typically have 800:1 ratios for all these services.

Unlike community colleges, all of the occupational colleges devote substantial resources to job placement, separate from the other counseling and advising functions. Job placement offices are well staffed with low student-to-staff ratios, ranging from 90:1 to 122:1 at all these colleges. In contrast, none of these community colleges have any full-time staff devoted to job placement, and other research suggests that may be typical (Grubb 1996; Brewer and Gray 1999). Occupational colleges believe these investments are essential to their mission of helping students complete degrees and get good jobs.

Fifth, in contrast with community colleges, at occupational colleges, instructors communicate with advisors to exchange information about students' progress. Advisors are regularly informed about departmental requirements and faculty talk with advisors about particular students, a simple process given the highly explicit organization of programs.

Quick Detection of Mistakes

Sixth, in contrast to the difficulty of detecting student mistakes at community colleges, occupational colleges require students to meet with their advisors frequently—usually every term. At one college, students must meet with their advisor three times each term.

Occupational colleges also tend to have good student information systems that keep advisors informed about students' progress or difficulties. At several occupational colleges, attendance is regularly taken, advisors are quickly informed of absences, and students are contacted by their advisors before the problem gets serious. After midterms, instructors notify advisors of those students who are performing poorly in class. If the student seems to be having problems, the advisor is responsible for mediating between student and teacher to find a solution to existing problems and make sure the student receives academic support. Through the scheduled interactions, students get to know their advisors on a personal basis, and they are more likely to approach them for help even when they are not required to do so. This is a stark contrast to the more anonymous community college system of advising.

Reducing Conflicts with Outside Demands

Seventh, occupational colleges make efforts to alleviate external pressures that increase the chances of dropping out. These schools have adapted to students' needs by compacting the school year. In an old study, Wilms (1974) estimated that proprietary schools have competitive cost-benefit ratios, despite much higher tuitions, because of their speed at getting students to a degree that raises their earnings sooner. If an associate's degree raises students' wage rates, and if completing school increases students' work hours each week, then getting the degree nine months earlier increases earnings in two ways.

In addition, many students face strong pressures from parents, spouses, children, and jobs to complete schooling quickly. Private occupational colleges respond to these pressures by creating year-round schooling, which leads more quickly to degrees. Several schools have altered their school year to consist of year-round courses with only two one-week vacations in December and July. Students attend classes year round, and in one school, they can obtain a fifteen-month associate's degree.

Since disadvantaged students face many pressures and crises that cause students to lose the benefit of their prior work for the term, occupational colleges reduce the cost of such discontinuities by shortening the length of the school term. If outside pressures force students to suspend their studies and lose one term, it is a relatively short term, and they can resume their studies in a very short time. In addition, prospective students do not have to wait long before a new term begins. Instead of offering classes in relatively long semesters, one school has altered the school year so that it now consists of a series of five ten-week terms, and several other schools have short terms.

While the answer is not to turn community colleges into occupational colleges, community colleges can better help students by borrowing some lessons from occupational colleges.

Moreover, unlike community colleges, which have complex class schedules in noncontinuous time slots, occupational colleges schedule two courses back-to-back that would typically be taken in a program. This blocking of courses decreases commuting time and makes it easier for students to attend school while they continue to work. Also, while community colleges' class schedules change from term to term, occupational colleges offer the same time schedules from one term to the next. As a result, work and child care arrangements made for one term will continue to work out in the following term.

In addition, while community colleges offer so many courses that they cannot promise to offer needed courses each term, occupational colleges preplan sequences of courses for each program, and they make sure that every program has the courses necessary to make progress every term. Obviously, when all students in a program are taking the same courses, this is relatively easy and economically efficient, but the commitment of these colleges goes beyond that. In several cases, a few students fell out of their cohort's sequence in their course taking, and the colleges offered classes with only three students, just so students could finish their degree within the promised time frame. This is very expensive, but the colleges prized their promise that students can complete the degree in the customary time. In the community colleges, classes below a minimum enrollment were routinely cancelled.

In contrast to community colleges' futile attempt to downplay students' jobs, occupational colleges essentially turn what is viewed as something negative into something that can advance students' career goals. Students receive detailed guidance on how to combine their need to work with their educational goals. These occupational colleges consider work a valuable experience related to their degrees, and they help students find relevant jobs, even if they may pay less. Advisors encourage students to get jobs related to their goals:

> We tell them in the first quarter . . . try to get a job, even if you're just answering the phone, let's say, at Arthur Andersen, but you're an accounting student. One day you can say, "Here's my resume, I want to see if there's something for me here." And then you can be a clerk, you know; you've just got to move your way up.

Instead of lamenting the reality of students' need to work, occupational colleges try to guide students toward using their work to advance their career goals.

Conclusion

While we have seen that community colleges pose some serious problems for students who lack know-how, some occupational colleges have found ways to address these problems. While the answer is not to turn community colleges into occupational colleges, community colleges can better help students by borrowing some lessons from occupational colleges—(1) creating clear curriculum structures, (2) vastly improving counseling, (3) closely monitoring student progress, (4) implementing an information system that would quickly show signs of student difficulties, and (5) alleviating conflicts with external pressures.

This article has addressed an issue in community colleges that may influence the outcomes of low-income, first-generation, and nontraditional students. We show how the structure of community colleges we studied creates a need for students to have extensive know-how about the college process. We have also found that by making the implicit explicit, some occupational colleges eliminate the know-how prerequisite that community colleges seem to require for students to be successful in completing their educational and career goals.

Although most people in our society must learn to cope with bureaucratic complexities eventually, students' ability to cope and learn from them may improve with experience—they may be able to adapt to complexities better as they proceed through college, after acquiring social know-how and academic successes.[8] An individual's capacity to adapt to complexities may depend on attainment of basic skills or increased maturity. It is also possible that procedures that gradually introduce the complexities in small steps may make them easier to manage, and strong advising and school supports may also make adaptation easier.

The occupational college model is not for everyone. Although these occupational colleges offer degrees in several fields, students' options are limited. On the other hand, community colleges offer a more diverse range of programs and courses. For students who have the know-how for making these decisions and who do not face strong external competing pressures, community colleges may provide an inexpensive version of a four-year college education that works very well. However, community colleges pose challenges that often require students to devote additional time (and tuition) obtaining information, puzzling among choices, exploring, and making false starts and mistakes in pursuit of a degree in this complex system. For students who lack social know-how, their attempts at college may amount to nothing more than a series of unrelated credit hours and failed dreams.

Notes

1. A more recent study by Shaw (1997) does compare institutional cultures and ideologies across several community colleges, and it is an excellent example of the value of such comparative qualitative work. Yet her focus is on remedial programs and not on the general experiences of credit-level students. Furthermore, her work does not specifically connect qualitative data with issues of persistence.

2. Surveys were administered to students in class; therefore, the response rate approached 100 percent. Classes were selected to target a cross section of credit-level students in comparable occupationally focused programs across the various colleges. Surveys asked about students' goals, background, attitudes, experiences, course-taking patterns, and perceptions. In both types of colleges, students' families are generally lower and middle income, with 41 percent of community college students and 45 percent of occupational college students reporting parents' annual incomes less than $30,000 (and nearly one-quarter less than $19,000 in each type of college). Approximately 83 percent of community college students and 89 percent of occupational college students have parents with less than a bachelor's degree. At community colleges, 25 percent reported grades of Cs or lower in high school, and at occupational colleges, 28 percent reported these low grades. Moreover, at both, students want similar things from college, with just less than 70 percent at community colleges and slightly more than 80 percent at occupational colleges indicating that they were in college to "get a better job." These findings confirm well-established findings of prior research (Dougherty 1994; Grubb 1996).

3. In the fall of 1999, 121,573 undergraduate freshman were enrolled, but only 57,670 undergraduate sophomores were enrolled in the fall of 2000. Since only 12,286 students were reported to have transferred from community colleges in that same semester and 4,391 transferred to community colleges, and freshman enrollments increased by only 799, these data suggest that roughly 45 percent of the 1999 freshmen did not return the following year as sophomores. Some, especially part-timers, may have returned as freshmen again, but since this same pattern persists from 1997 to 2000, it is likely that this percentage reflects attrition during the first two years. This percentage is likely to be higher than in longitudinal studies since it does not account for students' degree intentions or follow the same students over time.

4. Sophomores are 41.5 percent of the previous year's freshman enrollments, and the fall 2000 transfer percentage was doubled to 20 percent, assuming that each of the fall and spring semesters would include 10 percent of students transferring.

5. These colleges, which we termed "occupational colleges" (Deil and Rosenbaum 2001), are similar to what Bailey, Badway, and Gumport (2001) referred to as "Accredited Career Colleges." They have very low loan default rates, unlike many former proprietary schools that were closed as a result of new legislation. Two-year business colleges and technical colleges can be found in every major city and are widely advertised in local media.

6. Two of the colleges in our sample have their own accelerated bachelor's degree programs in business, computer, and technology fields.

7. This analysis includes only those students who had not attended a previous college.

8. While this entire discussion has focused on community colleges, similar issues arise at other levels of education, such as high schools, where students make choices about courses in increasingly complex "shopping mall high schools," where curricula are unstructured and implications of choices are unclear. For instance, failure to choose algebra by ninth grade precludes precalculus by twelfth grade, which makes science majors difficult in college, yet these implications of ninth-grade choices do not become apparent for many years.

References

Apling, Richard N. 1993. Proprietary schools and their students. *Journal of Higher Education* 64 (4): 379-416.

Bailey, Thomas. 2002. Director's column. *CCRC currents*, April.

Bailey, T., N. Badway, and P. Gumport. 2001. *For-profit higher education and community colleges*. Stanford, CA: Center for Postsecondary Improvement.

Bourdieu, Pierre, and John C. Passeron. 1977. *Reproduction in education, society and culture*. Beverly Hills, CA: Sage.

Brewer, Dominic J., and Maryann Gray. 1999. Do faculty connect school to work? Evidence from community colleges. *Educational Evaluation and Policy Analysis* 21 (4): 405-16.

Brint, Steven, and J. Karabel. 1989. *The diverted dream: Community colleges and the promise of educational opportunity in America, 1900-1985*. New York: Oxford University Press.

Deil, Regina, and James Rosenbaum. 2001. How can low-status colleges help young adults gain access to better jobs? Practitioners' applications of human capital vs. sociological models. Paper presented to the American Sociological Association, Los Angeles, 19 August.

Dougherty, Kevin J. 1994. *The contradictory college: The conflicting origins, impacts, and cultures of the community college*. Albany: State University of New York Press.

Grubb, Norton W. 1996. *Working in the middle: Strengthening education and training for the mid-skilled labor force*. San Francisco: Jossey-Bass.

Heckman, James J. 1999. Doing it right: Job training and education. *Public Interest* 135:86-107.

London, Howard B. 1978. *The culture of a community college*. New York: Praeger.

National Center for Educational Statistics. 1998. *Total first-time freshman enrolled in institutions of higher education and degree-granting institutions, 1955-1996*. Washington, DC: Government Printing Office.

Neumann, R. W., and D. Riesman. 1980. The community college elite. In *New directions in community colleges #32: Questioning the community college role*, edited by G. Vaughan, 53-71. San Francisco: Jossey-Bass.

Orfield, Gary, and Faith G. Paul. 1994. *High hopes, long odds: A major report on Hoosier teens and the American dream*. Indianapolis: Indiana Youth Institute.

Richardson, R. C., E. A. Fisk, and M. A. Okum. 1983. *Literacy in the open-access college*. San Francisco: Jossey-Bass.

Shaw, Kathleen M. 1997. Remedial education as ideological background: Emerging remedial education policies in the community college. *Education Evaluation and Analysis* 19 (3): 284-96.

Tinto, Vincent. 1993. *Leaving college*. Chicago: University of Chicago Press.

Weis, Lois. 1985. *Between two worlds: Black students in an urban community college*. Boston: Routledge Kegan Paul.

Wilms, Wellford W. 1974. *Public and proprietary vocational training: A study of effectiveness*. Berkeley, CA: Center for Research and Development in Higher Education.

Zwerling, L. Steven, and Howard B. London. 1992. First-generation students: Confronting the cultural issues. In *New directions in community colleges 80*. San Francisco: Jossey-Bass.

Work-First or Work-Only: Welfare Reform, State Policy, and Access to Postsecondary Education

By
CHRISTOPHER MAZZEO,
SARA RAB,
and
SUSAN EACHUS

As a result of the 1996 welfare reform—Temporary Aid to Needy Families (TANF)—the number of welfare recipients enrolled in postsecondary education has decreased dramatically. The new welfare law also gives states significant discretion to support and even promote postsecondary education for low-income adults; consequently, state policies regarding access vary widely. This study uses qualitative data from three states to examine the sources and consequences of state variation in access to postsecondary education for disadvantaged individuals. Our cross-state comparison shows that competing ideas about welfare, work and the role of education in the lives of welfare recipients help structure and shape political debates, and policy outcomes, in the each of the states. Ideas influenced policies via four key channels: the state human service agency; advocacy organizations; the persistence of the "work-first" idea within implementation processes; and the power of policy "signals" to drive state welfare reform.

Keywords: welfare reform; community colleges; state variation

It is almost a truism among educators, researchers, and policy makers that postsecondary education leads to long-term employment stability and economic self-sufficiency. Yet despite clear empirical evidence about the relationship between education and earnings (Levy and Murnane 1992; Kane and Rouse 1995; Grubb 1999; Meyer and Peterson 1999), the 1996 Personal Responsibility and Work Opportunity Reconciliation Act, otherwise known as welfare reform, explicitly shifted federal welfare policy toward a work-first philosophy, away from the

Christopher Mazzeo is a senior policy analyst at the National Governors Association (NGA). At NGA, Dr. Mazzeo's work focuses on state and urban school reform, community colleges, and policies impacting student and adult postsecondary educational success. He is the coauthor of A Governor's Guide to Creating a 21st-Century Workforce *and a recent Ford Foundation study,* Building a Career Pathways System: Promising Practices in Community College-Centered Workforce Development, *conducted by the Workforce Strategy Center. Dr. Mazzeo is also working with colleagues at the University of Pennsylvania and Temple University on a multistate*

DOI: 10.1177/0095399702250212

human-capital-building approach of prior programs such as Aid to Families with Dependent Children (AFDC) and the Job Opportunities and Basic Skills Training Program (Greenberg, Strawn, and Plimpton 2000; Weaver 2000; Gais et al. 2001).

While this new system of welfare provision does not expressly forbid states from allowing welfare recipients to pursue postsecondary education, it does include a number of regulations that discourage states from enrolling recipients in two- and four-year colleges and in degree-granting programs in particular (Greenberg, Strawn, and Plimpton 2000). Under the new federal welfare program—Transitional Aid to Needy Families (TANF)—states receive a block grant designed to provide temporary cash assistance and support to help families move into the workforce quickly. Under TANF, by 2002, states were required to have 50 percent of all families on cash assistance participating in thirty hours per week of work activity, or the states would face fiscal penalties. According to the federal rules, vocational educational training can count toward work requirements, but only for up to twelve months and for no more than 30 percent of the caseload. All recipients are also required to "engage in work" within twenty-four months of receiving cash assistance (Golonka and Matus-Grossman 2001). In short, TANF sends a clear signal to states that workforce attachment is the guiding principle of the new welfare law, with caseload reductions as the ultimate measure of state and local policy success (Gais et al. 2001).[1]

As might be expected, the initial evidence suggests that the number of welfare recipients enrolled in various forms of postsecondary education has decreased dramatically since 1996 (Institute for Women's Policy Research 1998; Jacobs and Shaw 1999). Of the 1.9 million adults in the Job Opportunities and Basic Skills Training Program in 1995, 136,000, or 16.7 percent, were enrolled in postsecondary education and not working in unsubsidized jobs. While fully comparable data do not exist for the Personal Responsibility and Work Opportunity Reconciliation Act,[2] what evidence there is suggests a notable decline in the number of TANF adults enrolled in postsecondary education programs. Lurie (2001) reported that by 1999, only 6.1 percent of TANF adults were engaged in education or training, and 2001 Department of Health and Human Services data show that, for the 2,273,554 families on TANF who count toward federal work requirements, only 50,103, or about 2 percent, were in vocational education or education related to employment (Administration for Children and Families 2001). At the state level, a seven-state General Accounting Office report found that between 1994 and

study examining the impact of changes in federal welfare and workforce policies on adult access to postsecondary education. He received his Ph.D. in social sciences, policy and educational practice from Stanford University in 2000.

Sara Rab is a doctoral candidate in sociology at the University of Pennsylvania. Her research interests include community colleges, poverty, and gender. She is currently working on a dissertation exploring the causes and consequences of complex undergraduate attendance patterns.

Susan Eachus is a doctoral student in sociology at the University of Pennsylvania. She is writing her dissertation on the effects of ideas and organizational patterns on welfare reform implementation.

1997, the percentage of welfare recipients enrolled in education and training activities declined in each of the states (General Accounting Office 1998).

The 1996 federal welfare law also gives states significant discretion to support and even promote postsecondary access for low-income adults. States, for instance, have latitude in defining the activities that can count toward work participation and activity requirements. If a recipient participates in a minimum of twenty hours of work, the remainder of work requirements can be filled through "job skills training related directly to employment" (Golonka and Matus-Grossman 2001, 7). While these federal rules govern how states count their overall participation rates, states are free to set different rules for individual recipients (Greenberg, Strawn, and Plimpton 2000). For example, in Pennsylvania, a recipient can count education as filling his or her work requirement for up to thirty-six months. To date, states have had little trouble filling their overall participation rates even when they allow activities that do not count under federal rules. States are also required to spend their own funds on welfare programs (maintenance of effort funds), and these monies are not subject to the restrictions attached to federal TANF dollars.

As a result of the discretion accorded to states under welfare reform, state policies regarding access to postsecondary education for welfare recipients vary widely. As of 2002, thirty states (and the District of Columbia) allowed participation in postsecondary degree programs to count toward work requirements for longer than twelve months. Fourteen of these states allow participation in postsecondary education to completely meet work requirements.[3] Five of these states sometimes allow participation in postsecondary education to fulfill the work requirement but may require that it be combined with other work activities.[4] In eleven states, postsecondary participation by students can fully or partially meet work requirements, but only for up to twelve months. In four states, postsecondary degree programs cannot count toward meeting state work requirements, save the 30 percent of the caseload allowed to participate in vocational education (Center for Law and Social Policy 2002).[5]

Research Questions and Method

The purpose of this study is to better understand the sources and consequences of state variation in access to postsecondary education for welfare recipients and the working poor. In what follows, we compare three states—Massachusetts, Illinois, and Washington—that have responded in different ways to federal welfare reform and thus potentially provide different amounts and kinds of access to postsecondary education (see Table 1):

- In Massachusetts, the TANF program is driven by a strict work-oriented philosophy with few postsecondary options made available to welfare recipients.
- In Illinois, a strong and vocal advocacy community convinced the governor to "stop the clock" on federal time limits for up to thirty-six months for recipients in approved postsecondary degree programs.

TABLE 1

STATE TRANSITIONAL AID TO NEEDY FAMILIES POLICIES TOWARD POSTSECONDARY TRAINING OR EDUCATION

State	A. Can Postsecondary Training or Education Count toward Work Requirement?	B. If Yes to A, under What Conditions?	C. If Yes to A, What Are Time Limits?	D. Does Time Spent in Postsecondary Training or Education Count against Time Limits on Assistance?	E. If Education Is an Allowable Work Activity at All, What Type of Education Is Allowed?	F. Is Transitional Education and Training Assistance Available to Former Transitional Aid to Needy Families Recipients?
Massachusetts	No[a]	—	—	—	—	Yes. If employed. Up to twelve months
Illinois	Yes	May have to be combined with other work activities[b]	Up to thirty-six months[c]	No[d]	Postsecondary degree, vocational training, General Equivalency Diploma, English as a second language—but clock will not always be stopped (see note 3)	Yes

147

TABLE 1 (continued)

State	A. Can Postsecondary Training or Education Count toward Work Requirement?	B. If Yes to A, under What Conditions?	C. If Yes to A, What Are Time Limits?	D. Does Time Spent in Postsecondary Training or Education Count against Time Limits on Assistance?	E. If Education Is an Allowable Work Activity at All, What Type of Education Is Allowed?	F. Is Transitional Education and Training Assistance Available to Former Transitional Aid to Needy Families Recipients?
Washington	Yes	Must be combined with other work activities, with exception for high-demand training	Up to twelve months	Yes	High-wage/high-demand training, preemployment training, vocational training, General Equivalency Diploma, English as a second language, and literacy	Yes, for those with incomes less than 175 percent of poverty line. Tuition assistance available. Must be working twenty hours per week or more

SOURCE: Center for Law and Social Policy (2002), independently gathered information during interviews, and the following state Web sites: Massachusetts, http://www.state.ma.us/dta/dtatoday/reform/Tanfpdf.pdf (State Plan Amendment 2000); Illinois, http://www.state.il.us/agency/dhs/tanfnp.html, http://www.state.il.us/agency/dhs/tanfqsnp.html, http://www.state.il.us/agency/dhs/tpoct01sept03.pdf (State Plan); Washington, http://www-app2.wa.gov/dshs/esa/wfhand/e_and_t_intro.htm (State Handbook).

a. The work requirement in Massachusetts only applies to 10 percent of the caseload, however. The remaining 90 percent, most of whom are not even subject to time limits, are allowed and encouraged to seek training. About 11 percent of the overall caseload is currently in some form of education/training.

b. If the recipient does not have a high school degree and is in a degree-seeking program (other than General Equivalency Diploma classes), it must be combined with twenty hours of work. Some exceptions may be made for those single parents in postsecondary degree program with GPAs of 2.5 or higher.

c. Recipients may participate in General Equivalency Diploma, Adult Basic Education, and vocational programs for up to twenty-four months without a work requirement.

d. The clock is stopped only for those full-time college students (they must have high school degree already) who are in degree-seeking programs and who have a GPA of 2.5 or better. The clock is not stopped until the GPA is established, that is, for the first semester.

- In Washington, the enabling legislation for TANF was titled Work First and initially sought to limit education and training to low-income workers seeking job advancement subsequent to leaving the welfare rolls.

In this article, we examine how and why TANF policies vary in these three states and how these policy differences affect the type and amount of education and training available to current and former welfare recipients. In particular, we are concerned with the role that ideas—problem definitions, beliefs, and values and causal theories—play in welfare and education policy making in the three states. Do the beliefs and causal theories policy makers and implementing agencies hold about welfare recipients and the role of education and training in their lives play a major role in structuring welfare reform and postsecondary access policies? If so, how do ideas influence state policy in each of the states?

Data for this article come from a six-state study of community colleges and their responses to local, state, and federal policy changes in the training and employment arena. Data were collected at several different levels of analysis using a mixed-methods case study design. As part of this larger study, interviews were conducted in Washington, Illinois, and Massachusetts with a range of state-level policy makers and advocacy organizations involved in welfare policy making and in shaping each state's response to federal welfare reform. We also interviewed individuals responsible for implementing welfare policies on the ground—including caseworkers and community college administrators and program operators. Interview data were supplemented with a comprehensive analysis of relevant policy and program documents.

Interview transcripts were analyzed using Hyperresearch software. Substantive codes were derived both inductively from our research questions and deductively based on issues we found emerging in the data. Coded data were then compared across states to investigate state policy differences.

Theoretical Framework

Traditionally, variations in state policy are accounted for with reference to political or institutional factors (see March and Olson 1995; Hall 1997; Levi 1997; Meyers, Gornick, and Peck 2001). On the political side, some argue for "inherent differences" in states rooted in political culture or ideology, while others point to shorter-term political factors such as the characteristics of key policy coalitions in power at the time of adoption (Levi 1997; McDermott 2001). Institutional perspectives point instead to the role of policy governance, specifically to the power of implementing agencies and the impact of "policy legacies" in shaping policy choices and state responses to the external environment (March and Olson 1995; Hall 1997).

Political and institutional factors are clearly important determinants of policy as reflected in our interview protocols and coding of the interview and documentary data. Like the research of others (Stone 1989; Kingdon 1995; Hall 1997;

McDermott 2001), this article concerns itself particularly with the role ideas play in influencing policy choices. In the social policy arena, prior studies have found a central role for ideas in welfare policy processes. The ideology of maternalism, for example, was crucial to shaping 1935 legislation that established a federal welfare program (Mink 1995). Katz (2001) has identified a set of publicly held ideas about work and citizenship as a key force in redefining the nature of the American welfare state.

The literature also suggests that ideas can work at two distinct levels—in policy development and in implementation—to shape the meaning of state policy for welfare recipients. As Ball (1994) pointed out, policies are "representations" that reflect compromise, ambiguity, and political struggle and are "decoded in complex ways via actors' interpretations and meanings in relation to their history, experiences, skills, resources and context" (p. 16). Policies do not tell implementers—whether state or local—what to do; rather, "they create circumstances in which the range of options available in deciding what to do are narrowed or changed, or particular goals or outcomes are set" (Ball 1995, 17). State and local policy processes still have significant space for creative responses rooted in the motivations, capacities, and collectively held values and beliefs of policy actors (Lipsky 1974; Lin 2000; Lurie, Meyers, and Riccucci 2001).

One implication of this analysis is that implementation can act in ways that run counter to the official rules of policy. Miller (1991), for example, found that a set of ideas embedded in the Work Incentive Program blaming unemployment on lack of effort by participants was decisive in how the program was delivered at the street level, even to the point of overriding formal policy rulings. A second implication is that implementation will vary greatly across states, organizations, and communities, and this variation will be dictated in large part by the meaning implementers attach to policy based on their own values, beliefs, and policy theories (Lin 2000; Mills and Hyle 2001). These values, beliefs, and theories are in turn shaped by the "terms of political discourse" (Jenson 1988; Hall 1989) that exist within states and the nation at large.

These features of the policy process demand an analytic approach that links ideas, events, and policy formation with implementation. So-called trajectory studies "trace policy formulation, struggle and response from within the state itself through to the various recipients of policy" (Ball 1995, 26) both over time and across space (Bowe and Ball 1992).

In the cases that follow, we describe the policy environment in each state at the time of welfare reform, focusing on the key actors and policy coalitions involved and the extant problem definitions in each state surrounding welfare policy, work, and the role of postsecondary education. We also examine the goals, purposes, and theory of action behind welfare reform in that state along with any changes that occurred in these since the passage of TANF. We examine some preliminary data on policy implementation, focusing on the ways in which implementation amplifies or runs counter to formal policy mandates and incentives. Finally, we examine the outcomes of policy in terms of access to postsecondary education, earnings, or other key indicators.

Massachusetts

Massachusetts's welfare reform legislation preceded the passage of the Personal Responsibility and Work Opportunity Reconciliation Act and is in many ways more restrictive than the federal legislation. Under the current program, the time limit for receiving welfare is twenty-four months out of every sixty months, compared to the sixty-month lifetime limit required by federal law. Postsecondary education cannot count toward meeting work requirements. On the other hand, those recipients exempt from work requirements—about 75 percent of the caseload—are allowed to enroll in educational programs without working for up to four years. In practice, however, the state has enrolled few recipients in community college training and even fewer in postsecondary degree programs. The newly renamed Department of Transitional Assistance (DTA) has strongly embraced the work-first approach, while community colleges and advocacy organizations have played a limited role in welfare reform.

In the early 1990s, Massachusetts's Democratic legislature passed several welfare reform laws that were vetoed by Republican Governor William Weld. The governor then proposed his own more restrictive welfare reform legislation, which was passed by the legislature (Kirby et al. 1997). Some observers credit high-profile evaluations of work-first programs such as Riverside, California's, GAIN program with persuading Democratic legislators to pass Weld's reforms. Massachusetts's current welfare legislation, Transitional Aid to Families with Dependent Children, was passed in 1995 and implemented beginning in December 1996.

During the 1990s, welfare officials in Massachusetts were concerned that their relatively generous AFDC policies had not worked, since despite a generally good economy, their caseloads were increasing. The mood throughout the department at the time was one of frustration. One administrator told us,

> I think that [my job] is more rewarding [since welfare reform]. I think the job prior to welfare reform was somewhat frustrating. . . . We found that in some cases—many, many cases—clients really did everything they could to get off of public assistance. Some clients really resisted that, and it became very, very frustrating for us. As much as we tried, we had difficulty trying to get that client involved with the program.

Another administrator said she felt that recipients "needed a kick in the butt" to get them to go to work. In this atmosphere, the welfare department welcomed Weld's reforms and implemented the new rules in a work-focused manner.

The current two-year time limit means that many more recipients in Massachusetts have reached their time limits than in most states. However, certain categories of recipients are temporarily exempt from the time limits, including those with a child younger than two, disabled recipients, and recipients who are noncitizens without work papers. When the program began, about half the caseload was exempt from the time limits; now about 75 percent are exempt. Recipients can get time-limit extensions in a few circumstances if they are in cooperation with DTA, but not to complete an educational program. Recipients whose youngest child is six or older are required to be in work activities twenty hours per week. Activities that count toward the work requirement include paid employment, job search, and programs that combine work with basic skills training.

During interviews early in the implementation process, officials at DTA reported that they thought it would be better if all recipients subject to time limits were also subject to some work requirements. And in March 2001, they got the changes they wanted—Republican Governor Paul Cellucci pushed through the legislature changes in the rules so that clients whose youngest child is between two and six (who had been subject to time limits but exempt from participation requirements) are now required to participate in some work or educational activity, though they have no minimum hours requirement (Kaye et al. 2001).

In sum, both official policy and implementation processes have conspired to strongly limit access to postsecondary education for welfare recipients in Massachusetts.

Education programs do not count toward the work requirement, but they do count as participation for those whose youngest child is between two and six years old. DTA provides support services, such as transportation and child care expenses, for education and training programs that are included in a recipient's Employment Development Plan. The main criterion for allowing education in a plan is that the recipient complete the program in less than his or her time limit. However, we were told that, in practice, recipients rarely are told that education is allowed, even when they have substantial amounts of time left and are now subject to the twenty-hour work requirement. Caseworkers are communicating only the work-first message.

The division of the Massachusetts Executive Office of Health and Human Services that administers welfare changed its name from the Department of Public Welfare to the Department of Transitional Assistance in 1996. The name change was intended to symbolize a shift in emphasis from determining eligibility to planning with recipients how they will attain employment while providing transitional support. The changes in welfare require caseworkers to use a more individualized approach in determining how the time limits apply to a particular recipient and setting an Employment Development Plan that can be completed in less than that time limit. This is presented as better, more personalized service than under AFDC, when all clients were informed of a standard set of services (including training programs and child care assistance). Welfare officials say that welfare reform has worked well in Massachusetts and has promoted the idea that recipients take more responsibility for their lives.

Welfare officials argue that work requirements and time limits are a big improvement over the old AFDC rules because they compel recipients to cooperate with caseworkers. They believe that this is a major reason for the greatly reduced caseloads and that it has pushed poor mothers to be better role models for their children. One respondent from the DTA argued that the new requirements are breaking the cycle of generations of dependency that she had observed during the preceding three decades: "I saw four generations where they had the wrong role model. And so I think that I'm pleased that this gives them what I consider a more appropriate role model." She felt imposing time limits has been a good thing for the recipients' children because they get to see their mothers go out to work. She argued that while it is fine for mothers who have private financial support to stay home, those who do not ought to go to work to be role models for children. Other respondents from DTA claim that time limits and work requirements have made recipients take job search and short-term training opportunities seriously. They credit the dramatic decrease in their caseloads to the work requirement and short time limits.

Welfare officials also connected the changes in welfare to changes in work patterns in society more broadly. They said that middle-class workers do not work at one corporation for their whole careers, and poor mothers should not expect to stay on welfare for a lifetime, nor should they expect to make a career out of their first job. These officials talked about time limits as motivation to take the initiative to get that first job.

While the state's formal policy rules allow substantial latitude and support for education, as of March 2001, less than 10 percent of the caseload was participating in education or training activities.[6] Those most likely to be in education and training programs were those subject to time limits but not work requirements. While approximately 18 percent of those subject to the time limit but not the work requirement were in education, training, or a combination of activities, fewer than 7 percent of those not subject to the time limits and of those subject to both the time limits and the work requirement were in education, training, or a combination of activities. Less than 2 percent were in college degree programs.[7]

Advocacy organizations have collaborated with the community college sector on efforts to win a larger role for postsecondary education in welfare reform, but with limited success. One major victory for the community colleges came in December of 1998, when the DTA agreed to count internships and work study jobs toward work requirements.

DTA has also worked with some community colleges on a program called Education That Works, designed to provide for the delivery of "intensive, high caliber, short-term academic skills training and employment services [so that] recipients can access employment opportunities that enable them to transition from welfare to successful Employment." Education That Works provides tuition assistance for noncredit course work, and community colleges that participate in this program are subject to explicit job placement outcome measures. The program requires job placement within four months and pays colleges for enrollment, job placement, and ninety-day retention.

Most of Massachusetts's community colleges have chosen not to participate in Education That Works.[8] Interviews with various individuals at several Massachusetts community colleges point to the job placement outcomes requirements attached to this funding as the key reason for their nonparticipation. While some argued that the rates DTA was willing to pay were not high enough to operate quality training programs, others objected on principle. As one community college administrator stated, "We're not an employment service. We're an educational institution. I don't think it's appropriate for the state to be subjecting us to such measures."

Local DTA offices have also blunted the impact of Education That Works by limiting referrals. Some community colleges have worked to build links between their Education That Works programs and their part-time General Equivalency Diploma, certificate, and degree programs; DTA, however, has resisted these efforts.

In sum, both official policy and implementation processes have conspired to strongly limit access to postsecondary education for welfare recipients in Massachusetts. Successive governors and the new welfare bureaucracy have strongly embraced the work-first idea and met little effective opposition from advocacy organizations or community colleges. Community colleges themselves have, in some cases, resisted providing short-term, job-oriented programs on ideological grounds, further limiting the enrollment of welfare recipients in the state.[9]

Illinois

Illinois is among those states whose welfare policies allow and enable some welfare recipients to attend community college while at the same time encouraging rapid labor force attachment. Several factors shaped Illinois's unique response to federal reform, including a reorganization of state agencies, the transition to a new governor during implementation, the efforts of a strong advocacy community, and the strength of the state community college system.

As a result, a small proportion of both current and former TANF recipients in Illinois are currently enrolled in both degree- and non-degree-seeking programs at community colleges. Some of these recipients receive supportive funds to help pay for their child care, their transportation, and the cost of books while they are in school. Others work while attending vocational certificate programs.

Prior to the move to TANF with the 1996 federal reform, Illinois had several education programs for welfare recipients, including a Job Opportunities and Basic Skills Training Program known as Project Chance that sent people primarily to adult education classes and a community college–based case management program called Opportunities. These programs were funded by the Illinois Department of Public Aid and were not required nor focused on outcomes. AFDC recipients were allowed to receive their welfare check and participate or not participate in these programs as they saw fit.[10]

But while these programs existed prior to reform, they did not necessarily reflect a strong commitment on the part of state policy makers to postsecondary education for welfare recipients. The Opportunities program enabled the Department of Public Aid to access additional federal matching funds that would have otherwise been inaccessible. Community colleges were happy to participate in the program since it increased their enrollment and funding somewhat and also fulfilled part of their mission to serve the community. Project Chance was reportedly somewhat less popular. According to one advocate,

> The sense was it was almost meandering; there was a sense that people could go and stay for a while, and there wasn't any real focus on outcomes. And I think welfare reform was in part a reaction to that type of program in which there was a lot of adult education done and very little of it focused on actual workforce outcomes.

When the advocacy community in Illinois became aware of the mandatory work requirements of the coming federal welfare reform, they lobbied for the inclusion of education and training as a work activity, and they were somewhat successful. Illinois has a sixty-month lifetime limit on benefits. These months do not include those when the recipient is working at least thirty hours per week. Clients must be involved in thirty hours per week to meet the required work participation, but permitted activities include on-the-job training, up to twelve months of vocational education training, job skills training directly related to employment, and up to two years of adult basic education or General Equivalency Diploma classes.

Coinciding with the passage of the legislation in 1997, there was a reorganization of state agencies, and the Illinois Department of Human Services (IDHS) was formed. Whereas AFDC was administered by the Department of Public Aid, the task of administering TANF was given to IDHS, now the largest agency in the state, and headed by Secretary Howard Peters. Peters fully embraced the work-first philosophy of the federal welfare reform. Under his direction, the state legislation that was intended to permit some education activities was interpreted as strictly work-first. Said one advocate,

> So although Illinois kept its plan, the same plan on paper, what has happened since is that essentially, very, very few people were allowed into education and training. . . . The prevailing philosophy was get a job, any job, and get it quick.

Peters believed that the goal of TANF was rapid labor force attachment, and this clashed with advocates and the Illinois Community College Board (ICCB) who believed that the goal should be economic self-sufficiency and that the best route to that goal was education. One advocate reported that "Howard Peters was single-mindedly driven by work-first and his whole thing was any job is better than no job, and that's what drove everyone there [at IDHS]."

The advocates and ICCB were frustrated with Peters, who seemed to cut them "out of the loop," and they lobbied the Governor's Commission on Women for a post-implementation policy change to promote education. They were successful. As one of his last acts before leaving office, Governor Jim Edgar issued a decree requiring the time clock on benefits to be stopped for up to thirty-six months to allow for participation in postsecondary education. "Howard Peters never wanted that, never liked it, and I believe never intended to implement it fully," said one advocate.

Beginning in January 1999, the five-year clock could be stopped for a TANF recipient attending "an accredited post-secondary education program full-time" with a cumulative GPA of 2.5 or better. The recipient did not have to meet the work requirement to participate in postsecondary education. However, since for the first semester of school the recipient does not yet have a GPA, he or she does not have to work, but her clock does not stop until the second semester. In addition, the clock resumes during the summer months when the recipient is not in class. The clock can be stopped for up to a lifetime maximum of thirty-six months (Peters 1999).[11]

One advocate attributed this progressive move in part to the work of advocates who understood that the state wanted to maximize the federal dollars and worked with officials to develop a way to spend the maintenance of effort dollars in a way that would help prevent a return to the rolls. She said,

> I think DHS [Department of Human Services] realized that they had the money to do some things that would help buffer them against people moving back onto the rolls. And they didn't want to see people moving back onto the roles,

In other words, postsecondary education was seen as little more than a tool to keep people working.

As a result of the stop-the-clock provision, postsecondary education is currently a formal option for welfare recipients in Illinois. However, a relatively small percentage of recipients in Illinois are actually accessing this education.[12] As of March 2001, approximately 3.5 percent, or 6,500 TANF recipients, were enrolled in some form of postsecondary education (not including Adult Basic Education or General Equivalency Diploma) in Illinois. But only 11 percent of these students were in a program that stopped the clock (general postsecondary or vocational postsecondary degree-seeking education with a GPA of 2.5 or better). The remaining 89 percent did not have their clocks stopped, and most were enrolled in vocational training leading to a certificate but not a degree.

A series of focus groups with Illinois welfare recipients, conducted by DHS in Fall 2001, revealed a desire for DHS to support education and that "all training and schooling should count towards work requirement hours." The recipients also wanted to see class study time counted as well. Some recipients also complained that they had been placed in job training programs for jobs they were not interested in (IDHS 2002).

During the initial implementation of TANF, Illinois operated a welfare-to-work program based at community colleges, known as the Advancing Opportunities (AO) program. AO was a collaborative effort of the ICCB and the IDHS. This program began as Opportunities in 1992, prior to TANF, and was revamped in response to TANF and the new work-first philosophy.

Prior to TANF, the focus of Opportunities was on providing AFDC recipients with "comprehensive education, training and counseling" (ICCB brochure n. d.). In response to TANF, the program emphasis was shifted to include a focus on "post-employment support and job upgrading" (ICCB brochure), and the program was renamed Advancing Opportunities. While AO retained its case management model, the training offered was short term and most often occupational or vocational in nature. In addition, funding for AO was based on performance outcomes, so completion and placement became more important to program directors.

A former director of AO at one community college expressed concern about recipients who took advantage of the program immediately after the shift to TANF:

> When it started to change, I think students felt like they were being forced into either education or work. And they chose education thinking it was the easier thing to do, and then they found out it wasn't. So there was probably some anger because they were forced to do something.

However, at the time of the interview in spring of 2001, she reported that recipients who want to enroll in AO had to struggle for it. "Now you have to prove to them [caseworkers] that you need training. . . . They have to fight for it."

AO operated in thirty-six of the forty-eight Illinois community colleges from 1998 to 2001, when Governor George Ryan sacrificed the $3.4 million program during budget cuts. As of spring 2001, AO was serving 3,900 current and former TANF recipients attending community college. Given that AO was recognized by many as a best practice program, its demise came as a surprise to some. "It does seem like a bit of a surprise to me that they would cut off their only education-focused program," said one woman at ICCB. According to a letter from the current heads of IDHS and ICCB (Baker and Cipfl 2001), the reduction in TANF caseloads caused the administration to reassess the delivery of training services. "As part of the transition from the Advancing Opportunities program, TANF individuals will be able to access educational programs directly through local community colleges with support services and case management provided by the local DHS offices," they wrote. This meant a shift in the location of these services from an office located on the community college campus to a DHS office off site, which was mentioned by some as a negative change since the DHS office treated the recipient as a TANF client, not a college student. But colleges will continue to receive a flexible welfare-to-work grant (the total pot of money for the grant is $3.7 million) to further the goal of ensuring "the welfare population has access to and receives education and training that will help them to succeed."

However, several representatives of the ICCB expressed concern about the ability of welfare recipients to access postsecondary education, especially after the end of AO. While AO was in operation, members of ICCB felt that "the staff at DHS really [had] an understanding of the value of education. . . . While they had a work-first policy to implement, they are committed to education and training." But they expressed concern that the end of AO meant that the administration at IDHS had succumbed to work-first pressures. A staffer at the ICCB noted:

> As educators, we truly believe that in order for people to get to their full potential they need skills training and education, not to just be put out in a job. . . . And we see our role as really fundamental to those kinds of improvements in people's lives. And welfare has taken a work-first philosophy that is just devastating to those outcomes for individuals,

Peters left his position as secretary of IDHS a year into Governor Ryan's administration, and the politically savvy Linda Renee Baker took over in 2000, continuing much of his agenda. "Linda is a lifelong politician," one advocate noted. "She understands the need to not totally embrace Howard's work-first, but she also understands the need not to totally just dump it either."

As a result of the discretion accorded to states under welfare reform, state policies regarding access to postsecondary education for welfare recipients vary widely.

One strong barrier to accessing postsecondary education appears to be IDHS caseworkers. Interviews with ICCB officials, community college representatives, advocates, and even members of IDHS revealed that the formal work-first philosophy is embraced by these street-level workers. One advocate said,

> You've basically got eligibility clerks that are now trying to do case management and employment, and we're talking about people who've been clerks for twenty-seven years and all of a sudden you want to make them a case manager or employment counselor?

The pro-education, stop-the-clock provision was apparently unpopular with some caseworkers and their supervisors, who failed to inform recipients of these new options. "It's very difficult, these caseworkers I think really embrace the notion of preaching about getting a job. . . . They did buy in well ideologically speaking, they support the [work-first] philosophy," said another advocate. He added, "The consistent message they get is caseload reduction, enter employment, and everything else is bullshit." According to this advocate, the Opportunities program existed as a way to draw additional federal matching dollars available under AFDC, and when

TANF took over, those matching dollars disappeared, and the motivation to maintain Opportunities declined. "The Department of Human Services understood that and made noises from the beginning about pulling Opportunities and the community colleges had gotten used to a pot of money and were pretty good at lobbying," and thus the program persisted for a while longer. He continued,

> But I think the department has started to take the attitude that they're not going to pay for education anymore to the extent they ever were. They're not going to pay for hard skills training and education, but they will pay for supports for people to be involved with that.

Another advocate reported hearing from recipients about difficulties in accessing education. "There are a lot of cases of people who said, 'I want to go to college,' and their workers say, 'You can't; you need to go to work.'" Caseworkers are not informing recipients about the stop-the-clock provision and are focused on reducing caseloads, not sending people to education, according to several advocates.

> They were measured by how many people got off the caseload, and they saw going to college as a thirty-six-month delay in getting someone off their caseload. And the overall message coming from the top was, Get people off, get people off, and education didn't fit in.

Illinois is a clear example of a state where the values, beliefs, and theories of action of key policy makers and administrative agencies have presented both opportunities and barriers to education for welfare recipients. Advocacy organizations and a community college system supportive of postsecondary education for disadvantaged women convinced a governor to stop the clock for recipients and allow them to receive benefits while in school. These groups clearly agree on the goal of promoting economic self-sufficiency through education and together have worked to enable several thousand welfare recipients to attend community college in Illinois. Yet, while the legislation is fairly permissive, implementation of that legislation strayed far from the written provisions. An agency director who believed rapid labor force attachment was the key to moving women off welfare was able to instill the work-first message in the bureaucracy and limit the number of recipients in college.

Washington

Washington's Work First legislation was passed by the legislature and signed by Governor Gary Locke in April 1997. The law—a collaboration between a Republican legislature and a Democratic governor—followed federal law in mandating a five-year lifetime limit on welfare benefits and requires work as a condition of public assistance. Among those in the state, there is near unanimous consensus that the initial law was "fairly narrow in terms of . . . work-first" and attempted to move away from previous welfare-to-work efforts in the state that focused greater attention on human capital building and skill development. As one interviewee put it,

> They (the governor's advisors) concluded that they had to put the labor market test first . . .
> that it had to be work-first. And they wanted to send that message very aggressively every-
> where. To clients, income maintenance workers, social workers, CSOs, advocates and leg-
> islators, this is where we're going to go.[13]

To ensure implementation of the new welfare law, the governor created a Work First subcabinet initially made up of representatives from his office, the Department of Human and Social Services (DSHS), the Employment Security Department (ESD), and the Office of Trade and Economic Development to work out the details. The initial implementation followed the tenor of the law. A client would first go to a DSHS case manager where he or she would complete an Individual Responsibility Plan that included a minimum work requirement of twenty hours per week. Then the client was sent to ESD to be placed for mandatory job search for up to twelve weeks. Under the initial interpretation of the law, only after twelve weeks of job search could clients enter postsecondary training of some sort. According to one advocate, case managers were discouraged from even mentioning education options because clients would more likely fail at the job search.

The consensus among advocates and others was that the state's new direction on welfare stemmed from the governor's own values and beliefs as well as the need to reduce public assistance caseloads. "I think he (the governor) believes in the work ethic strongly. . . . And he believes that, by George, you ought to go to work," noted one advocate. Work First was also influenced by reaction to previous welfare policies in the state, most especially the Family Independence Program. The Family Independence Program was an initiative of former governor Booth Gardner that used an aggressive human-capital-building approach to getting clients off of welfare. The consensus among many policy makers in Washington—Democrat and Republican—was that the Family Independence Program was a massive failure that raised caseloads, cost too much money, and created perverse "incentives that make welfare better than a job." This perception was shaped by a devastating Urban Institute evaluation of the program, noted one advocate.

> If you talk to a lot of the governors' advisors, they won't mention FIP [the Family Inde-
> pendence Program] necessarily, although they might, from time to time, but they'll say, we
> tried that in the old days, we tried education and training and it failed.

Yet within the first few months of Work First, there was a push from the governor's office to provide more education and training opportunities within the framework of the law. How and why this happened is a matter of some dispute in the state. According to a representative from the governor's office, from the beginning, the governor's staff recognized that "there was no practical way to expect large numbers of poor families to be able to get ahead unless they were able to build skills." Some advocates recognize that "this may have been the vision" from the start but was buried under the work-first rhetoric. As one advocate put it, "I think he (the governor) really believes in the theory . . . that once people make an effort, that we ought to help them with education and training and child care and so on."

To develop this component of Work First, the governor invited the State Board for Community and Technical Colleges (SBCTC) to sit on the subcabinet. The college system office was reticent at first, as was DSHS, reflecting the "clear difference in philosophy" between the two agencies regarding education access for welfare clients. On being included, the SBCTC did a data run and realized that a significant number of its students (around 9 percent) were current or former welfare recipients. As one advocate tells it, "While colleges and the college system were initially resistant to short-term skills training, they eventually realized that Work First wasn't going away and the only way they could keep their students was to embrace these kinds of programs." In August of 1997, the subcabinet unveiled a preemployment training (PET) initiative in collaboration with employers in Seattle and Spokane. The vision of the governor's office and DSHS was that PET would provide training in initial employment skills that would directly lead to employment. Although one senior DSHS staffer admits the training issue was initially raised by advocates and a high-tech business community concerned about skills shortages, DSHS fully supported the notion, as long as there were "assurances of a job at the end of training." In particular, they saw PET as a way for some of their higher-skilled clients—and former clients—to transition to a better-paying job. The initial contract provided $7 million to the SBCTC to develop PET programs.

Under the program, the SBCTC awarded colleges competitive subgrants to develop twelve-week, full-time PET modules. The DSHS model of a guaranteed job morphed into a sectoral strategy of industry-specific training and then, only after much back and forth between advocates, employers groups and the subcabinet. In practice, the local colleges run a boutique training operation for employers in key sectors experiencing job growth and skill shortages. Employers make no guarantee to hire PET graduates, which is still a bone of contention for DSHS since some regions have poor placement rates. In 2001, DSHS began to collect systematic data on PET placement rates, with a target goal of 50 percent successful placement (State of Washington, Work First 2001).

PET was the centerpiece of a $30 million allocation to the SBCTC that also included monies for colleges to (1) redesign programs and services to make it easier for students to access college, (2) provide tuition assistance to employed students, (3) offer workplace and family literacy services, and (4) provide evening and weekend child care for Work First participants attending college. Each of these programs was available broadly to low-wage workers at or under 175 percent of the poverty level. In the first two years of the program, 18,800 students received Work First training at the state's community colleges, with 3,170 of those students in PET programs specifically (SBCTC 2001). Indeed, since 1997, there has been a general extension of education and training services available to current and former recipients. In the summer of 2000, advocates and the SBCTC successfully lobbied to expand PET from twelve to twenty-two weeks. Just last year, a new high-wage, high-demand PET program was created, allowing up to one year of education in informational technology.

Some advocates are impressed with the evolution of DSHS on education and training while others grumble they have seen no "major movement in terms of education and training opportunities" and DSHS is merely doing what federal law allows (providing twelve months of vocational education toward work requirements) and have steadfastly refused to support stopping the clock for students attending community college full-time. DSHS for its part has made concrete changes in its policies since 1997, most concretely, changing performance reporting to allow PET training to be coded as a form of job search. The governor's subcabinet has commissioned researchers at the University of Washington to conduct a study of Work First, specifically looking at the impact of various program activities—including PET—on employment and earnings outcomes. Both DSHS and the subcabinet are concerned with the issues of retention and wage progression, particularly for former clients, and have developed the Washington Post-Employment Labor Exchange to provide two years of intensive retention and advancement services for former TANF clients.

In essence, the shorthand of "work-first" has become the guiding principle for state welfare policy and local implementation.

As the governor's subcabinet and DSHS evolved their message on education and training, they faced some daunting obstacles at the implementation level, particularly among the local welfare offices. In one sense, this was a predictable consequence of the strong work-first signal initially sent. As one advocate put it,

> They said okay, we have to change the culture of the welfare offices. We have to change this whole system from income maintenance to getting people into jobs. The only way we can do that is to send a very simple message: work-first. . . . (One of) the governor's advisors on Work First, he told me directly . . . he said this department DSHS is capable of doing one thing well, if that. We cannot, we can't send out multiple messages. . . . We can't say, But you know, they have to go to work, but they also need soft skills or they need ESL [English as a second language], or they might need short-term training. That was not a message they felt they could impart to the field offices and have them carry that out.

This message was reinforced by the legislation itself, which mandates job search for all clients who cannot be placed. Even though DSHS now counts PET as the equivalent of job search, many case managers require clients to go through twelve weeks of job search before promoting PET. Taken together, these factors have led to an underutilization of PET, to the dismay of one senior DSHS staffer:

> Here's where our problem was. When the governor says that clients would take the first available job, we knew that we were gonna send every able-bodied client to job search. . . . We didn't want to say, We will send everybody to job search where they'll take the first available job, but for a small portion of people, determined by us somehow, we'll divert those folks to preemployment training. What we thought was more equitable was to go to job search, and then from job search, every client will have the opportunities to go to preemployment training. . . . Okay, what's wrong with this picture? When you send people to job search, the ones that are most likely to benefit from preemployment training in the economy we've had for the last four years are also most likely to get placed in a job and exit. What is the job of the people running job search? It is to get people a job.

This unintended outcome has left PET both underenrolled and serving a harder-to-serve clientele than was initially envisioned. To address the enrollment problem, DSHS is now keeping data on whether local offices (CSOs) are maximizing their available PET slots. Nevertheless, the challenges in promoting education and training at the CSOs are daunting. For one, case managers still spend around 60 to 75 percent of their time on eligibility determination, despite DSHS efforts to have staff do more client assessment and referrals to PET or other programs as appropriate. DSHS staff repeatedly noted few training opportunities made available for case managers and extreme pressures from offices to reduce caseloads and raise placement rates. Many workers themselves are not convinced of the merits of education for their clients. One observer expressed shock at the "harsh" treatment of clients by DSHS eligibility workers and case managers.

Barriers to education are also present once clients are sent to job search and the ESD office. One job service specialist at ESD reported that she referred "maybe one client every three months" for education and training. The same employee noted there seem to be two kinds of case managers at ESD. "A certain group . . . they're of the philosophy that . . . we're not doing people any favors to be slack on them as far as job search and let the months roll by. . . . They want them to prove they're going to get a job first." The other group of case managers "is more liberal and takes the approach that training is an investment in the future, that if you can upgrade somebody's skills, (and) you can help somebody get a better job . . . it's worth the time and risk." These two sets of case manager beliefs and values are split evenly across the two offices she works in.

These problems were readily admitted to by DSHS, ESD staff, and representatives from the governor's office. Though the state community and technical colleges have raised similar concerns, they—spurred by the system office—have moved aggressively in recent years to collaborate with local DSHS and ESD staff, actively recruit current and former recipients, and reorganize college programs to make them more accessible. This attitude toward PET and short-term training was not there from the beginning. "When (Work First) happened, there was this attitude out there . . . Why should we have to do this when (our current) offerings are already working?" noted a member of the system office. While change was surely driven by the self-interest of earning a greater share of the Work First dollars available through the DSHS contract, many praise the leadership and commitment of the majority of colleges in embracing welfare reform and serving these students.[14]

"The colleges . . . didn't all make that change for some kind of narrow pecuniary interest. . . . I mean they saw (welfare reform) as part of a mission somewhere they're trying to do." The governor himself personally thanked colleges for their work with Work First clients in a speech last year to the state trustees association.

For their part, representatives of the governor are both "thrilled" and "surprised" with community colleges and their response to welfare reform. Still, while most colleges have come around, some still refuse to embrace either Work First or short-term workforce training programs. "The jury's still out," reported one senior SBCTC staffer.

Advocates too have seen their views evolve over time, some rooted in pragmatism ("it's not going away"), others in changing beliefs about education for welfare clients. As one well-respected advocate put it,

> My sense from the people I've talked to, including low-income people, is probably no more than 10 to 15 percent at the most would for a one- or two-year vocational postsecondary education and training program. . . . (Most) just say, Give me a job. . . . That's all I really want. . . . The reason I am saying that is I think that even if we were to open it up to a higher end, you know two years, four years, I don't think everyone would take advantage of that. . . . So in my own mind, I think that some of the short-term training does make sense.

Many of the state's advocacy organizations are now collaborating with local colleges to create more systematic career ladders that link short-term training with jobs with opportunities for advancement and additional educational credentials.

There is limited evidence about the impact these policy developments have had on postsecondary access in Washington State for current and former welfare recipients. What seems clear is that the number of welfare students in the state's community and technical colleges is beginning to rise again after decreasing each year since 1997. In the 2000-2001 academic year, 21,733 welfare-funded students were enrolled in the state's community and technical college, an increase of 5,839 students from the previous academic year (SBCTC 2001). While we do not know the breakdown of current clients, former clients, and the working poor, we do know that many of these referred to PET by DSHS are the hardest-to-employ segment of the client population. Although some interviewees suggested that colleges were "creaming" by serving the most skilled of the working poor, the system office claims that many colleges have been good in reaching out to current clients and the hardest to serve through their collaborations with the local DSHS and ESD offices.[15]

In summary, it appears a fragile ideological consensus on the role of education for welfare clients and poor adults is emerging in the state. Nevertheless, there are still tensions and unanswered questions. While the SBCTC is happy with evidence of the success of PET, they are uncomfortable with the program's being measured by its success in getting people off of welfare. DSHS, on the other hand, chides the colleges for poor record keeping and still is concerned about placement rates in some regions of the state. In 2001, the legislature has chimed in with a bill—as in

Illinois—to stop the clock on time limits for recipients in approved postsecondary programs, a bill neither DSHS nor the governor's office supports.

Perhaps what we are really seeing is a truce between philosophically opposed groups facilitated by a surplus of TANF dollars that were made available to support training. It will be interesting to see what develops in Washington as this surplus shrinks and the soft money training dollars slowly recede or even disappear.[16]

Comparing the Cases

Through a cross-state analysis, we are able to better understand both the sources and consequences of state variation in allowing access to postsecondary education for welfare recipients and the working poor. Not surprisingly, this article confirms that the discretion afforded by federal welfare reform policies led to significant differences in access policies across the three states. What the article also shows is that different and competing ideas about welfare, work, and the role of education in the lives of welfare recipients help structure and shape political debates, and ultimately policy outcomes, in each of the states. Ideas influence welfare reform policies in the three states through four key sources, or channels: via the state human service agency; via advocacy organizations; through the persistence of the work-first idea within implementation processes; and through the power of policy signals to drive welfare reform at the state level.

A central factor in determining the ways in which welfare reform affects access to education in each of these states is the role of the state human services agency in driving the work-first idea. In two of our three cases, Illinois and Massachusetts, it appears that the welfare department had a far stricter vision of work-first than the state legislation initially provided for. In one extreme case, the secretary of DHS in Illinois appears to have ignored the former governor's stop-the-clock provision and instead promoted his own agenda of rapid labor force attachment as the best solution.

Since the welfare department employs and trains the state employees who work most closely with welfare recipients, the caseworkers, the agency is most capable of setting the tone for implementation in a state. Liberal legislation, when implemented by caseworkers who are instructed to follow a work-first ideology or who believe in it themselves, is no longer liberal in practice. In Washington, it is clear that the actions of case managers followed the tone set by the department they work for. For example, initially, case managers rarely offered education to recipients since DSHS instructed them to focus on work. But over time, DSHS made policy changes allowing for greater access to education and training, and the state community and technical colleges embraced welfare reform. In 2000-2001, the number of Work First–eligible clients enrolled in community colleges increased markedly, after declining for the past four years. Clearly, the degree to which welfare departments embraced the work-first ideology and transmitted it to their caseworkers affected the degree to which welfare recipients were able to access training.

The advocacy community also plays an important role in shaping access policies within a state. The advocates in Washington State were successful in promoting education in welfare recipients in part because they were able to adapt their ideological approach to focus less on traditional postsecondary education than on short-term training linked to a long-term strategy for advancement. It is important to note that not all advocates in Washington have embraced this approach.

In Massachusetts, the advocacy community has been both less vocal and less effective in promoting educational access. Although the formal provisions of the welfare law allow up to four years of postsecondary training, only about 9 percent of the caseload are in education and training activities, and even fewer of those (less than 2 percent) in two-year community college degree programs.

The advocacy community in Illinois strategically targeted their efforts at the Governor's Commission on Women to gain the stop-the-clock provision. Since that time, advocates have actively fought, although sometimes unsuccessfully, to protect the AO program and other welfare-to-work programs in the state that facilitate access to education. Although Illinois advocates have had some success in affecting formal policy, only 3.5 percent of recipients are taking advantage of such training, with fewer than seven hundred students falling under the clock-stopping provision.

Our findings in Illinois—indeed in all three states—speak to the gap between the formal provision of educational access and its reality for clients. Surely, there are many personal and financial reasons current welfare recipients are not enrolling in college (Golonka and Matus-Grossman 2001). Nevertheless, even efforts like those in Illinois and Washington—to actively promote postsecondary access—are challenged by implementation problems, particularly at the level of frontline caseworkers and other street-level bureaucrats, who interpret and make these policies real for recipients on a daily basis. In all three of our states, we saw the beliefs and attitudes of caseworkers and other frontline employees about work and education consistently reinforced the work-first message coming from the welfare bureaucracy and others. Research in other states confirms that "frontline workers generally believe welfare recipients should work" as a precondition for receiving public assistance (Lurie 2001, 2).

The beliefs and values of frontline workers stand as only one barrier to educational access. Caseworkers also operate in an environment with limited opportunities to build their own professional capacities and strong pressures to reduce caseloads and get clients into the workforce as a measure of their job performance (Lurie 2001). Efforts to change the culture of the welfare office in places like Massachusetts, Illinois, and Washington have only added to the responsibilities of frontline workers without reducing client loads or subtracting responsibilities such as eligibility determination. Few frontline workers in these three states or nationally have the skills and formal credentials to engage clients about their lives, problems, and barriers to work or career advancement (see also Lurie 2001; Lurie,

Meyers, and Riccucci 2001), making real case management little more than the wishful thinking of welfare policy makers.

Although implementation poses significant barriers to access for current and former welfare recipients, in Washington, we saw that an aggressive community college sector can counter some of the tendencies within the welfare bureaucracy. This requires community colleges and college systems that are committed to serving these students, something we saw in all three states. Our initial evidence also suggests that this commitment necessitates a willingness to partner with the state human services agency around shorter-term training and workforce development. Of our three states, Washington's colleges—and state system office—were most willing to move in this direction, and only after some initial reluctance. This suggests that how colleges and college systems define their educational mission—traditional transfer, vocational education, short-term workforce development, or some combination of these—may dictate how aggressively and successfully they reach out to low-income populations.

One commonality across our three states is the power of federal welfare reform to drive change—both in formal law and in bureaucratic procedures. In each of our states, state human service agencies and other agencies have dramatically changed the ideological signals sent to clients and frontline workers about welfare (Gais et al. 2001, 9). These new signals stress the centrality of work to welfare, the personal responsibility of clients, and the time-limited nature of public assistance. In essence, the shorthand of work-first has become the guiding principle for state welfare policy and local implementation. The challenge states have faced is moving beyond this simple work-first signal to a more complex idea that embraces education and human capital development as a complement to workforce attachment strategies. Even when this message has captured policy makers (Washington, Illinois), implementation processes have remained steadfastly work-first in practice. Whether this is due to beliefs, incentives, inertia, or merely the challenge in implementing a more complex policy idea remains to be seen. To the extent TANF reauthorization seeks to enhance educational access, federal policy makers will have to grapple with these issues.

In summary, ideas work at the level of both formal state policy and local implementation to shape welfare reform outcomes in these three states. The power of ideas, especially in policy implementation, can lead to outcomes that might otherwise be unexpected. In Massachusetts, the efforts of the DTA produced postsecondary access policies significantly more limited than they were within the formal dictates of the law. In Illinois, work-first conceptions were able to significantly weaken the well-intentioned efforts of advocates and the governor to promote college access for welfare recipients. While in Washington, the work-first idea has given way to a greater focus on PET and a fragile new ideological consensus about the role of education among advocates, elected and appointed officials, and community colleges, efforts challenged by the persistence of the work-first idea within the welfare bureaucracy. In all three states, the meaning of welfare reform often overrode its formal policy mechanics (Stein 2001), making liberal policies more restrictive in practice and vice versa.

Conclusion and Next Steps

While educational researchers, especially those in the postsecondary arena, take for granted the importance of education in improving life chances, many are likely unaware of the contrary tendencies built into federal welfare reform. By examining state policy responses to TANF, this article has sought to provide a more fine-grained analysis of the impact of this new world of welfare on postsecondary access for low-income individuals. Such knowledge is crucial, we believe, for higher education researchers concerned with issues of access and degree attainment.

In particular, this article emphasizes the role that public policy ideas, and their influence on policy implementation, play in shaping postsecondary access. The new policy environment around welfare reform has brought with it a new discourse around education and labor market attachment for the clients of welfare programs. Given this fact, it is imperative that researchers look more closely at the access barriers and opportunities created by this new and dynamic ideological environment, along with the policy implementation structures (frontline workers, community colleges) that carry these ideas forward. Can states successfully alter policy signals to successfully promote education for current and former welfare clients? How do implementation-level factors (beliefs and incentives of frontline workers, mission/ideology of community colleges) shape the outcome of these efforts? Although we may be able to wrap our minds more easily around the barriers, future research must not ignore the success stories—those cases where federal-, state-, and institutional-level policies help welfare recipients and the working poor obtain meaningful access to community college degree and certificate programs and ultimately to economic self-sufficiency.

Notes

1. The Department of Health and Human Services reports that in 2000, less than 1 percent of federal Transitional Aid to Needy Families funds were spent on education and training nationwide (Greenberg 2001).

2. Since postsecondary education does not count as a work activity, it is not a reporting category. In other words, because it is not an allowable activity under the rules, the federal government collects no data on it.

3. The states are Arizona, Georgia, Iowa, Kentucky, Maine, Minnesota, Missouri, Nebraska, New Mexico, Rhode Island, Utah, Vermont, West Virginia, and Wyoming.

4. The states are Alabama, Arkansas, California, Illinois, and North Carolina.

5. Five states—Colorado, Florida, Maryland, New York, and Ohio—allow counties to decide if postsecondary education can help meet work requirements.

6. In March 2001, 92.4 percent of the caseload (more than 38,700 recipients) were either exempt from work requirements and time limits or nonexempt but subject to time limits only. At that time, 9.1 percent of the caseload was participating in "Education & Training" or a "Combination" of types of activities (Massachusetts Department of Transitional Assistance 2001b). Note that this is the same month the participation requirement went into effect for those subject to the time limit but not the twenty-hour work requirement. The new requirement presumably has increased participation and potentially educational enrollments.

7. Just 702 welfare recipients in Massachusetts were in two-year college programs, and just one recipient was in a four-year college program (Massachusetts Department of Transitional Assistance 2001a).

8. Ten of the state's fifteen community colleges have participated at some point. Eight initially implemented programs; at this point only five colleges have programs.

9. One possible reason for this is that community colleges in Massachusetts do not have a strong history of providing workforce development training. A recent impetus for change in this area has come from reports by the Boston-based MassINC (2000a, 2000b). Working with MassINC, community colleges were able for the first time to win funding from the state for contract training. Previously, they only received money for their for-credit courses.

10. See Brodkin (1997) for more details on Job Opportunities and the Basic Skills Training Program in Chicago. Under funding and evaluation pressures, caseworkers pushed the program more in the direction of job search and rapid labor market attachment.

11. The computer system used by caseworkers does not allow them to formally stop the sixty-month counter. Instead, local offices must identify clients who meet the criterion for having their clocks stopped and determine the number of months countered in error. Then they have to send paperwork to a central office to have the counter adjusted.

12. Welfare caseloads in Illinois are down substantially, from 663,000 recipients in January 1996 to 194,000 in March 2001 (for the latest available, see acf.dhhs.gov/news/stats).

13. CSOs are the regional offices of the Department of Human and Social Services in Washington.

14. Or the fear of losing these students otherwise. According to an interviewee, one campus in 1997 found that 33 percent of its students were current welfare recipients.

15. The first outcome analysis from the longitudinal Work First study found that participation in preemployment training had a statistically significant impact on rates of employment and earnings and did significantly better than other Work First activities such as job search and work experience (Klawitter 2001).

16. In June of 2002, funding for Work First training programs was reduced by $7.5 million, a smaller cut than many expected, given the state's budget woes (www.wa.gov/WORKFIRST/statestaff/WITQandA.htm).

References

Administration for Children and Families, Office of Research Planning and Evaluation. 2001. Available from http://www.acf.dhhs.gov/programs/opre/particip/im00rate/table4a.htm.

Baker, Linda Renee, and Joseph Cipfl. 2001. Letter regarding Advancing Opportunities program. Chicago: Illinois Department of Human Services.

Ball, Stephen. 1994. What is policy? Texts, trajectories and toolboxes. In *Educational reform: A critical and post-structural approach*, 14-27. London: Taylor-Francis.

Bowe, Richard, and Stephen Ball. 1992. *Reforming education and changing schools: Case studies in policy sociology*. London: Routledge.

Brodkin, Evelyn Z. 1997. Inside the welfare contract: Discretion and accountability in state welfare administration. *Social Service Review* 71:1-33.

Center for Law and Social Policy. 2002. Likely to cut access to postsecondary training or education under house-passed bill. Available from www.clasp.org.

Gais, Thomas, Richard Nathan, Irene Lurie, and Thomas Kaplan. 2001. The implementation of the Personal Responsibility Act of 1996: Commonalities, variations and the challenge of complexity. Unpublished paper. New York: Rockefeller Institute of Government, State University of New York.

Golonka, Susan, and Lisa Matus-Grossman. 2001. *Opening doors: Expanding educational opportunities for low-income workers*. New York: MDRC and National Governors Association Center for Best Practices.

Government Accounting Office. 1998. *Restructuring state welfare programs*. Washington, DC: Government Accounting Office.

Greenberg, Mark. 2001. *How are TANF funds being used? The story in FY 2000*. Washington, DC: Center for Law and Social Policy.

Greenberg, Mark, Julie Strawn, and Lisa Plimpton. 2000. *State opportunities to provide access to postsecondary education under TANF*. Washington, DC: Center for Law and Social Policy.

Grubb, W. Norton. 1999. *The economic benefits of subbaccalaureate education: Results from state and local studies*. Community College Research Center Brief no. 3. New York: Teachers College, Columbia University.

Hall, Peter. 1989. *The political power of economic ideas: Keynesianism across nations*. Princeton, NJ: Princeton University Press.

———. 1997. The role of interests, institutions and ideas in the comparative political economy of the industrializing nations. In *Comparative politics: Rationality, culture and structure*, edited by Marc Lichbach and Irving Zuckerman, 174-207. Cambridge, MA: Cambridge University Press.

Illinois Community College Board. n.d. *Advancing opportunities: A welfare to education to work program: Creating hope through education*. Springfield: State of Illinois.

Illinois Department of Human Services (IDHS). 2002. *TANF focus groups: Final report: What do TANF customers want to see in reauthorization?* Chicago: Illinois Department of Human Services.

Institute for Women's Policy Research. 1998. *Welfare reform and postsecondary education: Research & policy update*. Washington, DC: Institute for Women's Policy Research.

Jacobs, Jerry, and Kathleen Shaw. 1999. *Welfare reform and community colleges*. A proposal to the Atlantic Philanthropies. Unpublished Document.

Jenson, Jane. 1989. Paradigms and political discourse: Protective legislation in France and the United States before 1914. *Canadian Journal of Political Science* 22:235-58.

Kane, Thomas, and Cecilia Rouse. 1995. Labor market returns to two and four-year college. *American Economic Review* 85 (3): 600-28.

Katz, Michael. 2001. *The price of citizenship: Redefining the American welfare state*. New York: Metropolitan Books.

Kaye, Laura, Demetra Nightingale, Jodi Sandfort, and Lynne Fender. 2001. *Changes in Massachusetts welfare and work, child care, and child welfare systems*. Washington, DC: Urban Institute.

Kingdon, John. 1995. *Agendas, alternatives and public policies*. New York: HarperCollins.

Kirby, Gretchen, LaDonna Pavetti, Karen McGuire, and Rebecca Clark. 1997. *Income support and social services for low-income people in Massachusetts*. Washington, DC: Urban Institute.

Klawitter, Marika. 2001. *Effects of Work First activities on employment and earnings*. Work First longitudinal study. Seattle: University of Washington Press.

Levi, Margaret. 1997. A model, a method, and a map: Rational choice in comparative and historical analysis. In *Comparative politics: Rationality, culture and structure*, edited by Marc Lichbach and Irving Zuckerman, 19-41. Cambridge, MA: Cambridge University Press.

Levy, Frank, and Richard Murnane. 1992. U.S. earnings levels and earnings inequality: A review of recent trends and proposed explanations. *Journal of Economic Literature* 30 (3): 1333-81.

Lin, Ann Chih. 2000. *Reform in the making: The implementation of social policy in prison*. Princeton, NJ: Princeton University Press.

Lipsky, Mark. 1988. *Street level bureaucracy*. New York: Russell Sage.

Lurie, Irene. 2001. Changing welfare offices. In *The Brookings Institution, welfare reform and beyond*. Policy brief no. 9. Washington, DC: Brookings Institution.

Lurie, Irene, Marcia Meyers, and Norma Riccucci. 2001. Achieving goal congruence in complex environments: The case of welfare reform. *Journal of Public Administration Research and Theory* 11 (2): 165-201.

March, James, and Johan Olson. 1995. *Democratic governance*. New York: Free Press.

Massachusetts Department of Transitional Assistance. 2001a. *Commonwealth of Massachusetts, statewide client participation by component through January 2001*. Boston: Massachusetts Department of Transitional Assistance.

———. 2001b. *TAFDC caseload and participation breakdown as of 03/07/01*. Boston: Massachusetts Department of Transitional Assistance.

MassINC. 2000a. *New skills for a new economy: Adult education's key role in sustaining economic growth and expanding opportunity*. Boston: Massachusetts Institute for a New Commonwealth.

MassINC. 2000b. *Opportunity knocks: Training the commonwealth's workers for the new economy*. Boston: Massachusetts Institute for a New Commonwealth.

McDermott, Kathryn. 2001. Understanding variation in state assessment policies. Unpublished paper, University of Massachusetts, Amherst.

Meyer, Susan, and Paul Peterson. 1999. *Earning and learning: How schools matter*. New York: Brookings Institution/Russell Sage.

Meyers, Marcia, Janet Gornick, and Laura Peck. 2001. Packaging support for low-income families: Policy variation across the United States. *Journal of Policy Analysis and Management* 20:457-84.

Miller, Gale. 1991. *Enforcing the work ethic: Rhetoric and everyday life in a work incentive program*. Albany: State University of New York Press.

Mills, Michael, and Adrienne Hyle. 2001. No rookies on rookies: Compliance and opportunism in policy implementation. *Journal of Higher Education* 72 (4): 351-71.

Mink, Gwendolyn. 1995. *The wages of motherhood: Inequality in the welfare state, 1917-1942*. Ithaca, NY: Cornell University Press.

Peters, Howard A., III. 1999. Policy memorandum re: TANF 60-month limit and post-secondary education. 12 January. Chicago: Illinois Department of Human Services.

———. 2001. *Washington community and technical colleges: Academic year report, 00-01*. Olympia, WA: State Board for Community and Technical Colleges.

State of Washington, Work First. 2001. Local planning area performance measures report. Olympia, WA: Employment Security Department.

Stein, Sandra. 2001. These are your Title 1 students: Policy language in educational practice. *Policy Sciences*, 34 (2), 135-56.

Stone, Deborah. 1989. Causal stories and the formation of policy agendas. *Political Science Quarterly* 104:281-300.

Weaver, Kent. 2000. *Ending welfare as we know it*. Washington, DC: Brookings Institution.

Market Rhetoric Versus Reality in Policy and Practice: The Workforce Investment Act and Access to Community College Education and Training

By
KATHLEEN M. SHAW
and
SARA RAB

This article examines the impact of the Workforce Investment Act (WIA) of 1998 on access to community college education and training. The market-oriented, customer-focused rhetoric of WIA is compared to the realities of WIA implementation in three states: Rhode Island, Illinois, and Florida. The authors first discuss the emergence of WIA in the context of recent market-driven pressures on community colleges. Next, they provide an overview of the relevant components of WIA. Finally, they examine how the implementation and practice of WIA affects the ability of low-income populations to obtain postsecondary education. They find that WIA's rhetoric, intended to promote educational quality and increase customer choice, is not reflected in either formal policy or implementation. Important policy elements such as accountability measures and the focus on multiple customers have undercut the rhetoric of free choice. Thus, in practice, WIA has actually limited access to education and training at community colleges.

Keywords: community colleges; workforce development; market-driven education

Market-driven education (otherwise known as consumer-driven or outcomes-driven education) has become the clarion call heard throughout the educational system. This approach to education generally includes two major elements: first, an emphasis on the cus-

Kathleen M. Shaw is an associate professor of urban education in the Department of Educational Leadership and Policy Studies at Temple University. Her work focuses on educational policy and its effects on issues of access and equity. Much of her recent work examines how community colleges function within the K-16 educational pipeline and includes issues such as remediation and transfer. She is currently working on a book-length manuscript with Jerry A. Jacobs, Christopher Mazzeo, and Sara Rab on the effects of welfare reform and the Workforce Investment Act on access to community college for poor populations.

Sara Rab is a doctoral candidate in sociology at the University of Pennsylvania. Her research interests include community colleges, poverty, and gender. She is currently working on a dissertation exploring the causes and consequences of complex undergraduate attendance patterns.

DOI: 10.1177/0002716202250223

tomer, defined in various ways and second, the collection and dissemination of out-come or performance measures as a means through which customers can make informed educational choices. In theory, this approach standardizes outputs. But because it does not dictate the ways in which institutions are to achieve outcome goals, market-driven education is designed to create institutional autonomy and an entrepreneurial approach to delivering education. Underlying this perspective is the assumption that institutional autonomy leads to healthy competition among schools as they strive to produce the best outcomes and that educational customers are enabled to make free and informed choices regarding the educational institution or program that best suits their needs. When taken together, these market forces are designed to improve educational quality.

In recent years, these principles have become increasingly common in efforts to reform postsecondary education. The state of Tennessee was a pioneer in this movement, instituting performance-based funding and accountability measures for its colleges and universities as early as 1978. As is stated on its Web site, the system as it currently operates, rewards institutions that perform well on measurable outcomes with additional funding. Moreover, the beneficiaries are seen to be students themselves: "Tennesseans enrolled in public colleges and universities are the primary direct recipients of performance funding program benefits. . . . Students and faculty are at the heart of the performance funding program" (see Tennessee Higher Education Commission at www.state.tn.us/thec/academic/pf/page4.html).

Since then, accountability and other market-based, competitive principles have increasingly guided higher education institutions and systems across many states. Indeed, a recent state-by-state report card on higher education produced by the National Policy Center on Higher Education (2000) revealed that states are increasingly subject to comparison on such measures of success as preparation, participation, affordability, and completion. In fact, the number of states implementing accountability plans doubled between 1994 and 1997 (State Higher Education Executive Officers 1998). According to the most recent results of a national survey of State Higher Education Finance Officers conducted by the Rockefeller Institute of Government (Burke and Minassians 2001), performance reporting, budgeting, and financing have all become commonplace among state systems of higher education. While the bulk of financing for all public higher education institutions continues to be based on fixed costs such as faculty salaries and enrollment, "the increased use of performance budgeting and funding does indicate the growing belief in state capitals, but not on public campuses—that performance should somehow count in state budgeting for higher education" (Burke and Minassians 2001, 5).

Community colleges are particularly susceptible to market-driven educational reform efforts (Dougherty and Bakia 2000a). These institutions serve a critical function by serving as a link between the education and the employment sectors and between the K-12 and four-year college sectors as well. Their funding base is also relatively unstable and subject to various forms of political pressure. And perhaps most important, as the postsecondary educational sector that has traditionally served the most disadvantaged student populations, it is particularly vulnerable to measures of quality and success that focus on graduation, transfer, or stable employment. Indeed, the increased emphasis on workforce development approaches to education in the community college sector is a response to market pressures (an issue that we discuss in more detail below). Thus, for these reasons, community colleges provide an important site in which to examine how market-driven approaches to providing education and training might affect both the amount and type of education available to disadvantaged students.

The market-driven, outcomes-based philosophy that permeates postsecondary educational reform efforts at the state level is also fueling policy changes at the federal level that have direct impact on the delivery of education and training by community colleges. Most recently, it has been reflected in the Workforce Investment Act (WIA), a major piece of federal legislation that emerged in 1998. WIA embodies elements of a market-driven approach to delivering education and training to disadvantaged populations, measuring its success based on a set of outcomes that are designed to produce a more efficient, targeted, and ultimately successful approach to delivering education and training. Moreover, the outcome measures chosen are explicitly designed to address the concerns and needs of the "customer," which is variously defined as students, the business sector, and/or the state.

Yet despite the clear market rhetoric that drives this reform and the workforce-focused environment in which it operates, questions remain regarding the degree to which this philosophy is actually reflected in either the details of the policy itself or the practices of educational institutions as they respond to WIA. Moreover, the question of whether, and how, these policies actually serve the needs of students remains unanswered. The purpose of this article, then, is to address the following five questions: In what ways does WIA policy contain a market-driven approach to education? How do the elements of WIA interact with other market-driven educational trends, and in what ways are they contradictory? Does WIA reflect and enhance a market-driven approach to education that produces informed consumers with unlimited access to the education or training of their choice? If not, what factors impede the market-driven model that is supposed to be driving educational practices at community colleges? and What broad effects might WIA and market-driven policies more generally have on the role of community colleges in providing education and training to disadvantaged populations?

To address these questions, we first provide a context for the emergence of WIA by discussing more generally the market-driven pressures on community colleges that have emerged in recent years. Next, we provide an overview of those components of WIA that are designed to reflect a market approach to delivering education and training. Finally, the bulk of the article is devoted to a close examination of how the actual implementation and practice of WIA affect the ability of low-income populations to access postsecondary education and training.

Assumptions of Market-Driven Educational Models

The trend toward accountability-driven, customer-focused education is a reflection of an increasingly common approach to the educational enterprise in general (Gross, Shaw, and Shapiro 2002). It is driven by a free-market approach to democracy that is often associated with the University of Chicago economist Milton Friedman and more recently with the ideas of Chester Finn, Bruno Manno, and Diane Ravitch. This analysis places schools in the same category as other institutions in our economy—that is, organizations that must compete for customers who, at least theoretically, have free choice.

Yet the market-driven model of delivering education at the postsecondary level is based on a number of assumptions inherent in the accountability equation. First, although it is assumed that the needs of the customer can and should be met, the term "customer" is now frequently applied to two, and sometimes three, very different entities—students, the business community, and state legislators. In and of itself, the presence of multiple constituents is not new to the community college sector; indeed, Dougherty (1994) argued convincingly that community colleges have traditionally served multiple constituencies with considerable success, and this is still true today. As the National Council of Instructional Administrators (2002) stated, "inherent in the community college mission is a responsibility to be responsive to the needs of a wide variety of constituencies in the communities that are served" (p. 1).

Responsibility is increasingly achieved by accountability systems that are imposed on community colleges and are designed to track various types of outcomes defined as critical indicators of customer satisfaction. Taken alone, accountability is not inherently bad or detrimental to community colleges. Indeed, given the fact that these institutions are funded so heavily with public monies, it makes good sense to track the ability of community colleges to meet the needs of their intended customers.

However, when accountability is combined with multiple constituencies, problems arise. First, most community colleges have neither the funding nor the expertise to produce the myriad of outcomes measures requested by their varied constituents (Alfred and Carter 2002). As we demonstrate below, some institutions are able to develop specific measures to address the concerns of a particular constituency. Yet others opt out of the accountability system entirely, having made the decision that the benefits of participating do not justify the costs of doing so.

Perhaps just as important, the outcomes desired by one type of customer may make it impossible to meet the needs of another. The National Council of Instructional Administrators (2002) pointed out that

> community colleges also have multiple "masters" to whom they are accountable: federal and state governments and agencies; state boards and/or higher education coordinating bodies; accrediting bodies; regulatory agencies; local boards of trustees; the communities which support them through taxes; business and industry which employ students and graduates; and other constituent groups. Each of these "masters" has requirements, formats, procedures and expectations unique to its needs. These are, unfortunately, generally incompatible with each other. (Pp. 7-8)

Because the interests of this growing list of constituents are not necessarily complementary, it is often difficult for the community college to successfully address the needs of all customer groups.

Second, market-driven education assumes that all customers have equal access to the information needed to make an informed choice. Yet the outcomes reported as a result of accountability measures are one important part of the information equation, but not the only one. Customers must be able to access the information that they will need to make rational decisions. Moreover, the model assumes that free choice is indeed present and that customers are unencumbered by factors that might constrain their choice, such as finances, time, or transportation. These would seem to be problematic assumptions for community colleges, which are designed to serve the most disadvantaged student populations. Literacy levels, language barriers, knowledge of the employment sector, and the ability to navigate a complicated and unfamiliar bureaucracy are all potential barriers to the information that an informed consumer would need to make a wise educational choice.

It is also assumed in the free-market model that the entity (in this instance, the community college) that delivers the product desired by the customer is unencumbered by bureaucratic or financial constraints that would inhibit the entity's ability to respond to the market. Yet as Cohen (2000) has pointed out, states have become increasingly involved in the educational functions of the community college and have sought to increase their level of control by developing larger and more complicated accountability systems and reporting requirements, and the federal government has utilized large funding sources, such as those available under the Perkins Vocational Act, to influence community college policy and practice. Finally, market-driven models of education assume that the accountability measures that are nearly always built into these systems will, in fact, have the expected effect—that is, they will assert pressure on the educational institution to better serve the customer whom it is designed to serve. Yet, such matters have a mixed record of success. In all these ways, the assumptions on which a market-based education model is based are violated to some degree.

Accountability and the Movement toward Workforce Preparation

Despite the flaws in logic that are inherent in market-driven educational models, the market is becoming an increasingly potent force in the community college sector (Bailey and Averianova 1999; Levin 2001; Alfred and Carter 2002). Moreover, the business community is by far the strongest market force in the community college arena. Other types of customers, students in particular, are being overshadowed by the political and fiscal power of the business community. As a result, in the past thirty years in particular, community colleges have become increasingly focused on workforce preparation, and the degree of emphasis on this function has increased greatly in the past several years (Cohen and Brawer 1996; Bailey and Averianova 1999). Partnerships with industry and local and state governments have resulted in the development of relatively short-term, certificate-oriented training programs (Dougherty and Bakia 2000b), and financial pressures and opportunities have rendered this sector of education increasingly entrepreneurial (Grubb et al. 1997). While the educational level of the labor force is almost certain to increase, much of the growth will occur via shorter-term, specialized, vocationally oriented programs of study.

While community colleges have traditionally been the primary providers of such programs, they are facing increased competition. As Alfred and Carter (2002) pointed out, entities such as the University of Phoenix, in-house corporate trainers, and electronic campuses are reshaping the postsecondary market (p. 3). Thus, if community colleges want to remain the primary providers of such education, they must find ways to justify and successfully market their activities and their results in an increasingly competitive, institutionally varied environment.

The outcomes desired by one type of "customer" may make it impossible to meet the needs of another.

Institutional response to these market forces most typically comes in the form of an increased emphasis on workforce development. Workforce development is commonly defined as an approach to community college education that focuses on providing a workforce that is educated to the specifications of the local labor market (Public/Private Ventures 2001). By developing curricula and training programs that are designed to meet the expressed needs of the local business community, community colleges can utilize a workforce development approach to education that provides a more direct link to a very lucrative customer—the business sector.

Contract training, as a subset of workforce development, is a case in point. More than 90 percent of community colleges offer some type of contract training (Dougherty and Bakia 2000b). Under such arrangements, businesses can contract with any educational vendor to provide the specific skills and training desired by the company. Contract training embodies a market approach to delivering education because it requires community colleges to compete to win these contracts. Thus, contract training and other forms of workforce development efforts require close, consistent collaboration with the business sector and the development of training or education programs that are tailored specifically to the needs of a particular employer, industry, or occupation. Often, such programs are offered to those already employed by the business (as in contract or on-the-job continuing training), and they may or may not carry college-level credit or be transferable toward the acquisition of a more traditional academic credential, such as an associate's or bachelor's degree.

While workforce development does not explicitly negate the needs of students, it is clearly designed first and foremost to address the needs of another customer—the business community. Short-term training programs designed to meet the precise needs of an individual company may be quite useful to an employee, particularly while he or she remains employed by the company that paid for the training. But because such training does not often carry college credit or a recognizable credential, it most often remains meaningful only within the context of a particular company.

Education and Training Policy under WIA

WIA has emerged within the context of this unmistakable movement toward defining the employment sector as the primary customer of the community college. Indeed, many elements of WIA reflect and reinforce this orientation toward the needs of the labor market. Perhaps most prominently, despite the fact that WIA promises to deliver education and training to unemployed workers, it employs a work-first philosophy that actively discourages the acquisition of either education or training and encourages states and educational institutions to link access to education with the needs of the local labor market. Moreover, WIA employs an outcomes-driven, market ideology in both providing and assessing the quality of education and training. Thus, the policy would seem to be consistently in line with market-driven educational reforms.

Yet rhetoric is not necessarily consistently reflected in either the details of formal policy or the implementation of these policies in states and educational institutions. How well are the assumptions of a market-based approach to education supported in (1) the conceptualization of WIA and (2) its implementation? Below, we address the first portion of this question by providing an overview of WIA and the rhetoric that shapes it. Next, we examine how WIA is being implemented to examine whether the rhetoric matches the reality, particularly with regard to the question of whether WIA does, in fact, address the needs of students as one of the policy's primary customers.

WIA: A Market-Driven Policy Initiative

WIA represents a distinct departure from previous workforce development federal policies, such as the Comprehensive Employment Training Act of the 1980s and the Job Training Partnership Act (JTPA) of the 1990s, in three important ways. First, WIA employs a work-first philosophy whose goal is to place as many WIA clients into employment as quickly as possible. Rapid workforce attachment is emphasized; education and training are de-emphasized. Second, WIA is designed to be a customer-driven policy, and customers are broadly defined to include both students and the employment sector. Third, a comprehensive accountability system is employed to collect information designed in part to help customers make informed educational choices. When taken together, these three factors are designed to create a market-driven approach to providing services to WIA clients. This approach has important implications for access to education and training for disadvantaged students.

According to a recent Department of Labor (2002) Web site, WIA is driven by "customer satisfaction," which is gauged by a series of customer (both students and employers) satisfaction and job placement measures. This is in distinct contrast to previous federal job training policies, which both provided more access to education and training and operated via vendor-driven policies through which community colleges competed to obtain grants from the Department of Labor to offer education and training programs specifically for JTPA clients (Barnow and King 2001). The competition for vendor grants was clearly an element of JTPA that reflected a market orientation, but funding was relatively plentiful. Under WIA, the vendor is not the central element in the equation; instead, two sets of customers—the business sector and the WIA clients who become students—drive the model. As the Department of Labor (1998) stated, "The most important aspect of the Act is its focus on meeting the needs of businesses for skilled workers *and* the training, education and employment needs of individuals" (p. 4).

WIA operationalizes its customer-driven orientation via the use of two tools: the voucher-like Individualized Training Account (ITA) and the accountability system. Under JTPA, community colleges and other educational institutions competed for federal dollars distributed by states via training contracts. On receiving a contract to, for example, provide a training program for office assistants, the community college would develop the program, staff it, and advertise the program and recruit to fill its classes. Thus, while there was an element of competition for these dollars, on receiving the contract, community colleges could be sure that they would receive a sizable contract for developing and staffing such programs if they could fill their classes.

The accountability measures present in WIA are evidence of a distinctly different relationship between the federal government and providers of education and training. First, while JTPA did not impose eligibility requirements on training providers, WIA requires that all providers be certified with the federal or state government. In addition, whereas there were no reporting requirements under JTPA, under WIA, all providers must "submit annual specified performance-based information relating to the outcomes of their students (i.e., completion rates, placement and earnings)" (Department of Labor 2002, 4). Moreover, to remain eligible, they must meet or exceed minimum levels of performance established by states and localities. And finally, evidence of customer satisfaction for both participants and employers must be collected by each training provider as well.

These outcome measures are then fed back to the one-stop career centers that are the mandated entry point for individuals wishing to access WIA services. The centers provide the outcome measures as a means through which WIA clients approved for training can examine the outcome measures and make an informed choice regarding which program is most likely to help them achieve their educational and employment goals.

According to the WIA model, clients are able to access this training via the provision of ITAs. WIA clients who are not able to obtain employment by simply utilizing the on-site resources of the career centers are theoretically able to obtain an ITA and then choose an appropriate educational or training program. This differs from the JTPA model in that programs are not developed specifically for WIA clients, as they were under JTPA. Rather, clients are able to choose any program for which a community college or other educational organization submits the requisite accountability information. Thus, community colleges are not competing for contracts to develop programs; they are competing for individual students. In much the same way that K-12 school voucher program models provide parents with the opportunity to shop for the best existing school, ITAs explicitly treat students as consumers and education as an open market.

With the adaptation of both mechanisms, WIA, at least in theory, embraces a market-driven model for the delivery of education and training. As Barnow and King (2001) pointed out, "WIA is quite clear about providing accurate, up-to-date performance information on providers to support informed consumer choice, an essential element in fostering reliance on market mechanisms" (pp. 7-8). They went on to say,

> It is no longer unusual to see proposals and provisions referring to both participants and employers as "customers" of workforce services and viewing service providers (such as state and local agencies, community colleges, and community-based organizations) as entities addressing their needs. (P. 8)

Indeed, materials from the Department of Labor itself describe WIA using similar language, stating that

> provisions of the Act promote individual responsibility and personal decision-making through the use of "Individual Training Accounts" which allow adult customers to "purchase" the training they determine best for them. This market-driven system will enable customers to get the skills and credentials they need to succeed in their local labor markets. (usworkforce.org/runningtext2.htm)

The Reality of WIA: Does the Rhetoric Match the Reality?

Yet WIA is not as consistent, or as seamless, in its market orientation as this rhetoric would suggest. In fact, several assumptions of a market-driven model are violated under WIA. In the following section of this article, we utilize data from community colleges, one-stop career centers, and state policy makers to examine whether the implementation of WIA reflects a consistent market philosophy that honors students, as well as the business sector, as legitimate customers.

The data presented in this article are a subset of a larger data set that was collected as part of a research project funded by the Atlantic Philanthropic Foundation, the Russell Sage Foundation, and the Annie E. Casey Foundation. The purpose of the research project is to examine the ways in which community colleges have responded to welfare reform and WIA, particularly with regard to maintaining access to education for low-income populations. We have collected data in six states whose responses to these policies vary—Florida, Illinois, Pennsylvania, Massachusetts, Washington, and Rhode Island. Within each state, we have examined responses to these policies in two to three community colleges.

Reporting requirements are so onerous to some community colleges that they reduce or eliminate the ability of colleges to participate in WIA.

In conducting our study, we utilized a nested comparative case study design, which is based on the methodological thinking of Ragin, Becker, and others (Ragin 1989; Ragin and Becker 1992) that explores ways in which comparative case study methods can be used to examine complex social phenomena. Our goal was to develop a pool of data that would allow us to do meaningful comparisons of the effects of these policies across different state and institutional contexts.

Data were collected at several different levels using a mixed-methods case study design. First, we interviewed a total of 110 state-level bureaucrats in relevant departments (e.g., Education, Human Services, Employment and Training) and analyzed formal policy development and implementation utilizing existing policy documents, policy analyses provided by a number of policy research houses as well as the agencies themselves. Next, we identified three community colleges in each of the six states and interviewed a total of ninety-six faculty members and administrators. We also conducted interviews and focus groups with groups of low-income workers such as welfare recipients and WIA clients. Finally, we interviewed thirteen welfare and WIA caseworkers. In addition, we have collected an extensive amount of secondary data regarding the implementation and outcomes of both policies, including state-issued enrollment data, reports by research houses and advocacy organizations, and reports generated by individual community colleges. In all, our data will allow us to paint a detailed and comprehensive picture of how community colleges are responding to welfare reform and WIA and, in particular, to discern how these policies are affecting the ways in which they provide education and training to low-income workers. In this article, we utilize data from Illinois, Florida, and Rhode Island to provide examples of the ways in which community colleges are responding to a variety of market-driven pressures.

It is important to note that market-based, competitive models of federal and state educational policy exert their influences in varied ways. The relationship between workforce development and WIA is complicated in these states, and each of them exerts certain types of market pressure on community colleges. It is beyond the scope of this article to provide a systematic, comparative analysis of the implementation of WIA across these states. Rather, we utilize our data to untangle the effects of these admittedly entwined factors and to illustrate how several aspects of WIA and workforce development affect access to education and training for low-income workers.

The Effects of the Work-First Philosophy: Barriers at One-Stop Career Centers

As the Aspen Institute, the Workforce Alliance, and others have pointed out, recent federal public policy has been increasingly focused on getting unemployed individuals into the employment sector as quickly as possible. Work of any kind, rather than education and/or training, is seen as the most efficient solution to the needs of both the employment sector and the unemployed worker (Aspen Institute 2002, 1; Workforce Alliance 2002, 1). WIA is no exception. As the Department of Labor indicates, WIA offers three levels of service. At the most basic level, core services are available in the form of access to computers, assistance in filing unemployment insurance claims, or assistance with job search and placement. Intensive services are available to adults who cannot obtain employment through core services and include assessment of skill levels, counseling, and development of an individualized employment plan. Training services, the top layer of services, are relatively rare and are available only to those individuals who have not obtained employment via core or intensive services. Thus, access to training is greatly restricted by virtue of the hierarchy of services available to WIA clients. Moreover, according to the Department of Labor, "Training services must be directly linked to occupations in demand in the local area or in another area to which the participant is willing to move." Thus, in important ways, the work-first philosophy that drives the development of this hierarchy of services is a critical violation of free-market models of education because it restricts access to education. Customers, at least in the form of students, are not freely able to choose whether and how they will approach education and training. Rather, the hand of the state—in this instance, one-stop caseworkers—determines whether WIA clients will have access to education.

We see this phenomenon in play in a number of our states, as colleges report a significant decrease in enrollment as a result of WIA. For example, in Illinois, the ideology of rapid labor force attachment was so clearly received by caseworkers at one-stop career centers that very few individuals received ITAs during the initial years of implementation. According to a director of truck driver training (a short-term training program appropriate for many WIA clients) at an Illinois community college, the college experienced a large decline in the number of clients served when the transition from JTPA to WIA occurred. He said,

> We had a very small number of folks that came through WIA. We had a great pool of people that should have been coming through WIA; I was interviewing people every day that were qualified. But they would not send them, they would not fund them.

His impression was confirmed by a one-stop career center employee, who said,

> You have to go through core and intensive services before you ever get to training services. I've been in meetings where it has actually been stated that nobody is ever going to get to training because everybody is going to get a job in core or intensive. Our clients that are going to be left as we get to the bottom of the caseload are people who have a lot of barriers they have to overcome before they can even get training. So at this point, the ITAs really aren't an option for that group of people.

It was not until the federal government began talking about rescinding unspent WIA dollars that states began to issue more ITAs. According to an Illinois caseworker interviewed shortly after rumors about the potential rescinding of funds came out,

> [Laughing] Originally when I first started, they explained that this program was a work-first type of program in that whole work-first philosophy. Just recently, within the past couple of weeks, I have been notified by my supervisors and other individuals that that's not really what they're wanting to gear this program towards and they're reviewing the policy and so forth.

Clearly, WIA employs a number of policies that prevent many WIA clients from ever setting foot on a college campus.

Accountability Measures Result in Creaming

According to the Department of Labor, WIA employs universal access to services—that is, anyone who walks through the door of a one-stop career center is eligible for services (Department of Labor 1998). However, WIA's accountability system is a major disincentive to providing universal access to services at one-stop career centers. Strictly enforced outcome measures in the form of job placement and wage rates of WIA clients encourage one-stop centers to provide services to only those clients who are most likely to produce successful outcome measures.

The result can be a phenomenon referred to as creaming. Creaming occurs when caseworkers select clients for training based on their perceived ability to complete training and find work rather than on their need for increased skills or education. Centers can and do decide which types of potential clients they will serve, as the following conversation with an employee in a Rhode Island one-stop career center revealed. He described a steady pressure to meet performance targets for wages and job placements, asserting that "the fewer of those people [low literacy] I have to deal with, the more I am ensuring that my performance will be in the higher level, the more acceptable level."

Question: So there's more outreach to [high-skilled workers]?
Answer: Yes.

The strategy used here is clearly designed to meet the performance targets by enrolling only the more advantaged customers and making quick job placements rather than sending them to training. The career center worker went on to detail the differences between what he sees as a desirable client versus an undesirable client. In describing the undesirable client, he said, "The person says, 'Yeah, I can collect for twenty-six weeks; I'll worry about it on the twenty-fourth week and go out and get a job.' That's not a motivated client."

A desirable client, on the other hand, is one who is highly motivated to get a job.

Somebody comes in and says, "I don't want to be here, I want to be working." . . . We're going to enroll you in WIA, yes. Because what do I have? I have a motivated client for which I can get an outcome. . . . Now if that sounds like creaming, it might be to an extent.

In other words, career center workers act strategically in these decisions in response to the outcomes-oriented funding formula.

This situation is exacerbated by the fact that WIA does not take into consideration the difficulties of placing high-risk clients. As another career center director in Rhode Island reported,

There is no regression model under these performance standards like there was under JTPA. Under JTPA, the more of the hard-to-serve that you served, the lower your standard of placement . . . and you looked at wages. Female was a criteria, because women get paid less. So the more females you serve, the outcome is probably going to be lower wages. So the more women you served, they gave you credit for that.

This type of consideration is not present under the current WIA policy in Rhode Island. Again, this places additional pressure on the one-stop career centers to serve the relatively easy to serve. Visits to career centers throughout our three states bear this out: the majority of WIA clients present tended to be older, white males, with a few exceptions in heavily urban areas.

We found additional evidence of creaming in Florida in response to accountability measures. Florida's twenty-four regional workforce investment boards are rated on their one-stop career center wage and placement rates in a document known as the "Red and Green Report." This report, which places each region into a positive (green) or negative (red) performance category, is quite controversial throughout the state. Workforce investment boards, in urban areas in particular, struggle to maintain good performance indicators while at the same time serving the state's most disadvantaged populations (as in Rhode Island, the JTPA regression methodology is no longer in place). In one region, the board felt intense pressure from the state to improve performance and in turn pressured the local one-stop career centers to improve their outcomes. The result was that many local career center workers, including those based at community college campuses, felt the need to cream clients—in this case, they did so by not entering those individuals into the record-keeping system whom they felt would not have good outcomes, as a dialogue with a one-stop career center caseworker revealed:

> Answer: The emphasis is placement, and we are supposed to register in the database only those people who are looking for work. Only serious job seekers, and they are looking more for quality, not quantity.
> Question: You are only supposed to register in the database serious job seekers?
> Answer: Yes, serious job seekers. Meaning that we have students because of where we're located [at a community college] that either don't have to work or they're working a job but they just come in here to look to see if there's something better.
> Question: But they don't want those people to be entered into the system in the first place?
> Answer: Because we're supposed to place one out of three people.
> Question: Oh right, it's for statistical purposes obviously.
> Answer: Yes.
> Question: So if you're entering too many into the system and you don't place all of them . . . your numbers don't look great.
> Answer: Yes.
> Question: But it's a little bit of number playing then?
> Answer: Oh well, you know, we just have to be careful who we enter because we need to be successful.

The manipulation of the numbers used to report outcomes has many obvious consequences, but perhaps most important, it affects the ability of some individuals to access WIA funds for training since those individuals never enrolled in the reporting system are not eligible for training vouchers. As these examples show, the accountability mechanisms inherent in WIA do not address the education and training needs of WIA clients, particularly those who are most disadvantaged. Thus, accountability measures functioning at the site of one-stop career centers violate the free-choice, open-access assumptions on which a market-based model of educational delivery is based.

The Effects of WIA Accountability Measures on the Community College

The assumption that WIA clients will have the capacity to choose among all qualified education and training providers that exist in a locality is proving to be false as well. In addition to the significant barriers to education and training that are erected at the career centers, an additional set of disincentives exist that make it difficult for community colleges to participate in the WIA system as training and education providers. In the case of community colleges, accountability measures once again function to restrict the ability of WIA clients to access a full range of education and training.

As was stated earlier, customer satisfaction is a primary element of WIA. Within the context of WIA training providers, customer satisfaction is measured by statistics on job placement, wages, and satisfaction measures for both students and employers. These data must be collected for every program in which even a single WIA client is enrolled, for every student enrolled in the program (not just WIA students), and for every employer who hires one of these students. These reporting requirements are so onerous to some community colleges that they reduce or eliminate the ability of colleges to participate in WIA, and they encourage community colleges to participate with only those programs that produce the best outcome measures.

A preliminary report on WIA implementation issued by Government Accounting Office (2001), as well as a recent study published by the Aspen Institute (2002), indicates that these requirements do, in fact, reduce participation in WIA among community colleges and other educational providers. Many providers that delivered education and training under JTPA are not doing so under WIA. Both reports point to what they see as excessive data reporting requirements, outcome measures that many providers believe are unfair, and a drastic reduction in the number of potential students who might enroll in these institutions via WIA. As the Government Accounting Office stated, "WIA data collection coupled with the few job seekers sent to training has, to date, resulted in training providers reducing the number of programs they offer" (p. 11). In some instances, the number of providers has been reduced by nearly half. Thus, the free choice that is a prerequisite of market-driven models of education has been seriously curtailed by burdensome reporting requirements that necessitate the construction of data collection systems that many community colleges are either unable or unwilling to develop.

We observed this effect in several community colleges across our states. While community colleges have improved relationships with employers and increased workforce development efforts over the years, they still have difficulties with WIA's requirements. A director at the Illinois Community College Board reported that the Illinois colleges harbor negative feelings about WIA. She said,

> We have worked for a year to build up understanding among the colleges about the value of WIA, and to convince them that WIA is not the ends, it is simply a means. If they thought that workforce development in the state was only going to be WIA, they would all be out of here.

As an Illinois career center worker stated,

> There aren't a lot of providers on the list [of approved vendors]. That's the complaint we hear a lot. And community colleges aren't putting all of their programs on; they're just putting a few of their programs on. And I think the reason for that is because . . . if somebody enrolls in, say, a nursing program, then the performance of everybody that's in that program will be measured because the whole ITA system is gonna be judged by their performance. It's not just the employment outcomes of the [WIA] student. It's the employment outcomes of everybody that was in that program. And, you know, a lot of those people take those classes or are in particular programs are taking them for different reasons. They may not all be taking them so they can get a job.

As this quotation illustrates, the WIA reporting requirements function in direct opposition to the broader community college mission of providing access to education for a wide array of students. In many instances, if community colleges are asked to choose between maintaining the ability to enroll the few WIA clients who actually receive ITAs and continuing to enroll a wide array of students in a wide array of programs, they will choose the latter. As a result, WIA greatly curtails the educational choice available to its clients, thereby violating another principle of a market-driven educational system.

Analyzing WIA in a Workforce Development Context

As discussed earlier in this article, there has been a growing emphasis on workforce development at community colleges. This approach to providing education envisions the business community as its primary customer; students are a distant second. This trend has occurred in part because of actions taken by states to improve their workforces and become more attentive to the needs of business in general, and because of the need for the entrepreneurial community college to sustain itself.

While workforce development preceded the implementation of WIA, WIA in many ways contributes to and advances the goals of workforce development. Thus, while it is difficult to untangle the individual effects of WIA and workforce development in certain states, it seems safe to say that when taken together, these policies have a cumulative effect on access to education for WIA clients. The following discussion of Florida and Illinois provides examples of the ways in which WIA, when combined with a strong workforce development context, can affect the mission and function of the community college.

Florida: Targeted occupations

Florida's workforce development system is among the most integrated in the nation. The state's recently enacted Workforce Innovation Act of 2000, which followed the passage of the federal WIA, merged state welfare-to-work and workforce development agencies and services. Currently, both welfare reform and WIA are administered by one agency, Workforce Florida Incorporated. This move to integrate agencies and streamline the provision of services clearly reflects the federal WIA, which called for the creation of one-stop career centers to reduce administrative hassles and implement one-line access to services.

Florida policy makers are very concerned with maintaining competition among training providers, which according to one legislator creates a "capacity for success." He elaborated: "Well, isn't that what we're in? The business of putting people to work. Isn't that our business? The business of training. The business of education. Aren't we in a business?"

Yet Florida does not provide a free-market environment in which these educational businesses can function. The market does not determine which types of education will flourish; the state does. Florida students cannot access training at a community college using WIA funds unless their chosen work is on the targeted occupations list. These lists are determined by an occupational forecasting conference that considers employment, job openings, program placement, and earnings data to determine a ranking of high-wage, high-demand occupations for each of Florida's twenty-four regions so that education and training can meet those needs. The lists are used to help identify vocational programs eligible for the state's performance-based incentive funding, and they are targeted for training by community colleges and local workforce investment boards. Therefore, if the regional labor market does not require workers for a specific job, individuals will not receive WIA dollars to be trained for it. According to a former legislative aide, the purpose of targeted occupations lists is to ensure that state and federal money is spent in ways that benefit the state economy:

> The Workforce Investment Act said, "You will have the right to choose." You can make some decisions about the career you want to get into. . . . The WIA choice issue [means] you have to fix your cost. . . . You get to decide what you want to be, say you want to be an airline pilot. . . . We don't know where you're going to get a job, and we're certainly not going to pay $25,000 to have you not get a job. The targeted occupations means our money is being put into your hands to be spent, and so we're going to put a condition on it—the condition is our workforce needs someone with those skills.

This approach to funding WIA education and training is in line with the state's increased emphasis on workforce education at community colleges in general and clearly limits the choices available to WIA clients. A dean of workforce development at one Florida community college, when asked whether there has been an increase in activity around workforce education at her school, said,

> Yes, since the state decided to fund us for those activities in a very focused way with the performance state funding. All of the new academic programs we've developed have in mind that kind of high-demand, high-wage focus.

The new programs developed by the community colleges are intended specifically to serve the needs of the high-skills/high-wages industry—businesses such as Cisco Systems and Lucent Technology. Fewer programs are created to train people for less high-tech jobs because those jobs are not on the targeted occupations list. And since they are not on the targeted list, the colleges do not receive extra funding to train people for them. The free choice that is the hallmark of a market-driven educational model is not present under WIA. Many times, the training offered is short term and nondegree because that is what is required for the targeted occupation. Since the research clearly shows higher economic returns for degree and certificate-bearing programs (Kane and Rouse 1999), the student consumer is generally not well served by the existing types of programs. Instead, the customer that benefits here is the business community, which in Florida's economy in particular sustains a demand for a supply of workers willing to work for low wages.

Illinois: The symbolic effect of WIA in the
workforce development context

In Illinois, the combination of existing workforce development efforts and the implementation of WIA appear to have transformed some community colleges from primarily transfer institutions to those that embrace workforce development as a primary mission that is equally if not more important than the academic mission. According to a career center director, at the colleges, "Business and industry services are taking an increasingly important role, and we are consciously supporting that and promoting that. . . . I think we're seeing a much more comprehensive college now."

WIA reporting requirements function in direct opposition to the broader community college mission of providing access to education for a wide array of students.

While WIA's training vouchers are not used at Illinois community colleges often enough to effect much change, individuals at several community colleges indicated that WIA has a rather strong symbolic effect. "The federal dollars, if you look at our total budget, it becomes only 6 percent, but I think the important part of the federal dollars is that it is kind of a lightning rod," said the vice president for workforce development at one college. "We can say, 'Hey, we need to do something differently, or here is a population we need to reach out to.' "

Illustrating the symbolic power that WIA can wield, the college reorganized its organizational structure, moving workforce development to a more prominent place in the hierarchy of the structure of the college. In the past, oversight of workforce development was housed in a dean's level position; since WIA, workforce development is overseen by an associate vice president of workforce development, who oversees all workforce development efforts, including degree and certificate programs, adult education and literacy, welfare-to-work programs, the business training institute, and all contract training. Enrollment trends at the college reflect this shift in emphasis: During the years following the implementation of WIA (1999 on), the college has seen an increase in the number of students in vocational and occupational skills programs (approximately 32 percent in fall 2001, up from 24 percent in 1999), although very few of them have been WIA clients. In contrast, the number of students in the general associate's degree (nontransfer) program has declined during that same period of time (from 25 percent to 14 percent).

Other aspects of WIA also appear to have increased the focus on the needs of the business community. For example, the required presence of members of the business community on the local workforce investment boards brought them into contact with community college administrators. As a result, business representatives have attempted to impress on the community colleges their need for more certificate and short-term training—a need most often met in Illinois by private training providers. Thus, the colleges are aware that either they can meet the needs of local industry to gain more students or local industry will continue to ignore them. As one business leader in Illinois put it, "I have no pressing need to work with community colleges."

Discussion and Implications

WIA is being implemented within the context of a broader, business-friendly workforce development environment in the community college. While our data are far from conclusive on this point, our research certainly suggests that the employment sector has emerged as the primary customer of WIA and of community colleges in general. Moreover, this fact creates systematic and chronic tension with the free-market, consumer-driven rhetoric that describes WIA in official federal- and state-level documents, ensuring that there is considerable distance between the free-market rhetoric of WIA and its implementation on the ground.

In this article, we have identified several mechanisms through which this orientation plays out in the implementation of WIA and results in a reduction in educational access. First, the work-first philosophy creates a number of barriers to education and training, resulting in a sharp decrease in both the quantity and the quality of education and training available to WIA clients. Moreover, WIA's accountability measures focus on job placement and earnings, resulting in pressure for one-stop career centers to cream their clients and enroll only those clients who are likely to produce positive results on these outcome measures. WIA's accountability measures have negative effects on community colleges as well. Because all approved educational vendors must collect extensive outcome data, many community colleges have opted out of the WIA system either due to lack of resources needed to collect the data or because the outcome measures are viewed as unfair.

When examining WIA within the broader context of a workforce development environment, we have uncovered additional implementation factors that can affect access to education. In some states, tying WIA funding to targeted occupation lists greatly reduces clients' choice of education. And in other states, the mere presence of WIA seems to have a symbolic effect, moving community colleges closer to a workforce-centered philosophy than they might have been otherwise.

Despite the rhetoric that suggests that WIA is a market-driven policy fueled by the needs of both WIA clients and the business sector, our analysis clearly shows that several assumptions of a market-driven educational policy are violated in both the design and the implementation of this policy. This is true because several elements of the formal policy undercut free-market philosophy. The work-first approach to providing services to WIA clients reduces their access to education and training of any type, and accountability measures limit the types of clients who will receive education, as well as the type of education they will receive. In fact, WIA does possess the two elements of what is generally considered a market-driven educational model—that is, an emphasis on the customer and the provision of information so that customers can make informed choices. However, accountability structures designed to provide this information actually work at cross-purposes, undercutting the ability and the willingness of both one-stop career centers and community colleges to serve the needs of at least one of their primary customers—WIA clients. Under this model, institutional autonomy is constrained rather than increased, and the competition that is supposed to lead to an improvement in quality according to the market model is reduced.

The free choice that is the hallmark of a market-driven educational model is not present under WIA.

Moreover, the policy reflects and exists within an environment that clearly favors the needs of one particular customer—the business community. However, there are elements of WIA that thwart the influence of the business community as well. Again, the presence of what are broadly perceived to be onerous reporting requirements discourage community colleges from offering a wide array of education and training options to WIA clients. As a result, the training needs of the business community may not be fully met either.

What effects do such factors have on access to education and training, especially for disadvantaged populations? Some of our data help us to begin to answer that question. Clearly, the educational options available to the other named customer of the policy—that is, WIA clients—are being diminished in significant ways. Operating in a business-friendly, workforce-development context, WIA strongly encourages both one-stop career centers and community colleges to pay very close attention to ensuring that they can achieve success as measured by specific outcome measures. Since most times, the outcomes are employment and earnings measures and because barriers to employment and earnings are not taken into account, there is a pervasive and significant incentive to serve only those who have the most likelihood of succeeding. Barriers to access exist both at the entry point to WIA, the one-stop career centers, and at community colleges as well. As a result, the hardest to serve—that is, those with low literacy rates, spotty employment histories, women (especially those with young children), even the handicapped—may not receive the same kind of access to education and training as do the more advantaged. Because our data are descriptive of the implementation of these policies and it is too early to thoroughly assess the comprehensive impact of WIA on enrollment, we do not have the ability to say with certainty that this policy is having an adverse effect on access to education for the disadvantaged. But there are clear signs pointing in that direction that require careful attention.

It is important to point out that the type of education available to WIA clients is shifting as well. There is nothing inherently wrong with developing education and training programs designed to address the needs of the labor market; community colleges have been doing so for years and in fact have prided themselves on their close connection to the business world. However, when the only education available to WIA clients is that which suits the needs of local employers, student choice will be severely constricted despite the free-market philosophy that would, in theory, provide the customer with more choices rather than fewer. And again, it is important to note that this lack of flexibility has the most serious ramifications for those students who most need flexibility—students with young children, transportation barriers, or remedial educational needs. The free choice that is the hallmark of a market-driven educational model is not present under WIA, at least for WIA clients.

Conclusion

Despite the rhetoric that surrounds WIA, it is difficult to characterize this piece of federal policy as market driven, except insofar as it encourages community colleges to respond to the needs of one particular customer, the business community. As community colleges face increased pressures from multiple sources to become more business focused, it will continue to be important to develop a better understanding of how these institutions respond to local, state, and federal factors affecting the training and education available to all WIA clients, particularly high-risk clients. Our data suggest that, overall, as the ties between community colleges and the business sector have tightened, the influence of the workforce development model has increased. Business-friendly training and education has increased as access to credit-bearing, degree-granting education has decreased, as has the autonomy of many who seek education and training in general. Although it is still early in the life of WIA, our analyses suggest that the market-driven, customer-focused rhetoric that surrounds WIA is not reflected in either the details of formal policy or the implementation of the policy.

References

Alfred, Richard, and Patricia Carter. 2002. *Contradictory colleges: Thriving in an era of continuous change*. Washington, DC: American Association of Community Colleges.

Aspen Institute. 2002. *Measuring up and weighing in: Industry-based workforce development training results in strong employment outcomes*. Washington, DC: Aspen Institute.

Bailey, T. R., and I. E. Averianova. 1999. *Multiple missions of community colleges: Conflicting or Complementary?* Community College Research Center brief. New York: Teachers College, Columbia University.

Barnow, Burt S., and Christopher T. King. 2001. Publicly funded training in a changing labor market. In *Improving the odds: Increasing the effectiveness of publicly funded training*, edited by Burt S. Barnow and Christopher T. King. Washington, DC: Urban Institute.

Burke, Joseph C., and Henrik Minassians. 2001. *Linking state resources to campus results: From fad to trend. The fifth annual survey*. New York: Nelson A. Rockefeller Institute of Government.

Cohen, A., and F. Brawer. 1996. *The American community college*. 3d ed. San Francisco: Jossey-Bass.

Cohen, Arthur. 2000. Governmental policies affecting community colleges: A historical perspective. In *Community colleges: Policy in the future context*, edited by Barbara K. Townsend and Susan B. Twombly, 3-22. Westport, CT: Ablex.

Department of Labor. 1998. Key features of the Workforce Investment Act as compared to current law. Available from http://usworkforce.org/archive/sideby810.htm.

———. 2002. The Workforce Investment Act. Available from www.doleta.gov/usworkforce.

Dougherty, K., and M. Bakia. 2000a. Community colleges and contract training: Content, origins, and impact. *Teachers College Record* 102 (1): 197-243.

———. 2000b. *The new economic development role of the community college*. Community College Research Center brief no. 6. New York: Teachers College, Columbia University.

Dougherty, Kevin J. 1994. *The contradictory college: The conflicting origins, impacts and futures of the community college*. Albany: State University of New York Press.

Government Accounting Office. 2001. *Workforce Investment Act: New requirements create need for more guidance*. Statement of Sigurd R. Nelson, director, Education, Workforce, and Income Security Issues, GAO-02 94T. Washington, DC: Government Accounting Office.

Gross, Steven Jay, Kathleen M. Shaw, and Joan Shapiro. 2002. Deconstructing accountability through the lens of democratic philosophies: Toward a new analytic framework. *Journal of Research for Education Leaders*.

Grubb, W. N., N. Bawdy, D. Bell, D. Bragg, and M. Russian. 1997. *Workforce, economic and community development: The changing landscape of the "entrepreneurial" community college*. MDS-1094. Berkeley, CA: National Center for Research in Vocational Education.

Kane, Thomas J., and Cecilia E. Rouse. 1999. The community college: Training students at the margin between college and work. *Journal of Economic Perspectives* 13 (1): 63-84.

Levin, John S. 2001. *Globalizing the community college*. New York: Palgrave Macmillan.

National Council of Instructional Administrators. 2002. *Reframing the conversation about student success*. Washington, DC: National Council of Instructional Administrators.

National Policy Center on Higher Education. 2000. *Measuring up 2000*. Denver, CO: National Policy Center on Higher Education.

Public/Private Ventures. 2001. *States of change: Policies and programs to promote low-wage workers' steady employment and advancement*. Philadelphia: Public/Private Ventures.

Ragin, Charles C. 1989. *The comparative method: Moving beyond qualitative and quantitative strategies*. Berkeley: University of California Press.

Ragin, Charles C., and Howard S. Becker, eds. 1992. *What is a case? Exploring the foundations of social inquiry*. New York: Cambridge University Press.

State Higher Education Executive Officers. 1998. *State Survey on Performance Measures 1996-1997*. Denver, CO: State Higher Education Executive Officers.

Workforce Alliance. 2002. *Comment on Workforce Investment Act reauthorization submitted to the Employment and Training Administration, U.S. Department of Labor*. Washington, DC: Workforce Alliance.

Welfare Reform and Enrollment in Postsecondary Education

By
JERRY A. JACOBS
and
SARAH WINSLOW

Temporary Aid to Needy Families (TANF) has dramatically decreased welfare rolls, but has it reduced the college attendance rate of welfare recipients or limited the college enrollment of those who might have been on welfare without this policy change? The authors examine whether the work-first emphasis of welfare reform has reduced postsecondary education enrollment, principally in community colleges. Second, they consider whether welfare reform has increased enrollment in short-term, noncredit programs at the expense of degree-granting curricula. Third, they assess whether states with more restrictive formal policies regarding higher education have lower enrollment of welfare recipients than those with less restrictive policies. Finally, they examine whether welfare reform has affected the enrollment rates of young single mothers who might have been on welfare in the absence of TANF. They review enrollment data from a variety of sources and present original analyses of data on postsecondary enrollment patterns from multiple national data sets.

Keywords: welfare reform; Temporary Aid to Needy Families (TANF); postsecondary education enrollment

W elfare reform has been remarkably successful in reducing welfare rolls, far more successful than either supporters or critics expected. As a result, the current work-first approach enjoys broad political support.[1] But the reality of reform for those who have left wel-

Jerry A. Jacobs is Merriam Term Professor of Sociology at the University of Pennsylvania. He has written extensively on opportunities for working women during the past two decades. His research has addressed a number of aspects of women's employment, including authority, earnings, working conditions, part-time work, and entry into male-dominated occupations. His book on working time and work-family conflict, The Time Divide: Work, Family and Policy Post-Industrial America, *with Kathleen Gerson, will be published in 2004 by Harvard University Press. He is also working on a study of women in higher education as both students and faculty.*

Sarah Winslow is a Ph.D. candidate in sociology at the University of Pennsylvania. Her research interests focus on gender, the life course, and the intersection of work

DOI: 10.1177/0002716202250224

fare and those who remain on the rolls is much more complex. Academic and policy researchers have raised many concerns about both the short-term and the long-term consequences of welfare reform. Some welfare recipients have obtained jobs but have not kept them. Many are not better off financially after taking low-wage jobs, once the costs of child care, commuting, and health insurance are taken into account (Hays 2003; Peterson, Song, and Jones-DeWeever 2002; Brauner and Loprest 1999; Loprest 1999; U.S. General Accounting Office 1999; U.S. Department of Health and Human Services 1999). And the long-term consequences remain far from clear. Even now, the five-year cumulative time limits have not been reached in many localities, or they have not yet been enforced. Consequently, studies have yet to fully document how welfare recipients will fare during the current economic downturn.

Moreover, the long-term well-being of welfare mothers depends on their gaining the basic education and employment-related skills needed to obtain jobs that pay a sustaining wage. Yet, as we discuss below, recent policy reforms have limited the chances of welfare mothers to pursue higher education. As a result, welfare reform may have the effect of reducing the chances of welfare mothers to obtain a secure foothold in the mainstream of American society.

This article examines the impact of welfare reform on access to higher education. We will assess the impact of welfare reform on college enrollment, for both welfare recipients and other poor single mothers. We examine enrollment by the type of program—short term and noncredit versus degree granting—as well as the overall extent of participation in postsecondary education. The majority of welfare recipients who are enrolled in higher education attend community colleges, as we will see in more detail below.

The article is organized as follows. In the next section, we explain how the current welfare system has restricted access to higher education. Next, we review the available information on enrollment in higher education, pre-reform and post-reform. We proceed to explain how the Temporary Assistance for Needy Families (TANF) regulations adopted in 1999 allow a surprising degree of flexibility on the part of states in their approach to higher education.[2] We review variations in policies among states, which raises the question of whether welfare recipients in some states have more access to higher education than welfare recipients in other states. Then, we present longitudinal analyses of data from the Current Population Surveys (CPS), the National Household Education Surveys (NHES), and the National Postsecondary Student Aid Surveys (NPSAS). This report is one facet of a broader study of welfare reform and higher education that involved case studies of welfare reform and community colleges in six states. See Mazzeo, Rab, and Eachus (2003 [this issue]) and Shaw and Rab (2003 [this issue]) for more detail on the case-study components of this project.

and family. She has written about trends in work-family conflict from the 1970s through the 1990s and is currently working on a study of faculty working time. Her dissertation examines the work and family patterns of couples from both a historical and a contemporary perspective, with special attention to the impact of these decisions on individual well-being and marital stability.

Welfare Reform and Barriers to Enrollment in Higher Education

The 1996 Personal Responsibility and Work Opportunity Reconciliation Act (PRWORA) ended the federal guarantee of support for needy families and imposed time limits on the receipt of welfare. This act also replaced Aid to Families with Dependent Children (AFDC) with TANF block grants to states. To qualify for full TANF support, states had to demonstrate that 35 percent of welfare recipients worked in fiscal year 1999, a figure that gradually rose to 50 percent by fiscal year 2002. Under these new laws, states must place an increasing proportion of their welfare caseloads in work activities to avoid financial penalties. Moreover, beginning in the year 2000, a single mother must work at least thirty hours a week to be officially counted as an individual engaged in work activities (Cohen 1998).

This new system of welfare provision does not expressly forbid states from allowing welfare recipients to pursue postsecondary education. However, it does include a number of regulations that discourage states from enrolling recipients in college, in degree-granting programs in particular. First, the legislation encourages a work-first approach to moving welfare recipients off the rolls. In many cases, welfare recipients may be eligible for education and training services only after they have failed to find a job during a specified search period (Mazzeo, Rab, and Eachus 2003). Second, TANF caps enrollment in school at 30 percent of recipients. Third, this education cap may include those seeking to complete high school or obtain a General Equivalency Diploma, thereby further limiting the number of those seeking to enroll in higher education. And finally, recipients enrolled in postsecondary education for longer than a twelve-month period are, for the most part, excluded from a state's calculation of its work participation rates (Greenberg, Strawn, and Plimpton 1999). When taken together, these disincentives can greatly reduce welfare recipients' access to meaningful postsecondary education.

The Center for Law and Social Policy (CLASP) analysis suggests that states have cut educational opportunities much further than federal legislation requires, a theme we discuss in greater detail below. However, whether it is federal legislation, state and local implementation, or simply the overzealous commitment of caseworkers to the work-first ideology, many welfare recipients have been closed out of or otherwise steered away from schooling that had been promoted by the Job Opportunities and Basic Skills initiative of the late 1980s and early 1990s and other programs.

Enrollment of Welfare Recipients in Community Colleges, Pre- and Post-PRWORA

Data on whether PRWORA has reduced the overall enrollment of welfare recipients in postsecondary education remain spotty. Available data at all levels—national, state, and institutional—have serious limitations. Nonetheless, when taken together, these data suggest that there has been a decline in the enrollment of welfare recipients in degree-based programs throughout higher education. Below, we briefly review the available data and their limitations and outline new analyses that can add to our understanding of this trend.

National data. Five years after the PRWORA legislation became effective, there was a 56 percent decrease in the number of TANF recipients (U.S. Department of Health and Human Services 2002). Thus, the number of welfare recipients enrolled in higher education can be expected to decline because of the shrinking welfare rolls. Consequently, it is important to distinguish between a declining enrollment rate of recipients and a steady rate that produces declining numbers. It is also important to know at what rate former recipients are pursuing schooling.

The federal government did not collect specific data on the number of welfare recipients enrolled in community colleges and other institutions of higher education prior to welfare reform, and it does not collect such data now. Selected information regarding participation in broad activities related to postsecondary education is available for years preceding the adoption of PRWORA. However, federal data on the enrollment of welfare recipients in postsecondary education are not available since the enactment of PRWORA because it is not an approved work activity and thus is not a reporting category.

Available data suggest that about 136,000 welfare recipients were enrolled in higher education through the Job Opportunities and Basic Skills program in 1995. In contrast, post-PRWORA data indicate that only 54,000 recipients are engaged in any type of activity that could include postsecondary education. Comparing these two data sources implies a two-thirds reduction (or 100,000 people) in the enrollment of welfare recipients in higher education.[3] Furthermore, analysis of data from the Urban Institute's National Survey of American Families reveals that in 1996, when PRWORA was passed, high school graduates who were recipients of AFDC were 13 percent more likely to pursue postsecondary education than were other women (Cox and Spriggs 2002). Less than two years after the implementation of TANF, welfare recipients were 7 percent less likely than other poor women to go to college.

One other indicator of enrollment trends is data from financial aid applications. Between 1996-97 and 1998-99, the number of applicants for Title IV Student Aid who reported receiving AFDC/TANF benefits fell from 580,000 to 359,000, a 38 percent decline. In the same time frame, the overall number of student aid applicants increased from 9.3 million to 9.6 million (Friedman 1999). This is not a perfect indicator of enrollment, since not all those who enroll apply for aid and not all those who applied for aid enrolled.[4] Nonetheless, the trend line for this indicator is down, and its slope is remarkably steep. We explore this issue further below in original analyses of the 1996 and 2000 NPSAS, which allow us to consider what type of programs students are enrolled in.

Drawing on data from the Survey of Income and Program Participation, Peterson, Song, and Jones-DeWeever (2002) reported that the proportion of low-income single parents with some college education declined after the implementation of TANF, particularly among welfare recipients (from 24 percent to 17 percent). This finding suggests that the most educated welfare recipients were the most likely to leave the welfare rolls, but Peterson, Song, and Jones-DeWeever also maintain that it is consistent with the fact that welfare recipients have limited access to higher education.

State-level data. We also examined available state reports of enrollment of welfare recipients in community colleges pre- and post-PRWORA. Although the data are not comprehensive, they are consistent with national data suggesting a reduction in enrollment in postsecondary education among welfare recipients since 1996.

The results indicate that those states that allow postsecondary enrollment as an approved work activity for welfare recipients have higher enrollment rates than those states that do not allow enrollment.

For example, a 1999 General Accounting Office report based on data from seven states revealed a decline in the percentage of welfare recipients enrolled in higher education. In California, the enrollment rate dropped from 77 percent in 1994 to 53 percent in 1997; Maryland reported a drop from 65 percent to 11 percent; and Texas recorded a drop from 75 percent to 36 percent during the same time period. In Cuyahoga County, Ohio, the percentage of adults participating in welfare-to-work activities who were enrolled in postsecondary education fell from 49 percent in 1993-1994 to 9 percent in 1999-2000 (Brock, Nelson, and Reiter 2002). The Institute for Women's Policy Research (1998) reported that the Massachusetts Community College system experienced a decrease in welfare recipient enrollment of 47 percent from 1994 to 1997.

The available statistics in the six states we studied in depth all indicate low levels of enrollment of welfare recipients in postsecondary education. Official Massachusetts data indicate that 9.1 percent of welfare recipients were enrolled in postsecondary education (including basic education and skills training in addition to two-year and four-year colleges) in 2001, but less than 2 percent were enrolled in degree-granting programs. Illinois data indicate that only 3.5 percent of welfare recipients were enrolled in postsecondary education in 2001 (see Mazzeo, Rab, and Eachus 2003). Furthermore, the number of Illinois welfare recipients pursuing associate's degrees dropped from 4,430 in 1995 to 1,831 in 1998 (Applied Research Center 2001). Florida statistics are reported by the year that recipients first received welfare. The data indicate very low levels of enrollment of welfare recipients and a dropoff between the AFDC and TANF periods. In 2000, 7 percent of recipients who began AFDC in 1995-1996 were enrolled in postsecondary education, while only 3 percent of TANF recipients who became recipients after 1996 were enrolled (Florida Education and Training Placement Information Program 2001). In Pennsylvania, 6 percent of welfare recipients are enrolled in postsecondary education (Pennsylvania Office of Income Maintenance 2002). Washington State is the only state in our study that showed a trend toward more education. The enrollment rate of welfare recipients increased from 5.3 percent in 1998 to 10.1 percent in 2001 (Washington State Department of Social and Health Services 2002).

Institutional-level data. Data on TANF recipient enrollment in individual community colleges are scarce and largely anecdotal; two-thirds do not track students on public assistance (American Association of Community Colleges 1999). Yet the Institute for Women's Policy Research reports consistent decreases in enrollment in institutions that do collect data on welfare recipients. Baltimore City Community College experienced a 29 percent decrease from 1996 to 1997, City University of New York reported a decrease from 27,000 to 5,000 between 1995 and 2000, and at Milwaukee Area Technical College, enrollment of students on welfare dropped from 1,600 to 250 (Cox and Spriggs 2002; Pierre 1997).

Even for those few welfare recipients who are actually receiving some type of postsecondary education, both the quantity and quality of this educative experience have considerably shifted in response to the new federal legislation. This is true despite the fact that short-term training does not serve the long-term educational needs of this population. There can be little doubt that many welfare recipients lack the basic education and skills needed to succeed in the job market. One study (Carnevale and Desrochers 1999) found that 31 percent of welfare recipients lack the basic skills needed to attain a job that offers a living wage and that the other two-thirds would benefit from additional skills and educational credentials as well.

Research on welfare recipients shows that postsecondary education significantly increases earning potential. In a study of 4,500 working mothers, Spalter-Roth et al. (1995) found that more education increases both the hourly wages of welfare recipients and the chances of leaving welfare. Moreover, women receiving welfare who achieved a bachelor's degree are far more likely to be employed ten years after graduation than women who did not receive a degree (Gittell, Schehl, and Fareri 1990). And a 1997 survey of AFDC recipients in Maine revealed that as the level of formal education increases, so too does the percentage of women employed and their median hourly wage. Whereas only 20 percent of those with a high school diploma or General Equivalency Diploma were employed, 89 percent of those with a bachelor's degree had found work (Seguino and Butler 1998).

We also know that teenage mothers often return to school, not just for a period of weeks or months. Over a period of years, they can accumulate a substantial amount of schooling. For example, the cumulative educational experiences of Frank Furstenberg's sample of Baltimore teenage mothers is truly astonishing (Jacobs and Rich 1998). In 1970, several years after giving birth as teenagers, nearly three-quarters of this group had still not completed high school, and few had enrolled in college. By 1995, a full 80 percent had completed high school, more than one-third had enrolled in college, and 10 percent had completed college. Data of this sort suggest the desirability of encouraging long-term investment in schooling rather than channeling welfare mothers into eight- or twelve-week job search sessions. Lavin's (2001) thirty-year follow-up of students enrolled in the City University of New York in 1970 also documents significant additional schooling completed years and even decades after initial entry into college.

Evolving TANF Regulations

It is important to note that federal regulations with regard to PRWORA change often, particularly at the state level. When PRWORA was originally enacted in 1996, many of the details of the regulations regarding postsecondary education were unspecified, but analysts were in agreement that TANF would place harsh restrictions on welfare recipients' access to postsecondary education. Yet the final regulations issued by the Department of Health and Human Services in April of 1999 were not as harsh or as uniform as was previously anticipated. In fact, a state wishing to use both TANF and its own maintenance-of-effort funds to support the participation of low-income parents in postsecondary education may do so.

States also can provide access to college in a number of ways. For example, while recipients must be "engaged in work" after twenty-four months of receiving assistance, it is "entirely permissible for a state to count participation in postsecondary education (or other education or training activities) as being engaged in work" (Greenberg, Strawn, and Plimpton 1999, 1). This is because the final regulations leave the interpretation of work activities to the states.

States also have leeway to promote education, even without defining education as work, because states have far exceeded their participation-rate requirements, as Greenberg, Strawn, and Plimpton (1999) noted. PRWORA reduced the work requirements for those states with sharp declines in welfare rolls. Since most states have experienced dramatic declines in the number of welfare recipients, no state is in jeopardy of reductions in federal support levels. A final consideration is that the sharp decline in welfare rolls has left many states with considerable unspent funds targeted specifically for welfare programs. Consequently, advocates for the educational option maintain that states have the freedom to promote education for welfare recipients.

The CLASP analysis of the final TANF regulations suggests that states may support access to postsecondary education in a variety of ways (Greenberg, Strawn, and Plimpton 1999). Among them are the following:

- A state may decide to define postsecondary education as a work activity for the purposes of meeting the twenty-four-month requirement.
- A state can structure its policies so that months in which a parent participates in postsecondary education do not count against the sixty-month total time limit for assistance imposed by the federal government.
- A state can use TANF funds to provide support for postsecondary education by, for example, funding work study, child care, or transportation benefits that would enable recipients to attend college.
- A state can fund a parallel but separate state program for needy families that provides access to higher education, using its required matching maintenance-of-effort funds, without facing an elevated risk of TANF penalties.
- A state may allow TANF recipients to engage in postsecondary education regardless of whether the activities count toward participation rates, so long as the state meets the overall federal participation rate standards.

Yet, while these new regulations substantially expand the possibilities for fitting degree-based higher education under the rubric of welfare reform, policy variations across states will persist or even increase. These variations may be due to a variety of factors, including newfound flexibility in federal regulations, state legislative philosophy regarding welfare recipients, budgetary considerations, and the ability and willingness of individual community colleges to respond to the new regulations in innovative and creative ways. Below, we provide a brief overview of the variations in response to TANF across states.

State-Level Responses to TANF

Despite the overall reduction of welfare recipients' access to degree-granting postsecondary education that has resulted from PRWORA, states have wide latitude in the ways in which they respond to the federal TANF regulations. Moreover, strategies to accommodate these regulations continue to develop as new regulations are written and new legislation is introduced, at both the national and the state level. The variation that has resulted is critically important because we can both document the range of policies in place and ultimately track their effect on women's access to degree-granting postsecondary education and their success on the labor market. In fact, Cox and Spriggs (2002) found that state policies account for 13 percent of the post-TANF reduction in the probability of college enrollment among welfare recipients relative to other low-income women. Below, we provide a brief overview of variations in access to postsecondary education for welfare recipients at the state level.

Analyses of state-level policies regarding access to postsecondary education for welfare recipients indicate a great deal of variation regarding the degree and type of support offered to this population. The CLASP data suggest that states' level of support for access to postsecondary education falls into two basic divisions—allowance and time limits—each containing three basic categories. On the low end of the allowance scale are those states that offer little or no incentives or support for welfare recipients to obtain degree-granting postsecondary education.[5] This category includes eight states that do not count postsecondary education as an activity that satisfies work requirements;[6] moreover, they provide no additional support to help those electing to pursue postsecondary education, such as the provision of child care or transportation. Occupying the middle allowance category are twenty-five states that allow participation in a two-year degree program to satisfy work requirements as long as this educational activity is combined with some work. At the high end of the allowance scale are fourteen states that allow participation in a two-year degree program as a stand-alone work activity. The remaining four states have educational allowance policies that are set on a county-by-county basis. See Appendix A for the listing of the states that fall into each of these categories.

Young single mothers, some of whom might have been welfare recipients in the absence of policy changes that significantly reduced welfare rolls, are falling behind relative to other women in accessing postsecondary education.

In addition to allowance policies, states can be classified according to the length of time welfare recipients can participate in approved educational activities. At the low end of this scale are eleven states that allow postsecondary education to count toward the work requirement for just twelve months. Seventeen states have a time limit ranging from twelve to thirty-six months; these states occupy our middle time limit category. Finally, the high end of the time scale is occupied by thirteen states that place no time limit on participation in postsecondary education. The remaining states have no time limit classification because they do not allow any participation in postsecondary education. See Appendix B for the listing of states with respect to educational time limits.

Clearly, there is considerable variation in the ways in which states and institutions are responding to TANF regulations. This variability was evident in the six states included in our study. Rhode Island's relatively liberal welfare policies have resulted in strong and proactive involvement in maintaining access to postsecondary education on the part of the Community College of Rhode Island. In contrast, the state of Massachusetts will fund programs for welfare recipients in community colleges only if these institutions agree to track employment placement for participants. Individual community colleges vary in their response to these provisions, and so participation across institutions is inconsistent. The state of Illinois instituted a "stop the clock" provision for welfare recipients enrolled in postsecondary education, but the implementation of this policy has been spotty; the state of Washington's initial attempt to sharply restrict postsecondary education opportunity has softened in the past several years, and enrollment levels appear to be increasing. Clearly, at both the state and institutional level, variability is an important theme. This is consistent with the broader emphasis on devolution that has emerged at the federal level and is designed to provide more autonomy to state and local actors in the implementation of policy while maintaining rigid outcome requirements.

A Statistical Analysis of Enrollment Trends

Variations among states are important to understand if we want to know how welfare reform is working. To this end, this section of the article will assess the impact of welfare reform on the enrollment of current recipients and those demographically similar to them. Specifically, we seek to determine the trends in postsecondary enrollment of current and potential welfare recipients. We also examine whether welfare recipients in states with more generous policies are more likely to enroll in higher education than are those who live in states with more restrictive policies.

Despite the lack of uniformity, the available data consistently suggest that PRWORA has resulted in significant reductions in the number of welfare recipients enrolled in community colleges. But this provides only one piece of the puzzle. It is also important to assess whether former welfare recipients, and single mothers in general, are enrolling at steady or declining rates. To estimate an enrollment rate, we need data on those who are not enrolled in college as well as those who are enrolled.

To better understand the impact of welfare reform on trends in enrollment in higher education, we analyze data from several sources. Our first source of data is the Current Popular Survey. The CPS is a large and consistent data source that can be used to track enrollment trends. Our sample includes slightly less than 9,000 respondents in 1995 and slightly less than 8,000 respondents in 2000. By comparing enrollments in 1995 and 2000, we can ascertain what the impact of TANF has been on enrollments. The CPSs also allow us to examine the enrollment patterns of young single mothers in addition to welfare recipients. Finally, the CPS samples are large enough to allow us to examine variations across states.

The October CPS series has more detailed information on schooling patterns but unfortunately does not include information on family receipt of government programs. The March CPS data have more information on earnings and program receipt but less detail on schooling. Another important limitation of the March CPS data is that the school enrollment question is only asked of respondents aged twenty-four and younger. While this group of young welfare recipients is an important one, and includes the age group most likely to attend higher education, we sought additional data to examine enrollment trends across a wider age spectrum.

The National Household Education Surveys (NHES) were designed to track enrollment patterns for adult learners as well as for traditional-aged college students. NHES was administered in 1995 and 1999 and thus provides enrollment data pre- and post-TANF. Slightly less than 11,000 respondents were surveyed in 1995 and slightly less than 4,000 were surveyed in 1999. Unfortunately, the public-access data that we analyzed do not include state-level codes, and thus we were not able to examine the impact of state-by-state variation in access to higher education. In addition, the NHES data do not include a direct measure of parental status and thus are not ideal for examining the enrollment patterns of single mothers.[7] Nonetheless, we will examine these data to corroborate the results of the CPS and to examine whether the patterns differ among those older than twenty-four.

Our analysis proceeds as follows. We begin by comparing the enrollment rates of welfare recipients as well as nonrecipients before welfare reform (1995) and after welfare reform (2000) using the CPS data. We then conduct a multivariate regression analysis to assess the impact of welfare receipt and other factors on enrollment. Since enrollment is a discrete (0, 1) outcome, we estimate logistic regression models. We conducted the analyses separately for the before and after years and test for statistically significant changes between the years. We replicated the CPS results with the NHES data.

Individual-level factors include age (broken into the following categories: sixteen to eighteen, nineteen to twenty, twenty-one to twenty-two, and twenty-three to twenty-four, with nineteen to twenty serving as the reference category in the regression analysis), marital and parental status (single mothers, married mothers, married women without children, and single women without children, which was the reference category), and race and ethnicity (dummy variables for African American and Hispanic, with non-Hispanic white as the reference category).

We also examine the impact of state-level policy variables on enrollment rates.[8] We obtained a state-level measure of the dollar level of financial support for welfare recipients from data compiled by John Moffitt. We use the real benefit sum, which represents the maximum amount paid per month for a family of four. This total benefit is the sum of AFDC/TANF, Food Stamp, and Medicaid payments. In the regression analysis, we use the log of the benefit level, a standard statistical transformation used when income is included in multivariate models.[9]

We also constructed several variables to characterize state policies regarding access to higher education for welfare recipients. The first set of measures characterizes the status of education for welfare recipients. As noted above, in some states, education is not an approved work activity; in other states, education is allowed when combined with some work; while in still others, education is approved as a stand-alone work activity. We consequently constructed one dummy variable for those states where education may be combined with work and another for those where education is approved as a stand-alone activity. Those states where education is not an approved work activity stand as the reference category. We also include a dummy variable indicating that the policy is set at the county level for those states with decentralized policies.

A second variable was constructed for the time limits on education. States in which education is an approved work activity have leeway in setting the amount of time for which education may substitute for or complement paid work. Some states allow welfare recipients to participate in postsecondary education for twelve months, while other states have a more lengthy, yet still defined, time limit (these generally range from eighteen to thirty-six months). Still other states, used as the reference category in our analyses, do not place a limit on the length of time during which education may fulfill the work requirement. Appendices A and B display the classification of states for these two variables.

TANF has not only reduced access to higher education but also shifted enrollment to short-term, certificate programs and away from associate's degree and bachelor's degree enrollment.

The state classifications we used were based on the State Policy Documentation Project conducted by CLASP. We draw on the report issued in July 2000 that listed state policies as of October 1999. In this way, our measures of state policy correspond in time to the CPS enrollment data that we analyze.

The in-depth interviews we conducted in six states (see Mazzeo, Rab, and Eachus 2003; Shaw and Rab 2003) show that the state-level policy classification developed by CLASP does not completely correspond with the actual level of access to postsecondary education available to welfare recipients. Nonetheless, we expect that the CLASP measures should be related to enrollment patterns. In other words, a detailed, on-the-ground study in all fifty states would produce a classification scheme that would more closely match individual opportunities than that which CLASP has devised based on formal state policies. Thus, any effects we obtain will represent a lower-bound estimate of the impact of policy variation on access to higher education.

Since the National Postsecondary Student Aid Surveys (NPSAS) data only include those enrolled in school, we focus on the changing program composition rather than the enrollment rate when analyzing those data.

TABLE 1

PERCENTAGE ENROLLED IN POSTSECONDARY EDUCATION,
BY AGE AND SEX FOR HIGH SCHOOL GRADUATES

	All		Men		Women	
	1995	2000	1995	2000	1995	2000
16-18	55.26	59.73	52.71	57.16	57.49	61.60
19-20	51.91	55.63	49.41	52.19	54.16	58.86
21-22	41.61	42.85	39.69	43.83	43.41	41.89
23-24	23.38	21.96	24.08	22.89	22.68	21.02
Total (16-24)	40.42	43.60	38.83	42.37	41.91	44.77
Number of cases	8,954	7,961	4,205	3,825	4,749	4,136

SOURCE: March 1995 and 2000 Current Population Survey (annual demographic survey).

Results

CPS Data

In Table 1, we examine changes in enrollment of individuals aged sixteen to twenty-four in postsecondary education between 1995 and 2000. We restricted the data to focus only on those who had completed high school but had not yet completed college. This is the pool of potential students who are "at risk" of enrolling as undergraduates in two-year or four-year institutions. The overall enrollment rate increased during this time period, from 40.4 percent in 1995 to 43.6 percent in 2000, although this increase is not statistically significant. Women were slightly more likely to report being enrolled (44.8 percent for women vs. 42.4 percent for men) (again, this not a statistically significant difference), but the growth in enrollment during this period was similar for men (3.6 percent) and women (2.9 percent). Men and women differed in the age profile of enrollment, with women outdoing men in the younger years and men leading among older students. Until age twenty, women were roughly 5 percent more likely to be enrolled than were men, but by age twenty-three, men were slightly more likely to be enrolled than were women.

In Table 2, we examine the enrollment patterns of female welfare recipients. Welfare recipients who had graduated high school were far less likely to be enrolled in postsecondary education than were other young women. In 2000, roughly one-quarter of welfare recipients were enrolled in postsecondary education, compared with more than 40 percent of other women. These self-reports yield somewhat higher rates of enrollment than do official statistics, but this tendency to overreport should not affect the analysis of the trends over time in enrollment. The enrollment rate of welfare recipients was roughly stable during this period: 25.5 percent were enrolled in postsecondary education in 1995, and 24.5 percent were enrolled in 2000. (This change is not statistically significant in the

TABLE 2

PERCENTAGE ENROLLED IN POSTSECONDARY EDUCATION, BY AGE,
SEX, AND WELFARE RECEIPT FOR HIGH SCHOOL GRADUATES

	Women			
	Welfare Recipients 1995	Welfare Recipients 2000	Welfare Nonrecipients 1995	Welfare Nonrecipients 2000
16-18[a]	68.21	51.84	57.32	61.78
19-20	17.32	19.10	56.14	60.13
21-22	23.35	14.33	45.11	42.86
23-24	17.89	16.41	23.14	21.24
Total (16-24)	20.68	18.37	43.44	45.70

SOURCE: March 1995 and 2000 Current Population Survey (annual demographic survey).
a. Statistics for welfare recipients ages sixteen to eighteen in both 1995 and 2000 are based on very small ns because few students have both graduated from high school and become welfare recipients at these ages.

CPS data, but the NHES data presented below do reveal a statistically significant decline in enrollment among welfare recipients.)

Table 3 presents regression analyses of enrollment using the 1995 and 2000 CPS data. These figures represent the results of logistic regression models that estimate the odds of enrollment from individual-level and state-level measures. For both years, we examine the impact of a variety of demographic attributes on enrollment and one policy variable—the log of total welfare benefits—that varies between states. In 2000, we add two more policy indicators that vary between states to assess the impact of interstate variation in TANF policies on enrollment.

In both years, welfare recipients are less likely to be enrolled than are other young women. The size of the negative coefficient on receipt increases during this interval, but for the CPS data, this change is not statistically significant.

The regression analyses presented in Table 3 also include several important policy indicators that vary across states. First, the level of financial support provided to welfare recipients per se does not appear to be related to enrollment rates, either in 1995 or in 2000. However, policy measures more directly tied to enrollment opportunities do have a significant impact. Specifically, we examined whether postsecondary enrollment is not an authorized activity for welfare recipients (the reference category). As stated earlier, in some states, enrollment is an authorized activity when it is combined with some work, while in other states, it is approved as a stand-alone activity. Finally, in some states, such as Colorado, the policy regarding authorization is set at the county level.

The results indicate that those states that allow postsecondary enrollment as an approved work activity for welfare recipients have higher enrollment rates than those states that do not allow enrollment. However, the data do not indicate that

TABLE 3
WEIGHTED LOGISTIC REGRESSION OF COLLEGE ENROLLMENT

	1995	Odds Ratio	2000	Odds Ratio	2000	Odds Ratio
Intercept	1.106		0.505		0.854	
	(1.487)		(1.576)		(1.843)	
Welfare receipt	−0.474°°	0.622	−0.562°	0.570	−0.556°	0.573
	(0.167)		(0.243)		(0.243)	
Log of total benefits	−0.087	0.917	0.040	1.041	−0.073	0.929
	(0.219)		(0.233)		(0.270)	
Age						
16-18	0.006	1.006	0.080	1.084	0.082	1.086
	(0.120)		(0.122)		(0.123)	
19-20 (reference)						
21-22	−0.248°°	0.781	−0.514°°	0.598	−0.523°°	0.592
	(0.079)		(0.083)		(0.084)	
23-24	−0.992°°	0.371	−1.348°°	0.260	−1.351°°	0.259
	(0.089)		(0.102)		(0.102)	
Single mother	−0.867°°	0.420	−1.178°°	0.308	−1.175°°	0.309
	(0.116)		(0.115)		(0.115)	
Married mother	−2.037°°	0.130	−2.128°°	0.119	−2.129°°	0.119
	(0.149)		(0.187)		(0.189)	
Married without children	−1.300°°	0.273	−1.230°°	0.292	−1.226°°	0.294
	(0.120)		(0.143)		(0.144)	
Single without children (reference)						
African American	−0.316°°	0.729	−0.415°°	0.660	−0.440°°	0.644
	(0.092)		(0.102)		(0.103)	
Hispanic	−0.259°	0.772	−0.638°°	0.528	−0.675°°	0.509
	(0.110)		(0.118)		(0.121)	
Two-year education allowance						
Not authorized (reference)						
With some work					0.496°°	1.642
					(0.161)	
As a stand-alone					0.342°	1.408
					(0.174)	
Set by county					0.422°°	1.525
					(0.163)	
Education time limits						
None (reference)						
Twelve months					−0.133	0.875
					(0.119)	
Twelve or more to forty-eight months					0.115	1.122
					(0.113)	
χ^2 (percent explained)		0.124		0.150		0.154

SOURCE: 1995 and 2000 Current Population Survey (March annual demographic file).
NOTE: Current Population Survey values are in parentheses.
°$p < .05.$ °°$p < .01.$

SAGE Publications • 2455 Teller Road, Thousand Oaks, CA 91320 U.S.A. • Telephone:(800) 818-7243 (U.S.) / (805) 499-9774 (Outside of U.S.)
FAX: (800) 583-2665 (U.S.) / (805) 499-0871 (Outside of U.S.) • E-mail: order@sagepub.com • Website: www.sagepub.com

CALL: 800-818-7243   FAX: 800-583-2665   E-MAIL: order@sagepub.com   WEBSITE: sagepub.com

H00786

THE ANNALS OF THE AMERICAN ACADEMY OF POLITICAL AND SOCIAL SCIENCE – PAPERBOUND   *Frequency: 6 Times/Year*

□ **Please start my subscription to The ANNALS of the American Academy of Political and Social Science – Paperbound (J295)**
ISSN: 0002-7162

Prices	U.S.A.	Int'l / Canada*
Individuals	□ $71	□ $95
Institutions	□ $454	□ $478

PAYMENT

□ **Check enclosed.** (Payable to SAGE)   □ **Bill me.**

□ **Charge my:** □ MasterCard □ VISA □ AmEx □ Discover   (Phone number required) _____

Card # _____   Expiration Date _____

Signature _____

Name _____

Address _____

City/State/Zip Code/Country _____

Phone _____   E-mail _____

□ **Sign me up for SAGE CONTENTS ALERT (please include your e-mail address).**

Subscriptions will begin with current issue unless otherwise specified. Prices quoted in U.S. funds and subject to change. Prices outside U.S. include shipping via air-speeded delivery.
*Canadian customers please include appropriate GST and other provincial taxes.

SAGE Publications • 2455 Teller Road, Thousand Oaks, CA 91320 U.S.A. • Telephone: (800) 818-7243 (U.S.) / (805) 499-9774 (Outside of U.S.)

FAX: (800) 583-2665 (U.S.) / (805) 499-0871 (Outside of U.S.) • E-mail: order@sagepub.com • Website: www.sagepub.com

NO POSTAGE
NECESSARY
IF MAILED
IN THE
UNITED STATES

BUSINESS REPLY MAIL

FIRST-CLASS MAIL PERMIT NO. 90 THOUSAND OAKS, CA

POSTAGE WILL BE PAID BY ADDRESSEE

SAGE PUBLICATIONS
PO BOX 5084
THOUSAND OAKS CA 91359-9707

states allowing education as a stand-alone activity have higher enrollment than those requiring education combined with work.[10]

The data on time limits did not produce a statistically significant effect. In other words, those states with longer time limits on enrollment did not exhibit higher enrollments than those states with shorter time limits. These data suggest that the characterization of education as an allowable activity is more important than the dollar amount of welfare receipt or the presence of enrollment time limits on the enrollment of welfare recipients in higher education. An alternative interpretation is that the time limits, imposed in 1999, had not yet had an impact on enrollment patterns in 2000.

Another important finding in Table 3 is that the impact of being a single mother on enrollment increased during this period of time. (This difference is statistically significant.) In 2000, single mothers were less than one-third as likely to be enrolled as single women without children, which represents a decline from slightly more than 40 percent in 1995. In other words, these data indicate that young single mothers, some of whom might have been welfare recipients in the absence of policy changes that significantly reduced welfare rolls, are falling behind relative to other women in accessing postsecondary education.

But married mothers are even less likely to be enrolled than are single mothers. Being married reduces the chances of women's enrollment relative to being single, even in the absence of children; when combined with children, the effect is intensified. Marini (1978) and Teachman and Polonko (1988) reported that being married has an inhibiting effect on enrollment, which indicates that the positive effects of added financial resources stemming from marriage are not sufficient to counterbalance the negative effects of additional role responsibilities. This effect may be accentuated among the younger groups (younger than age twenty-five) included in the CPS sample (Jacobs and King 2002).

A number of other notable findings are evident in Table 3. African American and Hispanic women are less likely to be enrolled than their white counterparts. Enrollment declines with age. Both of these effects are consistent with those of previous studies (e.g., Jacobs and King 2002).

NHES Data

We repeated the demographic analysis using the 1995 and 1999 NHES. These results show a negative effect of welfare receipt on enrollment in 1999 but not in 1995. This finding is consistent with the expectation that the gap in enrollment between welfare recipients and other women has grown since the enactment of TANF in 1996. The odds ratio indicates that welfare recipients were about one-quarter as likely to be enrolled in 2000, compared to nonrecipients.

The NHES results indicate that enrollment declines with age, as would be expected. The findings also support the CPS finding that marriage inhibits enrollment for women, even when the marital role is not combined with the parental role. Married mothers are less likely to be enrolled than married women without children, and both are less likely to be enrolled than single childless women.

TABLE 4

WEIGHTED LOGISTIC REGRESSION ANALYSES OF COLLEGE ENROLLMENT

	1995	Odds Ratio	1999	Odds Ratio
Intercept	0.251°°		0.365	
	(0.093)		(0.210)	
Welfare receipt	0.136	1.145	−1.315°°	0.269
	(0.204)		(0.475)	
Age				
Younger than 20	0.510°°	1.665	0.037	1.037
	(0.171)		(0.261)	
20-24 (reference)				
25-29	−0.988°°	0.372	−1.365°°	0.255
	(0.133)		(0.268)	
30-39	−1.675°°	0.187	−1.642°°	0.194
	(0.123)		(0.216)	
40 and older	−3.196°°	0.041	−3.240°°	0.039
	(0.134)		(0.238)	
Single mother	−0.372°°	0.689	0.021	1.021
	(0.143)		(0.227)	
Married mother	−1.215°°	0.297	−0.905°°	0.405
	(0.131)		(0.238)	
Married without children	−0.577°°	0.561	−0.822°°	0.440
	(0.124)		(0.288)	
Single without children (reference)				
African American	−0.257°	0.774	−0.110	0.896
	(0.128)		(0.210)	
Hispanic	−0.295	0.745	−0.776°°	0.460
	(0.165)		(0.290)	
χ^2 (percent explained)	0.253		0.268	

SOURCE: 1995, 1999 National Household Education Surveys.
NOTE: Values for all ages are in parentheses.
°$p < .05.$ °°$p < .01.$

Several other results in the NHES data are not consistent with the CPS findings. The negative effect of being a single mother declined between 1995 and 1999 in the NHES data; the trend was sharply in the opposite direction for the CPS data. We place greater trust in the CPS findings on this particular point because the measure of parental status is not as precise in the NHES data.[11] There was no effect of being African American on enrollment for the NHES data in 2000 (there was a negative effect in 1995), but CPS data indicated a consistently negative effect in both years. These inconsistencies remind us of the idiosyncrasies of survey findings and the need to bring as many different sources of data together as possible to support a particular conclusion. We repeated this NHES analysis for those younger than twenty-five and found the same patterns reported in Table 4. In other words, the differences between the CPS and NHES results are not due to the restricted age group included in the CPS sample.[12]

NPSAS Data

One important limitation of the analyses we present thus far is that they do not allow us to identify the type of program in which students are enrolled. Interviews conducted with state-level welfare officials, community college leaders, welfare-rights advocates, and others have indicated that welfare reform has increasingly shifted recipients toward shorter-term, noncredit programs and away from curricula that lead to a degree (Mazzeo, Rab, and Eachus 2003; Shaw and Rab 2003).

To explore this issue further, we obtained data from the 1996 and 2000 NPSAS. These are two large surveys of students enrolled in college, with more than 30,000 respondents in 1996 and more than 40,000 respondents in 2000 (National Center for Education Statistics 1997, 2002). In 1996, slightly less than 1 percent (0.9 percent) of students enrolled as undergraduates reported having received some financial support from welfare during the past year; by 2000, this fraction had declined to 0.6 percent. This one-third decline is very much in line with the data indicating a decline in financial aid applications noted above. Both of these sources suggest a more modest decline than our calculations based on the Job Opportunities and Basic Skills data discussed above.

The NPSAS data also allow us to consider the type of program in which students are enrolled. Between 1996 and 2000, there was a sharp increase in enrollment in short-term, certificate programs. In 1996, 27.5 percent of welfare recipients were enrolled in certificate programs; by 2000, this figure had jumped to 43 percent of welfare recipients enrolled in postsecondary education. This change occurred despite no overall change in the incidence of enrollment in certificate programs. (In 2000, 12.1 percent of all postsecondary enrollment was in certificate programs vs. 12.2 percent in 1996.)

This growth was matched by a decline in the enrollment of welfare recipients in both associate's degree programs (a 7 percent decline) and bachelor's degree programs (a 6.7 percent decline). By 2000, welfare recipients were markedly overrepresented in certificate programs (welfare recipients were 3.6 times more likely to be enrolled in these programs than were other students); slightly overrepresented in associate's degree programs (1.06 times as likely to be enrolled); and markedly underrepresented in bachelor's degree programs (only 0.34 times as likely to be enrolled). The NPSAS data thus confirm what we have found in interviewing state welfare and community college officials: that TANF has not only reduced access to higher education but also shifted enrollment to short-term, certificate programs and away from associate's degree and bachelor's degree enrollment. This trend is consistent with other studies that suggest a growing concentration of students with limited resources in the lower echelons of postsecondary education (Institute for Higher Education Policy 2002).

Discussion

It seems clear that in a general sense, the result of welfare reform has been to reduce overall access to postsecondary education for welfare recipients and to reduce as well the quantity and quality of education available.

The data from all sources indicate a decline in the number of welfare recipients attending institutions of higher learning in the United States in the period after the enactment of TANF. However, much of this decline is due to the decline in the size of the welfare population. Has the rate of enrollment of those on welfare declined as well? The data on this point are not entirely consistent. Some sources, such as NPSAS data on college students, indicate that the declines in enrollment were somewhat smaller than the declines in the TANF caseload. The CPS data show that the odds of enrollment of welfare recipients younger than twenty-five declined between 1995 and 2000, but this decline was not statistically significant. The NHES data, in contrast, do indicate a statistically significant decline in the enrollment of all ages of welfare recipients between 1995 and 1999.

The CPS data indicate a relative decline for single mothers versus others, while the NHES data do not corroborate this result. Taken together, both data sets show a decline for either single mothers or welfare recipients.

The NPSAS data make it clear that the enrollment of welfare recipients shifted markedly from degree-based programs to short-term, certificate programs. Welfare recipients are now substantially overrepresented among students in certificate programs. At the same time, their traditional overrepresentation in associate's degree programs is eroding, and their underrepresentation in bachelor's degree programs is growing.

As we have seen, TANF is a decentralized system that allows for states to design their own systems, within certain restrictive constraints imposed by the federal government. Do formal differences in policies between states actually translate into differences in enrollments? The CPS data provide support for the conclusion that state policies matter. Those states with the most restrictive policies regarding welfare recipients had lower enrollment rates than states with more expansive options. The data suggest that it is not time limits per se or the level of welfare funding that is most relevant but rather policies regarding whether access to higher education is allowed as a stand-alone activity, is allowed combined with work, or is not allowed.

In our multistate research project (see Mazzeo, Rab, and Eachus 2003), we have found that policies on the ground do not fully correspond to the formal state-level policies that the researchers at CLASP have so thoroughly documented. The results of this article do not dispute this conclusion and are actually fully consistent with this finding. Rather, the results presented here merely suggest that the distinctions made by CLASP do indeed make a difference in terms of access to higher education. If we had a more fine-grained measure regarding the policies in practice in each state, we believe that this indicator would be an even more powerful predictor of enrollment variation than that presented here.

We believe that it is important to note that policies regarding access to higher education continue to evolve. As a result, it will continue to be important to estimate how these policy changes will affect enrollment. Notably, in a 2002 CLASP report, the number of states allowing welfare recipients to pursue higher education increased. This is an important change because the states that did not allow access had the lowest enrollment rates in our analysis of enrollment patterns in 2000.

APPENDIX A

TABLE A1
EDUCATIONAL ALLOWANCE CATEGORIZATIONS

Allowed as a Stand-Alone Activity	Allowed in Combination with Work	Not an Authorized Work Activity	Policy Set by County
Alaska	Alabama	West Virginia	
Florida	Arizona	Connecticut	Colorado
Georgia	Arkansas	Idaho	Montana
Illinois	California	Mississippi	New York
Iowa	Delaware	Oklahoma	Ohio
Kentucky	District of	Oregon	
Maine	Columbia	South Dakota	
Minnesota	Hawaii	Washington	
Nevada	Indiana	Wisconsin	
Pennsylvania	Kansas		
Rhode	Louisiana		
Island	Maryland		
Utah	Massachusetts		
Vermont	Michigan		
Wyoming	Missouri		
	Nebraska		
	New Hampshire		
	New Jersey		
	New Mexico		
	North Carolina		
	North Dakota		
	South Carolina		
	Tennessee		
	Texas		
	Virginia		

NOTE: These classifications are based on formal state-level policies as compiled by the State Policy and Documentation Project in July 2000.

APPENDIX B

TABLE B1
TIME LIMIT CATEGORIZATIONS

Twelve-Month Time Limit	Twelve or More- to Forty-Eight-Month Time Limit	No Time Limit
Alaska	California	Alabama
Arizona	Illinois	Arkansas
Florida	Iowa	Colorado
Indiana	Kentucky	Delaware
Kansas	Maine	Georgia
Louisiana	Maryland	Hawaii
Michigan	Minnesota	Massachusetts
Nevada	Missouri	Montana
New Mexico	Nebraska	New Jersey
North Dakota	New Hampshire	Ohio
Texas	North Carolina	Tennessee
	Pennsylvania	West Virginia
	Rhode Island	Wyoming
	South Carolina	
	Utah	
	Vermont	
	Virginia	

NOTE: These classifications are based on formal state-level policies as compiled by the State Policy and Documentation Project in July 2000.

Notes

1. For example, in a poll conducted by the Pew Center for the People and the Press in the spring of 2002, 46 percent of respondents said that the current welfare system works better than the system in place before 1996, while 17 percent said that it was worse. On the other hand, the 2002 Packard Foundation poll found that a majority (56 percent) felt that the best way to move people from welfare to work is for the government to help recipients develop the skills to get better jobs, versus 39 percent who felt that moving recipients into jobs as quickly as possible was best. The Packard poll also suggests that the public is concerned about the impact of welfare reform on children. Polling data were accessed at the Polling the Nations Web site: http://poll.orspub.com/poll/lpext.dll?f=templates&fn=main_h.htm.

2. The final Temporary Assistance for Needy Families regulations (64 Fed. Reg. 17720-19931) were released on 12 April 1999 and became effective as of 1 October 1999.

3. During fiscal year 1995, 1.9 million people, 43 percent of all Aid to Families with Dependent Children adult recipients, participated in the Job Opportunities and Basic Skills program nationwide. For fiscal year 1995, the average monthly percentage of Job Opportunities and Basic Skills participants enrolled in a self-initiated higher education program was 7.5 percent. The percentage enrolled in an assigned higher education program was 9.2 percent. Twenty-three percent were enrolled in a high school, General Equivalency Diploma, English as a second language, or remedial education program, and 7.8 percent were enrolled in vocational training (U.S. Department of Health and Human Services 1999, 482-83). These numbers are U.S. totals and were not broken down by state. These figures suggest that about 136,000 welfare recipients were enrolled in higher education through the Job Opportunities and Basic Skills program in 1995.

Following reform, the comparable information provided at the federal level by the U.S. Department of Health and Human Services is based on the number of Temporary Assistance for Needy Families families that meet all family work requirements by participating in an approved work activity. For fiscal year 1997, this number of participating families was 520,237. We analyzed the Department of Health and Human Services data on the activities of these individuals. Adding all of the categories that potentially involve higher education (vocational education, job skills training, education related to employment, satisfactory school attendance, on-the-job training), other than job search, yields a total of 54,000 enrolled in higher education. Comparing this figure to the 1995 total suggests a sharp reduction in the enrollment of welfare recipients in higher education, on the order of a two-thirds reduction, or a decline of 100,000. This estimate is more conservative than that offered by David Manzo (1997), who estimated that welfare reform may eliminate about 300,000 welfare recipients from educational programs across the country (p. 15). (Manzo's figure may include secondary as well as postsecondary education—it is not clear from his account what types of schooling are included.)

4. Part-time students are typically ineligible for financial aid. Thus, a large fraction of disadvantaged students, namely those who enroll in college part-time, will not appear in the financial aid statistics.

5. These breakdowns are based on a 2000 State Policy Documentation Project/Center for Law and Social Policy report, which was updated in 2002. We use the 1999 figures here because we sought to examine the impact of state policies on enrollment in 2000.

6. Eight states do not allow participation in two-year programs, while seventeen do not allow participation in a four-year program.

7. The 1999 National Household Education Survey asks for only the ages of all individuals living in the household. The 1995 National Household Education Survey does have a variable indicating whether there are children younger than ten in the household. However, in both cases, we are unable to determine whether the children belong to the respondent.

8. The Center for Law and Social Policy released a revised list of state policies in June 2002, which was based on a May 2002 survey of states. We did not use this revised classification in our analysis because it did not correspond in time with our enrollment data.

9. Moffit has compiled a very useful, state-level welfare policy database. More information can be found at www.econ.jhu.edu/People/Moffitt/Datasets.html.

10. In additional analyses not shown, we included these policies retrospectively for 1995. We found a statistically significant effect, but the coefficients were smaller than those for 2000. This finding suggests that the same states that had more liberal policies toward welfare recipients in 2000 had other policies in effect in 1995 that also encouraged enrollments.

11. In the National Household Education Surveys analyses, in 1995, we coded women with children younger than ten in the household as mothers. In 1999, we classified as childless those for whom questions about children were coded as "inapplicable," and we assigned the balance to the category of parent. These are both imprecise measures but are the best we could do given the data limitations discussed in note 4.

12. The effect of being African American is negative in the younger age group but not in the National Household Education Surveys sample as a whole. This difference may be related to the high rate of returning to school among African American women noted above. The explanatory power of the equation is greater for the entire sample than for the sixteen to twenty-four age group because the age measures explain more of the variance for the full sample.

References

American Association of Community Colleges. 1999. Community college involvement in welfare. Available from www.aacc.nche.edu/research/welfare.htm.

Applied Research Center. 2001. Welfare reform as we know it. Oakland, CA: Applied Research Center.

Brauner, Sarah, and Pamela Loprest. 1999. Where are they now? What states' studies of people who left welfare tell us. Washington, DC: Urban Institute.

Brock, Thomas, Laura C. Nelson, and Megan Reiter. 2002. Readying welfare recipients for work: Lessons from four big cities as they implement welfare reform. New York: Manpower Demonstration Research Corporation.

Carnevale, Anthony P., and Donna M. Desrochers. 1999. Getting down to business: Matching welfare recipients skills to jobs that train. Princeton, NJ: Educational Testing Service.

Center for Law and Social Policy (CLASP). 2002. Forty states likely to cut access to postsecondary training or education under House-passed bill. Available from http://www.clasp.org/pubs/jobseducation/Postsec_survey_061902.htm.

Cohen, Marie. 1998. Postsecondary education under welfare reform. *Welfare Information Network Issue Notes* 2 (8). Available from www.welfareinfo.org.

Cox, K. L., and W. E. Spriggs. 2002. *Negative effects of TANF on college enrollment.* Washington, DC: National Urban League Institute for Opportunity and Equality.

Florida Education and Training Placement Information Program. 2001. *Annual outcomes report. Fall 2000 data.* Tallahassee: Florida Department of Education.

Friedman, Pamela. 1999. Post-secondary education options for low-income adults. *Welfare Information Network Issue Notes* 3 (12). Available from http://www.welfareinfo.org/postseced2.htm.

Gittell, Marilyn, Margaret Schehl, and Camille Fareri. 1990. *From welfare to independence: The college options.* New York: Ford Foundation.

Greenberg, Mark, Julie Strawn, and Lisa Plimpton. 1999. *State opportunities to provide access to postsecondary education under TANF.* Washington, DC: Center for Law and Social Policy.

Hays, Sharon. 2003. *Flat broke with children.* New York: Oxford University Press.

Institute for Higher Education Policy. 2002. *The policy of choice: Expanding student options in higher education.* Washington, DC: Institution for Higher Education Policy.

Institute for Women's Policy Research. 1998. Welfare reform and postsecondary education: Research and policy update. Available from http://www.iwpr.org/wnn10.htm.

Jacobs, Jerry A., and Rosalind B. King. 2002. Age and college completion: A life history analysis of women aged 15 through 44. *Sociology of Education* 75:211-30.

Jacobs, Jerry A., and Lauren Rich. 1998. Returning to school: Determinants and consequences. Unpublished manuscript, Department of Sociology, University of Pennsylvania.

Lavin, David. 2001. Unpublished tabulations, Department of Sociology, City of New York Graduate Center.

Loprest, Pamela. 1999. *Families who left welfare: Who are they and how are they doing?* Washington, DC: Urban Institute.

Manzo, David. 1997. The influence of federal and state welfare reform on adult education. ED412-332. Available from http://www.edrs.com.

Marini, Margaret Mooney. 1978. The transition to adulthood: Sex differences in educational attainment and age at marriage. *American Sociological Review* 43 (4): 483-507.

Mazzeo, Christopher, Sara Rab, and Susan Eachus. 2003. Work-first or work-only: Welfare reform, state policy, and access to postsecondary education. *Annals of the American Academy of Political and Social Science* 586: 144-71.

National Center for Education Statistics. 1997. *National Postsecondary Student Aid Study. 1995-96 (NPSAS:96) methodology report.* Washington, DC: Government Printing Office.

———. 2002. *National Postsecondary Student Aid Study. 1999-2090 (NPSAS:2000) methodology report.* Washington, DC: Government Printing Office.

Pennsylvania Office of Income Maintenance, Bureau of Employment and Training. 2002. PA TANF all family and post-24-month caseload and activities report for March 2002. Harrisburg: Pennsylvania Department of Human Services. Available from http://www.state.il.us/agency/dhs/comtx899.htm.

Peterson, Janie, Xue Song, and Avis Jones-DeWeever. 2002. *Life after welfare reform: Low-income single parent families, pre- and post-TANF.* No. D446. Washington, DC: Institute for Women's Policy Research Publication.

Pierre, Robert. 1997. Trading textbooks for jobs. *Washington Post*, 29 December, p. A1.

Seguino, Stephanie, and Sandy Butler. 1998. Struggling to make ends meet in the Maine economy: A study of former and current AFDC/TANF recipients. Joint Project of the Women's Development Institute and the Maine Center for Economic Policy. Available from http://www.mecep.org/report-endmeet.htm.

Shaw, Kathleen M., and Sara Rab. 2003. Market rhetoric versus reality in policy and practice: The Workforce Investment Act and access to community college education and training. *Annals of the American Academy of Political and Social Science* 586: 172-93.

Spalter-Roth, Roberta, Beverly Burr, Heidi Hartmann, and Lois Shaw. 1995. *Welfare that works: The working lives of AFDC recipients*. Washington, DC: Institute for Women's Policy Research.

State Policy Documentation Project. 2000. Work requirements: Postsecondary education. Available from http://www.spdp.org/tanf/postsecondary.PDF.

Teachman, Jay D., and Karen A. Polonko. 1988. Marriage, parenthood and the college enrollment of men and women. *Social Forces* 67 (2): 512-23.

U. S. Department of Health and Human Services, Administration for Children and Families, Office of Planning, Research and Evaluation. 1999. *Second annual report to Congress on the Temporary Assistance for Needy Families (TANF) program*. Washington, DC: Government Printing Office.

———. 2002. *Second annual report to Congress on the Temporary Assistance for Needy Families (TANF) program*. Washington, DC: Government Printing Office.

U.S. General Accounting Office. 1999. *Welfare reform: Information on former recipients' status*. GAO/HEHS-99-48. Washington, DC: Government Printing Office.

Washington State Department of Social and Health Services. 2002. Economic Services Administration ESA briefing book state fiscal year 2000: A reference for programs, caseloads, and expenditures. Available from www.wa.gov/dshs/esa/briefingbook.htm.

Community Colleges and the Equity Agenda: The Potential of Noncredit Education

By
W. NORTON GRUBB,
NORENA BADWAY,
and
DENISE BELL

While community colleges pride themselves on their inclusiveness, they tend not to enroll many of the lowest-performing students leaving high schools, most of the disconnected youth who have dropped out of high school, and many low-income adults. This article explores the possibility of using noncredit education as a bridging mechanism to allow such students to enter the community college. Noncredit programs have many advantages including lower cost; greater accessibility, flexibility, and responsiveness; and greater access to immigrants. Some noncredit centers have worked hard to develop smooth transitions to the credit programs of their colleges. While noncredit education has great promise as a mechanism for expanding access to community colleges, it also faces familiar problems: inadequate funding, low status, inadequate support services, and developing in adequate articulation mechanisms with credit programs. Finally, community colleges cannot by themselves resolve the problems of inadequate schooling and poverty, and a variety of complementary social and economic policies must also be developed.

Keywords: community colleges; noncredit education; equity

Community colleges have prided themselves on their inclusiveness. The rhetoric about the people's college and democracy's open door has signaled the willingness of these institutions to serve lower-income students, immigrants, students whose parents have never been to college, older students including women returning to the labor force, and other nontraditional stu-

W. Norton Grubb is a professor and the David Gardner Chair in Higher Education at the School of Education, University of California, Berkeley, where he is also the faculty coordinator for the Principal Leadership Institute. He received his doctorate in economics from Harvard University in 1975. He has published extensively on various topics in the economics of education, public finance, education policy, community colleges and second chance programs, and social policy for children and youth. He also consults extensively with high schools, community colleges, and public policy groups about both institutional and policy reforms. He is the author most recently of Honored but Invisible: An Inside Look at Teaching in Community Colleges *(1999, Routledge),*

DOI: 10.1177/0002716202250226

dents. This inclusiveness is part of an old and glorious tradition in American education dating from the nineteenth century, the tradition of the common school that extended public support of education to everyone—initially for political purposes and then for occupational reasons. At their best, community colleges and their faculty are committed to their varied students and are supportive of them in many ways. As an economics instructor described this mission,

> I find [the community college] very rewarding, exciting, challenging. I tend to think it's probably one of the most important parts of higher education in that, as far as I'm concerned, it's the last real opportunity for many people in our community. You can be a high school dropout, you can have all sorts of problems or issues of your past and as long as the community college is there for you, there's still that hope. (Grubb and Associates 1999, 4)

In practice, however, community colleges have never reached the neediest individuals in any great numbers. The younger students coming right out of high school have tended to come from the middle of the distribution—with middling grades, middling income levels, middling (and sometimes inchoate) aspirations for their futures.[1] Many older students are experienced workers seeking to upgrade their skills; some have been sent by their employers, who tend to support only the most promising workers; and those seeking retraining, to find new occupations because of dislocations in the economy, tend to be experienced.

And so while community college students are nontraditional compared to four-year college students, they still tend not to include those who need further education the most: low-income individuals; those with no experience in the labor market, or with employment in low-wage jobs with marginal employers where upgrade

Learning to Work: The Case for Re-Integrating Education and Job Training (1996, Russell Sage), Working in the Middle: Strengthening the Education and Training of the Middle-Skilled Labor Force (1996, Jossey-Bass), and Education for Occupations in American High Schools (1995, Teachers College Press), on the integration of academic and occupational education.

Norena Badway is the director of the Community College Cooperative at the Graduate School of Education, University of California, Berkeley. She received her doctorate in education policy from Berkeley in 1998. Her research focuses on access to higher education and aspects of community college organization, curriculum, and teaching. She conducts evaluations of federal and state grant-funded programs and consults with secondary schools and community colleges about curriculum reform, assessment, developmental education, accreditation, and integrated program design.

Denise Bell is the director of assessment at Worcester State College and the program effectiveness coordinator at the University of California, Berkeley. She is currently a Ph.D. candidate in the School of Education at University of California, Berkeley. She received her Ed.M. in administration, planning, and social policy from Harvard University in 1987. Her research interests include performance funding in higher education, educational policy, community colleges, and assessment and planning in education. As a consultant, she has conducted numerous program evaluations for the Math, Engineering, Science Achievement program; Lucent Technologies; the Massachusetts Cultural Council; the Winnick Foundation; and Florida community colleges.

NOTE: This article has been supported with funds from the David Gardner Chair in Higher Education and with additional funding from the Metlife Foundation to Jobs for the Future. Jim Jacobs and Bob Gabriner provided helpful comments on an earlier draft.

training is unlikely to be provided; recent immigrants, without workable English or much familiarity with employment opportunities; those with serious family problems; welfare recipients and the long-term unemployed, many of whom have multiple barriers to employment; and those with criminal records or with physical or mental disabilities. These are potential students who have been served, if at all—and often, we will argue in the What Is the Alternative? section, they are ill-served—by adult education, welfare-to-work programs, and short-term job training including the Job Training Partnership Act and now the Workforce Investment Act (WIA). For simplicity, we will refer to them as low-income or low-wage students, but it is important to remember that they do not constitute a single group, and both the personal and the social sources of their needs vary substantially.

So the equity agenda would involve community colleges in a series of reforms to increase access among these potential students, as well as improving their progress through college, so that they too could have the benefits of postsecondary education. There are many different elements of a fully developed equity agenda, particularly since access without progress is an empty promise—and so issues like the improvement of developmental education, the reform of guidance and counseling and other student services, and better approaches to the work-family-schooling dilemma (which we explore in the Limits of the Equity Agenda and Education Reform section) would be necessary. For this article, however, we examine a form of education that could expand access for many of these poorly served students. Some colleges—not that many, we suspect, but enough to clarify a pattern and suggest a model—have developed programs of noncredit education that are in every way more welcoming of low-wage students and more supportive of their short-run goals while maintaining their long-run hopes. These noncredit programs constitute a precollege or bridging mechanism, helping individuals who might not otherwise gain access to community colleges make the transition into mainstream education. These programs are more flexible, less impersonal and bureaucratic than the credit divisions of community colleges, and more likely to be in community-based facilities, closer to where low-income students live. And under the right circumstances, they may be able to distinguish carefully among different types of low-income students and tailor programs to their specific needs—for example, the issues of recent immigrants, welfare mothers, or high school dropouts. We outline the advantages of these noncredit programs in the Advantages of Noncredit Education section, the heart of this article, based on research in four states.

However, noncredit education cannot escape the dilemmas of community colleges generally—the inadequate funding, the overuse of adjunct faculty, the low respect. As we clarify in the Endless Differentiation of Postsecondary Education section, again based on evidence from four states, noncredit education in community colleges represents yet another form of stratification within postsecondary education, with elite universities at the top, various gradations of progressively less selective universities below them, the credit programs of community colleges above the noncredit divisions, and various short-term job training and adult education programs at the very bottom. This is what we might term a huge inequity structure. It means that improving noncredit programs and enhancing the equity agenda in large numbers of community colleges requires confronting and over-coming the fundamental inequalities of funding, of status, and of attention in all of higher education.

However, to us, there is no other choice than to improve these aspects of com-munity colleges because the alternatives—the freestanding basic skills programs in adult education and the short-term job training efforts in welfare-to-work pro-grams and WIA—are so ineffective, as we argue in the What Is the Alternative? section based on the evaluation evidence available. They are also poorly linked to the mainstream educational opportunities, including the community college, that provide the best chances of getting out of poverty. If we as a country are serious about providing equity through education for a range of low-wage individuals, then the community college is the place to do it, and improvements in college are neces-sary to do so.

Finally, it is crucial to remember that education cannot achieve equity by itself—that equality of opportunity through education has never become a reality and cannot possibly be realized when the overall economy sputters. We need to understand the limitations of equality of educational opportunity as well as its promise and to develop other social and economic policies complementary to edu-cation policies. In The Limits of the Equity Agenda and Education Reform section, therefore, we outline some noneducation policies that can strengthen the effec-tiveness of the equity agenda and of community colleges, in an attempt to go beyond the limits of education alone.

The Advantages of Noncredit Education

We first became aware of the potential power of noncredit education as part of a sixteen-college study being undertaken by the Community College Research Center at Teachers College, Columbia, wherein one of the sixteen has a particu-larly active noncredit division serving low-income groups. Unfortunately, the information about noncredit programs is sparse.[2] For this article, we have con-ducted additional research in four states—California, Florida, North Carolina, and Wisconsin—that have relatively large amounts of noncredit education. In each state, we selected three to four colleges that we knew, based either on reputations or on the basis of state data, to have relatively large noncredit enrollments. We then administered open-ended phone interviews with directors of noncredit education and institutional researchers in thirteen community colleges, asking about the types of noncredit offerings, the numbers and types of noncredit students, the dif-ferences between credit and noncredit students, the availability of data on the sub-sequent education and enrollment of noncredit students, and the role within these institutions of noncredit divisions. We also interviewed state officials in each state and reviewed both state and local publications and data where available. In addi-tion to information from these thirteen colleges, we have also drawn on evidence collected in the sixteen Community College Research Center case studies. The Advantages of Noncredit Education and The Endless Differentiation of

Postsecondary Education sections rely almost entirely on this research, while the What Is the Alternative? and The Limits of the Equity Agenda and Education Reform sections use other kinds of evidence to interpret the potential as well as the limits of noncredit education as a bridging mechanism for low-income individuals.

. . . the equity agenda would involve community colleges in a series of reforms to increase access among these potential students, as well as improving their progress through college, so that they too could have the benefits of postsecondary education.

Noncredit education in community colleges serves several different purposes. Some courses offered in noncredit divisions[3] are clearly intended for upgrade training, including many at highly sophisticated levels; some are for retraining, for individuals who want or need new careers; some are designed to prepare for licensing exams in areas such as real estate, accounting, and human resources; some are plainly avocational or hobby-related courses or other forms of community education; and some colleges include customized training for specific employers in their noncredit divisions. It is often difficult to perceive which noncredit offerings focus on the equity agenda rather than upgrade training or retraining, although basic skills courses, English as a second language (ESL) classes, and lower-level occupational courses are usually intended for low-wage students. For example, one large noncredit program includes occupational programs in appliance repair, catering, electronic assembly and cabling, school bus driving, sheet metal work, and the ubiquitous early childhood programs—all entry-level positions that can be achieved with relatively short programs. The ambiguity in the purposes of noncredit education reflects a basic problem categorizing students as well: a student in upgrade training may be an experienced technician needing to learn a recent electronics process or an M.B.A. needing a specific accounting course, but he or she might equally be stuck in a low-paid service or medical job and seeking upgrade training to work his or her way out of poverty. So noncredit programs can be quite extensive without serving an equity agenda. On the other hand, they may serve this role in and among other purposes.

For similar reasons, it is difficult to answer the apparently simple question of how much noncredit education there is and especially how much of it supports low-income individuals. There are no national data on noncredit students, and the state-level data vary enormously in their definitions and coverage. Wisconsin's figures illustrate the problems of learning about magnitudes: enrollment in "vocational-adult," which includes all noncredit courses, was 264,320 on a headcount basis in 1999-2000, out of a total of 453,668, therefore representing 58 percent of all students. But because noncredit students typically enroll for short periods of time, they accounted for only 4,225 out of 58,074 full-time equivalents (FTEs), or only 7.3 percent. Furthermore, from discussions with Wisconsin colleges, the vast majority of noncredit enrollments are for upgrade training, not the equity agenda. In North Carolina, which has much better data than most states, "extension" (noncredit) programs represent 74.5 percent of all students but only 5.8 percent of FTE students (for 1999-2000); this implies that noncredit students are crucial to the community-serving mandates of these colleges but trivial in terms of the resources they generate. Of the noncredit students, 29 percent of all enrollments (but 40 percent of noncredit FTEs) are in basic education and programs for the long-term unemployed, 48.3 percent in occupational courses at various levels, 8.3 percent in firm-based training, and 14.4 percent in community service and avocational courses. Therefore, a substantial chunk of these noncredit enrollments—but again, a trivial fraction of FTEs—serves the equity agenda. For the moment, then, the magnitude of noncredit education in the country remains elusive, although the pattern from the two states with decent data seems reasonable: noncredit enrollments are often quite large, but much smaller in FTE terms, with much of this coming from occupational courses that have more to do with upgrading than with equity.

When college administrators refer to their low-income, noncredit students, they describe students who are tentative, uncomfortable with big bureaucracies, perhaps unsuccessful in prior efforts to get back into school, and uncertain about their identities as students. Noncredit programs allow them to "get their feet wet" or provide a "first step into college"; there are "no grades, no pressures," reducing the anxieties these students have about college. Noncredit programs are the "last best hope for lots of students," as one director in California declared. Another in North Carolina noted the clear difference between credit and noncredit students:

> It certainly is a different population we're serving. Curriculum [credit education] is serving those who want to pursue a degree. They have the academic ability to do that. Ours [noncredit students] have some gaps in their academic abilities, and we're trying to bring them up. Many do not have high school diplomas. The primary difference is education level already attained, and maybe even their objectives. Noncurriculum [noncredit] folks, many of them, it's a goal to read, or trying to retool and get a skill.

The major advantages of providing noncredit courses and programs for low-wage students comprise quite a long list—most of which, we should remember, have also been cited for community colleges as a whole.

Cost. Noncredit programs cost nothing at all, or considerably less than credit courses. In some cases, certain types of courses—basic education, for example—

are free, while others—hobby courses, usually—require students to pay the full costs. For low-income students, even the modest tuition costs of credit courses may be a serious deterrent, and so reduced tuition may be an important way of increasing access.

Open enrollment. Noncredit enrollment usually involves a simple sign-up procedure, without the more complex enrollment process, mandatory placement tests, and counseling referrals that some colleges have instituted for their regular programs. The problem is that these matriculation procedures are intended to help students find the right courses and programs, although they also operate to discourage potential students who are uncomfortable with impersonal bureaucratic procedures.

Flexibility. Noncredit courses very often start every week or two, rather than at the beginning of conventional semesters. They also tend to be provided at various times of the day and sometimes on weekends for working adults.

Responsiveness. While community colleges think of themselves as being responsive to new trends and demands, compared to four-year colleges with their bureaucratic procedures, noncredit programs are much more responsive than the credit programs of community colleges. They typically do not have to go through faculty and Senate approval, state approval mechanisms, or other delays that can take two years or more for credit courses. One noncredit director in North Carolina clarified the procedural differences between credit and noncredit approval process: "If it's something we haven't done before, we make it happen. If you ask one of my curriculum [credit] directors about approval, they moan and groan" because the approval process by the campus, the system office, and the state board takes from one year to eighteen months. The principal importance of flexibility is that noncredit division can put new programs into place when a specific community need arises or when a particular kind of occupational course becomes hot.

Location. In colleges with large noncredit divisions, individual centers are located throughout a city, often in community centers, centers for the elderly, community-based organizations (CBOs), churches, and other places familiar to the populations they are trying to reach. Not only are these centers physically closer and thus more accessible to low-income adults, but they are widely described as being small scale and more comfortable than the large central campuses of urban community colleges. More to the point, they can take on distinctive identities: in one city, for example, there are distinctive centers in Latino, in Chinese, and in black neighborhoods, each with a bilingual director and many bilingual staff, with a variety of support services specific to each community. Under these conditions, noncredit centers become what some CBOs aspire to be, except that they are also part of a larger college and can therefore provide access to more advanced programs that CBOs cannot provide.

Under these circumstances, neighborhood centers can identify and serve precise needs that might not be identified in other centers. For example, in the Latino population, a substantial fraction of immigrants (about 20 percent, according to a center director) have had substantial education and were professionals in their home country; their problems are quite different from those of immigrants with little formal schooling, little or no literacy in their native language, and prior employment only in subsistence agriculture. And so neighborhood-based centers can understand their students in ways that would be much more difficult in the large, heterogeneous classroom of regular credit courses.

Access to immigrants. One adult education program in a heavily Latino city noted that prospective students need only a U.S. address to enroll. They do not need to have a green card or to fill out other paperwork, and this is widely known in the Latino community that is nervous about its immigration status and contact with the Immigration and Naturalization Service.[4] In this way, the more informal procedures of noncredit programs reduce the barriers, real or perceived, to enrollment.

Support services. Many community colleges we examined allow their noncredit students full access to all the support services they provide, including child care, guidance and counseling, and tutoring. (Financial aid is unavailable because it is allowed only for students attending credit programs at least half time; however, since noncredit courses are either free or have reduced fees, this is not usually an issue.) To be sure, these support services are often available only on a main campus, not in every community-based center, so in practice, low-income adults may not be able to take advantage of these services. But at least the intention of such programs is to make a full array of support services available. In other cases, however—especially in Florida, with an emphasis on upgrade training—there appears to be very little access to support services, and in this sense, noncredit students seem to be second-class citizens.

The transition to credit programs. Perhaps the greatest advantage of locating noncredit programs for low-income students in community colleges is that after students have completed a relatively short course, they can take other related courses and, at the end of an appropriate sequence, transfer into credit courses of the community college. As their own desire, time, and life circumstances permit, they can continue with certificate and associate's programs, transfer to baccalaureate programs, and continue on to any form of graduate education. Indeed, there is a modern version of the rags-to-riches myth that sometimes emerges in welfare programs, of a woman who enrolls in noncredit developmental education and vocational courses to become a nursing assistant, continues to an associate's program in nursing, later transfers to a four-year college, graduates, and goes on to medical school! The point is not that this trajectory is likely; but it is possible within a well-articulated system of second-chance education.

The noncredit programs we reviewed vary substantially in their articulation with credit programs at the same college. In Florida, a final exam in a certain noncredit course can be used to earn credit; the Maricopa colleges also have a mechanism whereby noncredit courses are converted to credits. One institution has set up articulation agreements, just like those articulating two- and four-year colleges, promising that students who complete a specified roster of noncredit courses can join a credit program and have some of their prior course work count. This institution runs field trips for students from the various noncredit centers to visit the main campus, to familiarize them with the campus and the various administrative hurdles they will have to leap there. Counselors develop education plans with students and help them with the transfer process and with enrollment in credit programs for the first time. The centers are now reorganizing their counseling to concentrate on particular types of noncredit students (e.g., new students, continuing students, occupational students), with counselors developing greater expertise about the conditions such students face. This institution is one of the very few to keep track of how many students transfer from noncredit to credit every year; during the past few years, about 20 percent of their new students have enrolled from noncredit courses. The number who transfer from noncredit to credit programs represent about 6 percent of all noncredit students, although a transfer rate devised with longitudinal data would be somewhat larger. In this particular college, transfers come largely among students in transitional studies, earning a high school diploma or a General Equivalency Diploma (GED); among ESL students moving into credit programs; and among business students.

Another college with an active transfer policy is similarly establishing a series of articulation agreements with credit programs in three colleges within the same community college district. The district has also begun to track the numbers of students who transfer: about 2,000 to 3,000 students transfer every year, out of enrollments of about 57,000 in noncredit courses (excluding those for older adults), a number that surprised district administrators who thought it was much lower. But articulation at this district is still relatively new, and it is possible that the transfer numbers will increase as greater understanding of the possibilities for moving into credit programs develop. A third college has credit instructors recruit noncredit students by speaking to their classes and demonstrating what students will do in subsequent courses; they also have support services including counseling, pushing students aggressively to continue their schooling. About 15 to 20 percent of their credit students originate in noncredit courses, so among other things, the noncredit program is a recruitment mechanism—an important consideration in an enrollment-driven institution.

The mechanisms facilitating transfer from noncredit to credit programs are all easy to identify and quite familiar to colleges: student awareness of credit opportunities, articulation agreements, faculty advice and advertising, guidance and counseling, individual education plans, and support for students in the application and transfer processes. But the majority of the colleges we interviewed provided very few of these services. In most colleges, it was clear that if noncredit students could find a counselor interested in them, they can get help in the transfer process; but this is idiosyncratic rather than institutionalized and systematic. We could find no evidence of any sort—not even guesstimates—about the magnitude of transfers into credit programs in the colleges in Florida,[5] North Carolina, and Wisconsin. And so, as far as we can determine based on a limited sample, relatively few colleges use noncredit programs as a transitional stage into community college. This is especially the case where noncredit education focuses on upgrade training and retraining of the experienced workforce.

Several factors seem to account for colleges that have used their noncredit programs to serve low-income students. Most of them emerged from histories where the college (or a division of the college) had provided adult education in the region; as a result, a commitment to low-income students had developed, without competition from adult education programs run by K-12 districts. In addition, a couple of these programs have had strong individuals with clear and compelling visions to serve these students well. Finally, state policy has been permissive, if not particularly encouraging: these states fund noncredit education for equity-related purposes, albeit at lower rates than credit programs (in California, Florida, and North Carolina). As one local director noted, "What they fund is what drives what we offer." But in recessions—or, in Florida and California, where fiscal problems are pressuring programs to become self-sustaining—serving low-income students may become a lower priority.

From these few colleges, a model emerges of noncredit education as a way of addressing the equity agenda of community colleges. This model operates, in large part, by extending the advantages that community colleges already have over four-year colleges: these noncredit programs are lower in cost; more flexible in their schedules; physically closer to students; and more overtly community based, less bureaucratic, more open to immigrant students, and better able to respond quickly to emerging community and employment needs. Unfortunately, as we will see in the next section, noncredit programs are also heirs to many of the same problems that community colleges have suffered.

The Endless Differentiation of Postsecondary Education: The Dark Side of Noncredit Education

The community college represents one of many ways in which postsecondary education has been fragmented into institutions of different levels of selectivity and status, aimed at occupational preparation at different levels of the labor market. Based again on our interviews in four states, the development of noncredit programs focused on low-income students represents a further stratification within community colleges, and once again differences of funding, status, and pedagogy have emerged.

One obvious problem is that noncredit education is usually funded at substantially less than credit education. In California, for example, the funding per FTE student is $3,800 per course for credit students but $1,900 for noncredit students; in North Carolina, reimbursement for noncredit FTE is three-quarters of what it is for credit FTE. So funding, already low in community colleges, is even lower in noncredit programs.

One result is that noncredit programs use an even higher proportion of adjunct faculty than the credit divisions of community colleges do. While there is no systematic data, one of the noncredit programs we interviewed had 12 full-time instructors and 172 part-time or adjunct faculty. These are situations where the full-time faculty develop courses and hire part-timers, who are essentially treated as cogs in a big education machine; part-timers have little time for additional planning, office hours, or participation in staff development or governance committees. These are familiar problems in credit education as well, but they are worse in noncredit divisions.

*This model [of noncredit education
addressing the equity agenda] operates,
in large part, by extending the advantages
that community colleges already have
over four-year colleges.*

Under conditions where there is low funding and high proportions of adjunct faculty, the quality of teaching—a serious problem in many community colleges, despite their pride in being "teaching institutions" (Grubb and Associates 1999)— is likely to suffer. Adjunct faculty are usually hired off the street, with no preparation in teaching methods. They are unable to attend staff development; they have too little time to discuss teaching with their own colleagues or to reflect on and improve their own teaching. While we did not observe noncredit classes to examine the quality of teaching firsthand, the conditions necessary to improve teaching are absent in noncredit programs. As if to corroborate this, one institutional researcher referred to "shitty teachers, with lots of handicaps" in the college's noncredit program. In fact, it appeared that the noncredit ESL department had an active faculty, trying to develop a coherent departmental approach to ESL and regularly examining data about their success. The business department was trying to coordinate with other subjects. But the transitional studies department, designed to prepare students for transition to credit programs, was highly traditional, with older instructors not much interested in changing. This story indicates substantial variation within the noncredit division, which the college—whether through inattention, lack of resources, or lack of expertise—has been unable to improve. But it also implies that coherent programs and better teaching can be developed even with adjunct faculty and low resources, as long as there is sustained attention to the quality of teaching.

Furthermore, the large amount of developmental education in noncredit programs—a subject that is especially prone to dreary teaching—cannot possibly enhance the overall commitment to teaching. A great deal of developmental teaching follows the familiar pattern of skills and drills (or drill and kill), where complex competencies are broken into discrete, decontextualized skills on which students then drill. Another familiar pattern, one that we have directly observed in many developmental classes, is the practice of giving a great deal of emotional support to students to encourage their learning while not making any substantial cognitive demands on them lest that undermine their self-esteem—a pedagogy of loving students into failure that one often sees in adult education.[6] We have not directly observed teaching in noncredit programs and do not know whether these conditions in credit programs are also replicated in noncredit programs, but we fear that without substantial attention to the difficulties of teaching developmental education and ESL, the quality of teaching in noncredit programs is likely to be variable at best.

We also suspect that access to support services is less successful in practice than in theory. It is hard to imagine, given low budgets and lower enrollments in neighborhood centers, that noncredit programs can provide a full roster of services such as tutoring and child care. Guidance and counseling in most community colleges are inadequate in amount and dominated by academic counseling intended to provide students with information about requirements to complete credentials and transfer; the kind of career-oriented counseling that students unclear about their futures need is usually scant.[7] Support services are everywhere underfunded, in part because they do not generate revenues in enrollment-driven formulas. There is no reason to think that poorly funded noncredit centers can get around this problem.

Another systematic problem in noncredit programs is the issue of credentials. Noncredit programs tend to issue certificates of completion, but these certificates are not recognized by the states in the same way that one-year certificates, two-year associate's degrees, and baccalaureate degrees are. How local employers treat the certificates of completion issued by noncredit programs is anyone's guess. It is possible that certain local noncredit programs work closely with local employers, who then hire students completing these programs regardless of what credential they have, but it is equally possible that employers do not know much about local programs or that individuals move away, to areas where the college where they studied is not known. In general, certain kinds of certificates and most associate's degrees have substantial economic returns, compared to the earnings of high school completers, but the benefits for small amounts of course work are low and quite uncertain. The implication is that small amounts of noncredit education may not have much effect on employment and earnings.[8] If this is true, then the main benefit of completing noncredit education would be its value in gaining access to more advanced credit programs.

Particularly in North Carolina, a confusing discussion has taken place asserting that employers want "skills, not credentials"—that they value their employees for the skills they have and can demonstrate on the job, not for the pieces of paper they may have earned. Aside from the fact that this statement is based entirely on anecdotal evidence, it seems to justify teaching limited skills for entry-level jobs rather than coherent sequences of competencies that might prepare an individual for a career over a lifetime. In addition, the assertion that employers want "skills, not credentials" avoids the question of how an employer knows that a prospective hire has the skills necessary for the job. There are various indicators or signals of these skills including work experience, the recommendation of a prior employer, or the recommendation of a trusted instructor, but under normal circumstances, credentials are also one of the ways of signaling skills. (Otherwise, an employer would be forced to hire individuals at random and then let them go if they proved not to have the necessary skills—an inefficient and legally precarious hiring process requiring substantial turnover.) Without any direct evidence about the employment effects of noncredit education, it is likely that noncredit programs are effective only when individuals are completing courses directly related to their employment, which older students in upgrade training usually do, or when they give students access to widely recognized credentials. Many noncredit programs do so by providing GED preparation, high school equivalency programs, and courses preparing students for specific credentials such as Microsoft's MOUS or Comp TIA's A++ Computer Repair Technician credential or Network+ for networking applications.

Finally, there is the important issue of respect and status. Community colleges lack status relative to four-year colleges, of course; within them, the transfer programs have the greatest status, developmental programs have the least status, and noncredit programs have substantially less status than credit programs. As one administrator noted, "Credit education gets all the rah-rah"; many described noncredit education as the institution's "stepchild." Noncredit programs are often physically segregated from the rest of a college, in community-based centers or in a separate facility elsewhere in the community. They are then literally invisible as well as institutionally invisible; their faculties do not get a chance to meet faculty members teaching credit courses; and their students do not mingle either. Virtually every administrator noted the problem of low status, with noncredit programs being ignored in long-run planning, in faculty allocations, and in the overall sense of the college's mission. The only possible exceptions are continuing education courses for professionals, which are especially important in Florida.

Many administrators predict that noncredit enrollments will keep growing faster than credit enrollments, and this may rescue noncredit education from oblivion. However, it is likely that much of this growth—in enrollment as well as status—will come from professional continuing education, upgrade training, and customized training, where colleges can boast they are serving the large, economically important employers of their communities. If an administrator operates a noncredit division that combines contract training and continuing education with developmental education and other programs for low-income students, then the institutional incentives will always be to enhance programs working with wealthy corporations, not with the voiceless, powerless poor and unemployed. This is true in every educational institution, of course, but it is re-created even in the community college that prides itself as being the people's college.

In the end, extending and improving noncredit education so that it can better serve the equity agenda requires confronting a series of systematic issues that plague the credit programs of community colleges too: underfunding, the low political power of the poor and of the equity agenda in general, multiple barriers and higher costs in institutions sensitive to the costs and the revenues generated by different students, the need for student support services, and the need for improved developmental education. In all too many colleges, the equity agenda is at the bottom of the list of their many missions. Fortunately, there have been many experiments around the country, and many states and colleges have made progress on the issues of funding inequities, the use of adjunct faculty, the improvement of teaching, and the development of internally cohesive colleges—true community colleges. It remains to extend these experiments to the other colleges in the land.

What Is the Alternative? Adult Education, Job Training, and Potential Hybrids

For the low-income adults who need access to education and training, but do not live near a community college with active noncredit programs or other outreach activities, what are the alternatives? In the past, these individuals have been served in a motley mixture of local programs including adult schools administered by K-12 districts, usually offering Adult Basic Education, Adult Secondary Education leading to a GED, ESL, citizenship training, and sometimes limited vocational courses leading to entry-level occupations. In some states, area vocational schools provide adult courses, usually in short programs (fifteen weeks or less) leading to poorly paid entry-level jobs. Job training programs have been available to welfare recipients under Welfare to Work and to others under WIA, the successor to the Job Training Partnership Act of the 1980s and 1990s. In most local communities, there has been a wide spectrum of education and training alternatives, in most cases poorly coordinated with offerings in the educational system but providing potential routes into employment for the working poor, for immigrants, for dislocated workers, and for welfare recipients (Grubb and McDonnell 1996).

However, the quality of these offerings has been quite mediocre. Job training programs for welfare recipients and the long-term unemployed have consistently been found to have trivial effects on employment and earnings, not large enough to help individuals work their way out of poverty or welfare; some of them even have negative effects, especially for youth. Even programs that have positive effects in the short run turn out to be ineffective over five or six years, when the initial benefits of increasing the amount of employment dissipate.[9] Furthermore, WIA legislation took a mediocre job training program and made it worse, in at least three distinct ways. First, individuals wanting training have to go through two stages of job search before getting access to training, a requirement that transformed WIA into a work-first program with training only as a last resort and only for individuals who cannot find any kind of job on their own. Second, those who are eligible for training are given Individual Training Accounts, a kind of voucher that they can exchange for training from a list of approved providers. But the implementation of WIA has been slow, and at this moment, there have been very few Individual Training

If those of us within education stress the promises of education and equality of educational opportunity, we should also remember that other social and economic policies must change as well if our country is to be serious about the equity agenda.

Accounts granted (Javar and Wandner 2002; D'Amico et al. 2002). As a result, WIA has ceased to provide any substantial amounts of training. Third, many community colleges want nothing to do with WIA because the work-first requirements send them only the most difficult students, because the paperwork required to participate is extremely burdensome, because the performance measures necessary to participate in WIA are difficult to collect and narrowly defined, and because under the best of circumstances, WIA would not send colleges many students—at a time when most colleges are besieged with "regular" students. So many community colleges are not participating as approved providers (Javar and Wandner, 2002; D'Amico et al., 2002), thereby preventing WIA clients from gaining access to mainstream education.

Adult education is, by and large, in similarly miserable shape.[10] With the possible exception of ESL, where adult students are highly motivated, attendance in adult education programs is sporadic and usually too limited to make much progress. The teaching, often by part-time instructors hired off the street, is usually the most dreary kind of skills and drills. It is usually focused on getting students to pass the GED, a credential of dubious value in the labor market.[11] Even though adult education is often revered because of its saintly connection to literacy, there is virtually no evidence that any of its programs work. The few studies in the literature with positive results are seriously flawed,[12] and even these acknowledge that gains are small. For example, Diekhoff (1988) claimed that "there is little doubt that the average literacy program participant achieves a statistically significant improvement in reading skill" (p. 625), citing a 1974 study for the Office of Education that documented a half grade reading gain during a four-month period. But given the limited amount of time most adults spend in Adult Basic Education, with only 20 percent enrolling for longer than one year, most Adult Basic Education students improve by one year or less, and their gains—from a fifth- to a sixth-grade reading level, for example—are trivial in practical terms. As Diekhoff concluded,

> Adult literacy programs have failed to produce life-changing improvements in reading ability that are often suggested by published evaluations of these programs. It is true that a handful of adults do make substantial meaningful improvements, but the average participant gains only one or two reading grade levels and is still functionally illiterate by almost any standard when he or she leaves training. But published literacy program evaluations often ignore this fact. Instead of providing needed constructive criticism, these evaluations often read like funding proposals or public relations releases. (P. 629)

This literature confirms the information from our own analyses (Grubb and Kalman 1994)—of a large, unwieldy set of programs, lacking any systematic information about completion or progress, with virtually no evidence of success.

But the worst aspect of current adult education and job training programs is that they lead nowhere. Once an individual has completed a fifteen-week job training program, there is no natural next program—and since such short programs are inadequate to find meaningful employment (especially in a recession) the individual must begin the process of searching for training alternatives all over again. Individuals can stay for long periods of time in adult education, of course, and some of them do earn GEDs; but the effects on employment are small (Murnane, Willett, and Boudett 1995), and the benefits in gaining access to postsecondary education are similarly trivial (Quinn and Haberman 1986). So once again, the graduates of adult education and short-term job training programs are likely to be left behind in the low-skilled labor market, unable to earn enough to escape from poverty.

Given the failures of job training and adult education, the community college is the most obvious institution to serve low-wage workers. Then the precollege or bridging role of noncredit education becomes particularly important as a way of providing access for welfare recipients, the working poor, disconnected youth, and others who would not otherwise show up in community colleges. However, having described some of the problems of job training and adult education, it seems that there are at least three ways of creating bridging mechanisms:

- The first is for more colleges to create or extend their noncredit divisions to encompass the equity agenda. This requires, most obviously, providing an appropriate roster of developmental education, ESL, and entry-level occupational programs allowing individuals who must earn a living to get into employment quickly. Such programs must also create articulation agreements, guidance in developing educational plans, support in applying for credit programs, and the other linkages to credit education that we described in The Advantages of Noncredit Education section. This direction would locate the bridging mechanism entirely within the community college, strengthening the likelihood that transfer to mainstream credit offerings could take place smoothly.
- An alternative is for community colleges to articulate their credit programs with programs offered by CBOs and other providers within the job training system. Then the CBO would

provide initial recruitment, counseling, advocacy, and support while the college would provide developmental and occupational preparation; each draws on its own strength. Indeed, a few such efforts have been developed, especially Project QUEST in San Antonio profiled by Osterman and Lautsch (1996). In this case, a CBO recruited clients and provided more intensive support services. The program targeted high-growth jobs, particularly in health care and computer occupations, that are accessible to a population with relatively little education; the local community colleges provided remedial and occupational education in two-year programs, and participants earned credits so they could continue in other educational programs later. The division of labor between the CBO and the community college is instructive: the CBO provided a vision of the program, recruitment, various support services, and an advocacy role for its clients, while the colleges provided the educational components. Other examples of cooperation between colleges and CBOs have developed (Roberts 2002), although they clearly are not particularly common and WIA has made such partnerships more difficult to construct. But in some areas with strong CBOs, such partnerships may be more effective than noncredit divisions that may be created.

- Third, a similar form of articulation between publicly funded adult education programs (or area vocational schools) and community colleges seems possible. Students could then progress through adult education and then transfer to community colleges to work toward credentials with more value than the GED, again with articulation agreements and other bridging mechanisms to smooth the transition between the two. This approach might work in localities with especially strong adult schools or area vocational schools. Unfortunately, most community colleges that have approached local adult schools report being rebuffed, and we have never seen any examples where adult schools cooperate with community colleges to create ladders of educational opportunities.[13]

To develop any kind of precollege, several reforms should be started. The first step, as always, is to clarify to colleges the value of noncredit education—or of functional equivalents such as bridging programs in CBOs or adult schools—as an entry point. A second is to obtain funding, presumably from existing state and federal resources; in addition to clarifying the role of states in funding noncredit programs, existing funds for job training, for adult education, and for area vocational schools could be transferred to community colleges.[14] A third is to be sure that the quality of such programs is substantial, including the quality of the inevitable developmental education and ESL. Support services and articulation mechanisms with credit courses are also central. And the status of the equity agenda must be enhanced relative to the other, better-established missions of the community college. None of these is conceptually difficult, although efforts to put them in place would reveal the political complexities of the equity agenda.

The Limits of the Equity Agenda and Education Reform

The use of noncredit education specifically, or community colleges in general, to address the employment problems of low-income adults is part of an educational strategy that extends back at least a century. Around 1900, reformers tried to reduce high school dropouts and laggards (those falling behind in high school) as a way of reducing the likelihood that they would then go into dead-end, poorly paid jobs. Vocational education was part of the solution then, and it continues in the impulse to provide occupational forms of education and training whether in short-term training programs, traditional vocational education, nontraditional "education through occupations" in high schools (Grubb 1995), the occupational programs of community colleges, or the professional programs of four-year colleges and graduate schools. As formal schooling has become increasingly important for almost all employment—and especially for middle-level and professional employment—the centrality of equality of educational opportunity as a way of equalizing economic opportunities has grown.[15] Enhancing access to college through noncredit divisions and other bridging mechanisms is obviously one dimension of equalizing opportunities.

Unfortunately, equality of educational opportunity offers only changes in education as a solution to inequality, poverty, racial discrimination, and unequal opportunity. With the demise of other mechanisms of equalizing opportunities—the antipathy to welfare and the harsh measures of the 1996 welfare "reforms," the lackluster state of antidiscrimination policy, the inability to legislate serious revisions in health care, the lack of any coherent housing policy or urban development agenda, the demise of job training programs, and the weak state of unions—the improvement of education is almost the only antipoverty strategy that has much political power in this country.[16]

In their broadest claims, proponents of education reform sometimes claim that increases in education and changes in education policy can cure all ills, social and individual. Michael Bloomberg, the new mayor of New York, claimed recently that if schools are improved then "a lot of what Dr. [Martin Luther] King wanted to accomplish in our society will take care of itself."[17] But this is so clearly not true. Most obviously, of course, Martin Luther King promoted racial equity, social justice, freedom from the constraints of racism and poverty, and a clear moral vision that are difficult to develop through schooling alone, particularly through a vocationalized form of schooling. Partly, this kind of claim is untrue because the equity agenda remains chronically underfunded and underdeveloped, as inadequacies in noncredit education attest. Furthermore, even under the best of circumstances, reducing inequality, poverty, and other social problems requires more than what education can do. In the case of unemployment, for example, which has motivated many countries to increase education and training, such supply-side policies can reduce unemployment due to a mismatch of demand and supply, where there are shortages of certain high-skilled workers while there are surpluses of low-skilled workers, but they can do nothing about cyclical unemployment due to variation in demand, periodic shocks to an economy (like the recent concern with terrorism), or structural unemployment caused by inadequate growth.

In still other cases, the realization of educational reforms requires changes in noneducational policies, in social and economic changes that are complementary to educational reforms. Within community colleges, for example, at least three studies based on interviews with community college students indicate that the primary cause of dropping out, or making real progress, is the work-family-school dilemma—the fact that most community college students have jobs to support themselves and families who demand their attention (especially for women), all while they are attending college (e.g., Gittell and Steffy 2000; Matus-Grossman and Gooden 2002; California Tomorrow 2002). While some of them are more committed to college than to work, and have stay-in-school jobs to support their schooling, others reverse these priorities, trying to fit college around a demanding work schedule. The work-family-school dilemma means that students develop precarious arrangements for meeting their different obligations, but then any small change—different work hours, a change in a class schedule, a car breaking down, a family incident, the loss of child care—may cause the arrangement to break down. Schooling, the least pressing of these obligations, is usually the first casualty.

But community colleges by themselves can do little to resolve the work-family-schooling dilemma. Doing so requires income support policies—for example, expanded forms of student aid or support through Temporary Aid to Needy Families for extended education, something that has been missing under relentless work-first pressures. Solutions to the family component of this dilemma require expanding child care, but also coping with a range of other family problems including health issues and physical abuse—issues that might be addressed with a series of family support centers or comprehensive services centers in each community but that are broader than educational institutions can provide. And low-wage workers who want to enter noncredit programs need income support, sufficiently flexible hours of employment, or employment leave policies that allow them to attend school while they are working—again, policies that colleges by themselves cannot develop. And so the equity agenda requires educational reforms, to be sure, but it also requires a series of reforms in income support, child care, family policies, employment leave, and other employment policies—including the policies that Europeans call active labor market policies[18]—all of which are social goals in their own right but are also complementary to postsecondary education reforms.

Therefore, it is inadequate to emphasize education as the only solution to the problems of unemployment, low income, poverty, and integration into mainstream economic institutions. This is a good place to remember John Dewey and his opposition to framing debates in terms of polar opposites—in this case, reforming education rather than other social and economic policies, as equality of educational opportunity sometimes assumes, or conversely emphasizing greater economic equality without confronting educational inequities, as radical egalitarians sometimes propose. As Dewey (1938) said in his introduction to *Experience and Education*, "Mankind likes to think in terms of extreme opposites. It is given to formulating its beliefs in terms of Either-Ors, between which it recognizes no intermediate possibilities" (p. 17). In the context of discussing contrasting pedagogies, which he labeled traditional and progressive, he asserted that "the problems are not even recognized, to say nothing of being solved, when it is assumed that it suffices to reject the ideas and practices of the old education and then go to the opposite extreme" (p. 22). And so the equity agenda in this country surely requires educational reforms, but it also requires other social and economic reforms as well—a both-and strategy rather than an either-or approach. And if those of us within education stress the promises of education and equality of educational opportunity, we should also remember that other social and economic policies must change as well if our country is to be serious about the equity agenda.

Notes

1. See Grubb (1987) for these patterns based on the High School and Beyond study of 1980 high school graduates, results that are by now somewhat out of date. However, it is clear that these patterns still hold: Roughly 30 percent of high school graduates go to four-year colleges, 30 percent go to two-year colleges, and the remaining 40 percent tend not to go to any form of postsecondary education—of course, high school dropouts also tend not to attend any longer.

2. There is no national information about noncredit education since federal statistics do not include noncredit courses. Some states collect their own data since they must know about enrollments for funding purposes at a minimum; but even then, it is difficult to understand even the magnitude of noncredit education since the statistics are not comparable among states. For a handful of recent citations, see "The Role of Non-Credit Courses in the Future of Community Colleges" (2001). See also Cohen and Brawer (1989, chap. 10).

3. There are endless terminology problems, and we cannot clarify them in this short article. Colleges sometimes have divisions of noncredit education; others label this continuing education or community education. The Chicago colleges have bridge programs that play the same role. In some states (including North Carolina), contract education for specific employers is located within contract and continuing education divisions, combining programs for very different populations. In addition, in some institutions, there are noncredit courses, not-for-credit courses, zero-credit components of other courses (e.g., workshops and labs), credit courses that count for community college credentials but not for four-year college transfer, and credit courses that count for everything. Straightening out these technical complexities is, as they say, beyond the scope of this article.

4. However, a center serving a Latino population in another city denied that the lack of a green card was a particular barrier, although it might be a financial barrier because students without green cards would have to pay high out-of-state tuition.

5. Even though Florida has an excellent student tracking system, FETPIP, it is focused on credit students; following noncredit students is virtually impossible, even for counselors.

6. See especially Grubb and Associates (1999, chapters 1 and 5).

7. These results come from research in progress on guidance and counseling in sixteen community colleges, carried out by the Community College Research Center, Teachers College, Columbia University. See also Grubb (2001).

8. See Grubb (1999), also forthcoming in the *Economics of Education Review*. In these and all other statistical results, only credit courses are included, so strictly speaking, there has been no analysis of the economic effects of noncredit education.

9. There is a virtual industry summarizing the meager effects of training (see Grubb 1996; LaLonde 1995; U.S. Department of Labor 1995; Fischer and Cordray 1996; O'Neill and O'Neill 1997; Strawn 1998).

10. Adult education is so decentralized and so varied that some interesting programs can be found. However, in our experience they are usually idiosyncratic efforts disconnected from the main body of adult education programs.

11. The evidence suggests that completion of a General Equivalency Diploma (GED) has at best a very small effect on subsequent earnings compared to dropouts who have not earned a GED (see Cameron and Heckman 1993; Murnane, Willett, and Boudett 1995). Educators who have worked with the GED tend to report that it is the equivalent of an eighth- or ninth-grade education, not completion of a high school diploma—and this judgment is in effect confirmed by the evaluation results.

12. See, for example, Balmuth (1985, 1988), Darkenwald (1986), Kazemek (1988), and Sticht (1988). The exhaustive literature review by Solorzano, Stecher, and Perez (1989) included no outcome evaluations despite the authors' attempt to collect them. An evaluation of federally funded programs sponsored by the U.S. Department of Education has been undertaken by Development Associates, Arlington, Virginia, but it resulted in no outcome studies at all (see Young, Fitzgerald, and Morgan 1994). For a review with some posi-

tive findings, see Mahaffy (1983); however, most of the studies he cited have obvious validity problems because they depend on opinion surveys of Adult Basic Education administrators. Darkenwald (1986) cited a study by Kent examining pretests and posttests during a five-month period, with an average gain of 0.5 grade levels in reading and 0.3 grade levels in math (p. 7); another result, from an MDTA program, found increases of 0.4 grade levels after fifty-four hours of instruction. Paltry as they are, these gains may be due to selection effects, regression to the mean, practice effects, and other artifacts.

13. This information comes from the sixteen-college study being undertaken by the Community College Research Center. Other sources that found no evidence of adult education collaborating with other education programs include Grubb and McDonnell (1996), who investigated the complex of education and training programs in eight local communities, and Grubb and Kalman (1994), who examined all possible remedial education in other communities.

14. Obviously, we ignore the politics of such transfer. A favorite recommendation of ours in California has been to eliminate the area vocational programs—called Regional Occupation Centers and Programs—and transfer their resources to community colleges, but Master Plan Commissions in 1988 and 2001 were unable to broach this possibility because of political opposition.

15. The rise of occupational purposes throughout the twentieth century and its implications for schooling including conceptions of equity is the subject of Grubb and Lazerson (2002).

16. On the demise of the welfare state as an ideal and a reality, see Katz (2001).

17. See Richard Rothstein's (2002) column, "Linking Infant Mortality to Schooling and Stress."

18. While conceptions of active labor market policies vary, they usually include fiscal and monetary policy to reduce unemployment; labor matching efforts including job banks, sometimes career information and counseling, and apprenticeship policies; unemployment insurance; income support for low-income individuals, including direct funding (like welfare policies) as well as tax credits; legislation covering organized labor, wages, and working conditions, including minimum wage laws and employment leaves; health and safety legislation; retirement policies; antidiscrimination policies for women and minority groups; some aspects of trade policy, including tariffs on goods assembled abroad and efforts to prevent the export of jobs; the use and potential creation of tripartite groups (including business, labor, and government) to plan policies; and manpower policy covering job training (but not education). See also Esping-Anderson's (1990) conception of welfare capitalism, which covers the elements of active labor market policies.

References

Balmuth, M. 1985. *Essential characteristics of effective adult literacy programs: A review and analysis of the research*. The Adult Beginning Reader Project. New York: State Department of Education.

———. 1988. Recruitment and retention in adult basic education: What does the research say? *Journal of Reading* 31 (7): 620-23.

California Tomorrow. (2002). A new look at California community colleges: Keeping the promise alive for students of color and immigrants. Unpublished manuscript, California Tomorrow, Oakland, CA.

Cameron, S., and J. Heckman. 1993. The non-equivalence of high school equivalents. *Journal of Labor Economics* 11 (1): 34-56.

Cohen, A. M., and F. B. Brawer. 1989. *The American community college*. 2d ed. San Francisco: Jossey-Bass.

D'Amico, R., A. Martinez, J. Salzman, and R. Wagner. 2002. *An evaluation of the Individual Training Account/Eligible Training Provider Demonstration*. Research and Evaluation Monograph series 02-A. Washington, DC: U.S. Department of Labor.

Darkenwald, G. G. 1986. *Effective approaches to teaching basic skills to adults: A research synthesis*. Washington, DC: U.S. Department of Education, Office of Educational Research and Improvement. (ERIC Document Reproduction Service no. ED 325 631).

Dewey, J. 1938. *Experience and education*. New York: Macmillan.

Diekhoff, G. M. 1988. An appraisal of adult literacy programs: Reading between the lines. *Journal of Reading* 31 (7) : 624-30.

Esping-Anderson, E. 1990. *The three worlds of welfare capitalism*. Princeton, NJ: Princeton University Press.

Fischer, R., and D. Cordray. 1996. *Job training and welfare reform: A policy-driven synthesis*. New York: Russell Sage.

Gittell, M., and T. Steffy. 2000. *Community colleges addressing students' needs: A case study of LaGuardia Community College*. New York: Howard Samuels State Management and Policy Center, City University of New York.

Grubb, W. N. 1987. *The postsecondary vocational education of 1980 seniors*. LSB-87-4-10. Washington, DC: MPR Associates for the Center for Education Statistics, U.S. Department of Education.

———. 1995. *Education through occupations in American high schools*. 2 volumes. New York: Teachers College Press.

———. 1999. *Learning and earning in the middle: The economic benefits of sub-baccalaureate education*. Occasional paper. New York: Community College Research Center, Teachers College, Columbia University.

———. 2001. *"Getting into the world": Career counseling in community colleges*. Occasional paper. New York: Community College Research Center, Teachers College, Columbia University.

Grubb, W. N., and Associates. 1999. *Honored but invisible: An inside look at teaching in community colleges*. New York: Routledge.

Grubb, W. N., and J. Kalman. 1994. Relearning to earn: The role of remediation in vocational education and job training. *American Journal of Education* 103 (1): 54-93.

Grubb, W. N., and M. Lazerson. 2002. The vocational roles of American schooling: Believers, dissenters, and the education gospel. Unpublished manuscript.

Grubb, W. N., and L. McDonnell. 1996. Combating program fragmentation: Local systems of vocational education and job training. *Journal of Policy Analysis and Management* 15 (2): 252-70.

Javar, J., and S. Wandner. 2002. Use of intermediaries to provide training and employment services: Experience under WIA, JTPA, and Wagner-Peyser Programs. In *Job training in the United States: History, effectiveness, and prospects*, edited by C. O'Leary, R. Straits, and S. Wandner. Kalamazoo, MI: W. E. Upjohn Institute for Employment Research.

Katz, M. 2001. *The price of citizenship: Redefining the American welfare state*. New York: Henry Holt.

Kazemek, F. 1988. Necessary changes: Professional involvement in adult literacy programs. *Harvard Educational Review* 58 (4): 464-87.

LaLonde, R. 1995. The promise of public sector–sponsored training programs. *Journal of Economic Perspectives* 9 (2): 149-68.

Mahaffy, J. E. 1983. *Impact evaluation of adult basic education: Program outcomes*. Final report. Helena, MT: Office of Public Instruction.

Matus-Grossman, L., and S. Gooden. 2002. *Opening doors: Students' perspectives on juggling work, family, and college*. New York: MDRC.

Murnane, R., J. Willett, and K. P. Boudett. 1995. Do high school dropouts benefit from obtaining a GED? *Educational Evaluation and Policy Analysis* 17 (2): 133-48.

O'Neill, D., and J. O'Neill. 1997. *Lessons for welfare reform: An analysis of the AFDC caseload and past welfare-to-work programs*. Kalamazoo, MI: W. E. Upjohn Institute for Employment Research.

Osterman, P., and Lautsch, B. 1996. *Project QUEST: A report to the Ford Foundation*. Cambridge, MA: MIT Sloan School of Management.

Quinn, L., and M. Haberman. 1986. Are GED certificate holders ready for postsecondary education? *Metropolitan Education* 2:72-82.

Roberts, B. 2002. *The best of both: Community colleges and community-based organizations partner to better serve low-income workers*. Philadelphia: Public/Private Ventures.

The role of non-credit courses in the future of community colleges. 2001. Los Angeles: ERIC Clearinghouse for Community Colleges, University of California, Los Angeles. Information bulletin.

Rothstein, Richard. 2002. Linking infant mortality to schooling and stress. *New York Times*, 6 February, p. A20.

Solorzano, R., B. Stecher, and M. Perez. 1989. *Reducing illiteracy in California: Review of effective practices in adult literacy programs*. Report for the California State Department of Education, Adult Education Division. Pasadena, CA: Educational Testing Service.

Sticht, T. 1988. Adult literacy education. In *Review of research in education*, Vol. 15, edited by E. Rothkopf, 59-96. Washington, DC: American Educational Research Association.

Strawn, J. 1998. *Beyond job search or basic education: Rethinking the role of skills in welfare reform*. Washington, DC: Center for Law and Social Policy.

U.S. Department of Labor. 1995. *What's working (and what's not): A summary of research on the economic impacts of employment and training programs*. Washington, DC: U.S. Department of Labor, Office of the Chief Economist.

Young, M., N. Fitzgerald, and M. Morgan. 1994. *National evaluation of adult education programs, fourth report. Learner outcomes and program results*. Arlington, VA: Development Associates for the U.S. Department of Education.